A New Hitting System

DOUBLE-FORCE TENNIS STROKES

First Edition

by John D Borsos

Tennis As It Can Be

Third Level Books

Box 750   Matawan NJ   07747

Copyright @ 1994 by John D Borsos
First printing 1994

Publisher's Cataloging in Publication

Borsos, John D.
    Double-force tennis strokes / John D. Borsos
    p. cm.
    Includes index.
    ISBN 0-9624182-4-2

    1. Tennis.   I. Title.

GV995.B68472 1994   **796.342'2**
                                             QBI93-449

Library of Congress Catalog Card Number: 93-61856

Printed in the United States of America

Rotational inertia.

Chapter Five: Illusions vs Visualizations

Unreal goals. Awareness of what is vs what should be. Learning through satisfactions and feedback. Mental controls. Mental practice. Visualization, normal and slow-motion. Same faults in actual and visualized strokes. Mental anticipation and preparation.

Chapter Six: Compensations, Expedients, Deprivations, Circumventions, and Coercions

Levels of stroke elements. Instinctive adjustments and their by-products. The forces resisting change. Useful and harmful effects of compensations. Timing interactions. Harmless flourishes. Imagined problems. Reversion.

Chapter Seven: Follow-Through

A consequence, not the cause or cure of anything. End point misconceptions. Too short or too long. Direction during contact. The problem of the pose.

Chapter Eight: Roundhouse

The components of roundhouse motion. Relationship to stance, elbow-in, and body rotation. Origins.

Chapter Nine: Timing

Not just the racquet meeting the ball at the hitting point. Narrow view. Internal and external. Ripple effect of timing interactions. Swing controlled stroke. Timing of racquet attitude, backswing, and racquet momentum. Choice of early or late. Reverse variations. Deceptive ball velocity. Hitting on the move. Backhand timing.

Chapter Ten: Involvement of the Body.

Effect of reinforcement on racquet momentum. Timing reinforcement. Equal momentum loss for colliding bodies. Importance of reserve strength. Coordination of body and arm . Sans preparation, sans results. Grunting.

Controlling vs dependant elements. Obstacles to change. Retrospective analysis. Realistic expectations. Desperation reactions. The hitting point as internal to the swing. Centers of control. Learn to learn. Rate of deterioration vs improvement.

*chapter
one*

problems minus solutions

Tennis has unique advantages and interesting attributes, among them the feel of rhythm and power that comes with a well executed stroke; the exhilaration of competition; the priority of good technique over strength; the suitability for all age groups, types of physiques, and number of participants; the relatively small expense; and even the high level of difficulty that imparts an aura of artistry and achievement to those who are proficient.

There are few sports where size has as little importance. One drawback is that to be good at it requires spending a lot of time, regularly. But during that time a person obtains not only the satisfactions mentioned but also a quota and level of exercise that everyone needs and that cannot be delegated.

GETTING STARTED

Good strokes are not a matter of natural talent but acquired skills. A person need not be exceptional in either physique or athletic ability to become an accomplished tennis player. But it is not possible to learn to play an effective game of tennis without getting some type of instruction: either by taking lessons from a coach, watching instructional film, watching good players in action, reading books on tennis, or a combination of these.

Players who are not able to base their games on such beginnings are almost certain to develop makeshift styles with limited potential. Strokes of poor players range from atrocious idiosyncrasies to ostensibly fine patterns that are nevertheless highly artificial in execution. An athletically

built young man with wrong tennis habits may not be able to hit much more than ineffective push or slap shots, while a thin little girl may be able to hit deep and powerful drives.

THE DIFFICULTY OF INTRODUCING CHANGES

Players fall into status levels as determined by the kind of game they have. And it seems that improvement has been possible only within levels, leaving many devotees of the sport perpetually confined by an initial unfortunate choice of technique to corresponding levels of mediocrity and ineptitude. In other words, it has not been possible to become a player of a different type, only a slightly better or considerably worse player of the same type. The main aims of this book are to remove the limitations on progressive advancement from level to level, forestall the common and constant drift toward deterioration, and **introduce a new system, the "DOUBLE-FORCE" techniques, to improve everybody's ability to hit with ease, pace, and control**.

The rationalization that instructors often use in regard to a consistent failure to change mediocre or worse games to the game of anyone's dreams is that once students have taken suitable lessons then it is their own inflexibility and lack of talent that prevent then from mastering the techniques that

were described, demonstrated, and practiced during the lessons.

This excuse may have validity in some cases. However the experts are themselves bound by similar restrictions, albeit at a higher level, and have little or no more success with rebuilding their own games than the dubs do with theirs. It is necessary to uncover the ties that bind all levels of players to techniques and results that they themselves may detest, and to develop the means by which those ties can be broken.

The inner evaluation and acceptance of a technique are, of course, entirely up to the player. In the case of novices the coach can partly take over. But with experienced players the coach's most useful role is in guiding the player in the selection of things to try. These should usually include the somewhat undesirable along with the desirable.

Whether or not the ideas become a part of the player's game, or have any influence at all, is under the direct control of neither the player nor the coach. There has to be acceptance of the new elements by the inner controls, and then reconciliation with the retained elements as well as elimination of the conflicting. The teaching and practice methods have to satisfy those requirements.

CONFORMITY TO STYLE

At one time it was claimed that the single correct style for all players was the classic. But that was probably more the result of a desire to simplify and codify the teaching methods than to enable students to acquire some of the skills of the stars. Observation of top players shows that there is a great deal of variation in grip, stance, attitude of racquet, end point of swing, position of feet, use of wrist, etc.

An often used rationalization of this variation is that because of their exceptional talent the pros can get away with methods that would not be at all suitable for lesser players. This excuse neglects the fact that the athletically gifted players are apt to have a knack for recognizing what

is and what is not effective regardless of the degree of conformity to theory or tradition. They are skilled at being able to learn from each experience and to discard or modify anything they find to be ineffective, even if it happens to be one of the sacred traditions.

While many of the mannerisms of less talented players are well-known atrocities it is nevertheless unfair to require those fans to conform to elementary patterns, and thus in many cases actually deny them advantages that help the experts attain their superior level of play. Coaches now generally agree that it can no longer be assumed that all students must learn to do the same things the same way, even though a diversity of styles adds greatly to the teaching problems.

BAD HABITS
Although improvements are hard to come by, bad habits are acquired all too easily and imperceptibly, and soon become fixed all too permanently before there is any awareness of their existence.

The anomaly of the difficulty of learning a good habit compared with the great ease in acquiring a bad can be partly explained by the fact that the desired good habits are just observed external events, while the bad usually have internal origins. Many of the wrong techniques are often more or less automatic adjustments introduced to make up for more basic flaws, or for one's own presumed athletic limitations and inadequate early training.

While it is technique that delivers the ball it is habit that largely controls technique. Since it is true that repetition is instrumental in creating habit it is easy to assume, despite almost total evidence to the contrary, that the same type of repetition can also change habit. But although new strokes can be fairly easily acquired, such as the two-handed shot as a replacement for the single, almost all attempts at the more important task of making corrections to badly flawed games

have been marked by frustrating failure.

Explanations, analysis, demonstrations, emulation of patterns, breaking strokes down into components, use of video replay, etc., have neither individually nor in combination been very effective in redesigning flawed styles. This makes it appear that habit developed through an initial series of repetitions cannot be totally replaced by habit expected to emerge from a subsequent series of repetitions.

THE CONTROLLING FACTORS
Most player's strokes are controlled by a set of ideas, impulses, habits, and expectations that take over before the start of every stroke, rather than that they are controlled by conscious intentions, or by what might be expected to be learned from the appreciations and agonies experienced during and after countless previous strokes.

Some controlling factors can be readily identified: emotions, motives, gratifications, laziness, lack of confidence, misinformation, fanciful expectations, etc. They will be analyzed and discussed in detail later, together with how some can be used to enhance rather than prevent new learning. If the control exercised before a stroke by unreal expectations can be superseded at least in part by that based on the satisfactions generated by good techniques, then the major roadblocks to replacing bad habits can be removed.

Some elements that exert control over the way a person hits derive that influence partly just because of having priority in time, not because of considerations of importance or rationality. In this respect anticipations can assume undue importance because they come first, while appreciations derived from the manner of execution are ignored simply because they come last, when regret is one of the few remaining options. Mere repetitive practice is not very helpful, partly because new patterns are external in origin and therefor not inherently a source of much appreciation.

REPETITION RATIOS

There is also a problem of how to promote carry-over from practice into play, especially since most players are unwilling to risk new techniques during a game, even when it is merely social. Consequently the old methods are generally being used several times or even hundreds of times as often as the new. They are thereby being proportionately reinforced rather than progressively replaced.

In that event the desultory attempts to master new techniques often become nothing more than a source of confusion. The knowledge of the effect of repetition on retaining the old instead of learning the new may in itself be useful in inducing some players to change the repetition ratio in favor of the good habits, and thus increase the chances of new ideas being assimilated.

MAKING THE WRONG CHOICES

Even if repetition could change habit it is not at all certain that a particular technique or style being considered as a replacement, however classic and elegant or simple and rational, is any better. The old may be the more effective even if not exactly pretty. In choosing new techniques there is always the danger of lesser results and satisfactions in spite of improved appearance. In order to be able to adjust one's game in the light of experience it is necessary to develop at least some ability to recognize when the supposedly desirable is actually so, as well as when the supposedly bad is not bad in fact.

Since not everything is known, and even some "known" things are wrong, it is a wise player who can correctly decide which recommendations to listen to and which to ignore. There have been cases when even top tournament players with the best coaches made changes that had very negative consequences. An aim of this book is to develop sufficient guidelines so that such misfortunes are unlikely to occur even to average level players and coaches.

THE PROMISED REMEDIES

The remedies for this situation are inherent in the ideas in this book: the principles of hitting, the swing-controlled stroke, the mental control center, visualizations as mirrors of habit, self-monitoring, the reliability of satisfactions, the complexities and interactions of timing, fallacies in some dogma, the origin and nature of flaws and compensations, the force of habits and deprivations, the reasons for reversion, the problems with patterns, etc. They constitute guidelines that operate automatically and continually, and at the very least prevent technical decline.

In order to help make such discrimination possible a considerable examination of proper and improper influences and hitting techniques will be presented. The relevant principles of hitting, whose violation tends to be the trademark of the dub and whose observance that of the skilled tennis player, will be extensively examined.

The intent is to relate the problems that students have to the violation of related physical laws, and to base learning not on stroke patterns but on the satisfactions obtained by optimizing the processes basic to any stroke regardless of style. It is also necessary to be able to consciously recognize the unpleasantness that goes with doing things in a wrong way. Otherwise the subconscious and the muscles cannot be persuaded to forsake the familiar techniques.

A problem for both teachers and students is that the factors of a stroke are so interrelated that it may seem necessary to talk about everything all at once. An absolutely correct suggestion from the teacher may not have a positive effect for the student because the interpretation and execution are dependent on a level of athletic talent or experience that unsuccessful players are not apt to have. While it may be entirely impractical for the teacher to go through all the intricacies of a stroke it is somewhat of an impediment to success not to.

In an attempt to get at least a partial solution to this problem the sequence of topics in this book depends on the relatedness of concepts rather than on an orderly description of techniques. It is the principles of hitting that are being developed rather than the standard patterns and the "how-to" directions that go with them. Such directions are not the province of this book (except in the case of the new "DOUBLE-FORCE" strokes) since the concepts being presented are intended to apply to any tennis stroke in any style.

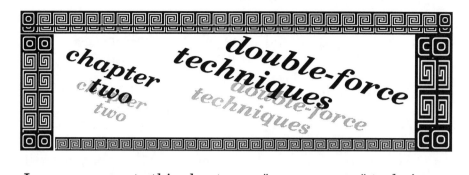

In some respects this chapter on "DOUBLE-FORCE" techniques should appear further on in this book: after the discussions of such topics as the behavior of elasticity, the principles of hitting, and the other factors that determine the effectiveness of tennis strokes.

But the rest of the book is concerned with the means to refine, not define, whatever strokes a player chooses to use. Hence it is necessary to make it possible to acquire a working knowledge of the new system. The information in the succeeding chapters can then be used to refine either the "DOUBLE-FORCE" techniques or the present strokes in the same way.

The abbreviation "DF", pronounced "D. F.", can be used in place of the full name.

TIME FOR A CHANGE

Some formerly taboo but now accepted techniques have actually been around for ages: two-handed shots, unorthodox grips, open stance, flying feet, elbow-first backswing, varying racquet attitude, circular follow-through. The long interval during which not much basically new appeared fits in with the remark made by a head of the Patent Office in the horse and buggy days that the Office ought to be closed because everything had been invented already.

However, the "DOUBLE-FORCE" techniques introduced in this book were not among the early departures from orthodoxy. Had the methods been used in the past they would likely be the standard today because of having all of the advantages of any previous style and none of the disadvantages. And the transition from any other method is not difficult.

The improvement in the effectiveness of ground strokes is great enough to reduce, and maybe even bring to an end, the dominant role of the "rush-to-the-net game". Small people may regain equality with the big and strong. Hackers can become respectable tennis players. Many people will probably come to regard the "DOUBLE-FORCE" backhand as the preferred shot instead of the one to avoid. Nobody need have a bad backhand, weak serve, or poor overhead.

The reader is invited to check these extravagant predictions after finishing this chapter and APPENDIX A, and then making use of the ideas on a tennis court or against a wall for just half an hour.

THE NATURE OF "DOUBLE-FORCE" STROKES

The general forms of the "DOUBLE-FORCE" strokes resemble those of the standard one-handed style, but with four major differences:

    1. Both hands are used for almost all strokes.

    2. The second hand applies its force to the racquet arm or hand, not to the racquet handle.

        a. By this means all the advantages of both the one-handed and two-handed strokes are realized, and all the disadvantages eliminated. This hand will be called the "**boost hand**" to distinguish it from the "**racquet**" hand.

    3. The "grip" of the "boost hand" is not always the same.

        a. It will vary freely both in type and point of application. The reasons will be made apparent in the discussions in this chapter.

    4. The "DOUBLE-FORCE" methods, unlike the standard

two-handed, are suitable for use on forehand, backhand, serve, and overhead.

    a. In fact they are easiest to apply, and make the greatest difference, on the backhand side.

Other terms that could be used instead of "boost" are "spare", "support", "assisting", "supplemental", "second", "complimentary", "reinforcing", "prop", "forcing", "auxiliary", "helping", "driving", "power", etc. Some, like "helping", have too many other connotations. Some, like "second", do not suggest the function. "Boost" has the advantage of being both reasonably short and descriptive.

Using two hands on both sides is not new in itself. The placement of the second hand on the handle is simply the natural thing to do when using any tool that requires the use of a lot of muscle. In tennis there is as much danger of using too much of the available strength as too little. Many players, even the strong, feel the need for more than what is available on one-handed backhands. The "DOUBLE-FORCE" techniques eliminate that feeling because they make ample strength available when and as needed.

The ordinary two-handed forehand (when both hands are on the racquet handle and the hands are not interchanged) is what in baseball is called a "cross-handed" shot. Two-handed forehands will probably change from being seldom used to being very commonly used, but only the "DOUBLE-FORCE" type, not the cross-handed.

The cross-handed forehand grip is uncommon in tennis but is being used, sometimes very effectively, which is the reverse of what might be expected. That does not change the fact that the location of the assist by the free hand (on the handle above the racquet hand) is about the most inappropriate that could be devised. The fact that it is being used shows that in some cases the extra strength and control obtained with two hands is important enough to outweigh the serious disadvantages. In baseball there apparently has been only one major league hitter who used it, a fairly good one at that.

A left-handed hitter in baseball uses the same position and grip as a   right-handed   tennis   player hitting a backhand. However, the relatively   heavy   bat   and   ball probably require the use of two hands   on   the   bat   handle.   So although the "DOUBLE-FORCE" tech-niques will find some use in that sport it will probably not be to a great extent.

Two-handed shots are used to improve <u>reinforcement and racquet momentum rather than to get higher racquet velocities</u>. Reinforcement increases racquet momentum because the <u>mass of the racquet is effectively increased</u> by putting <u>more of the weight of the body into the shot</u>, and the definition of <u>momentum is mass times velocity</u>.

The placement of the "boost hand" on the racquet arm enables swinging without clumsiness (as on the "cross-handed" forehand), without limitations on the reach (as on the ordinary two-handed strokes), and without the need to switch hands. An easy initial transition from a standard two-handed stroke is to simply grasp the racquet wrist or hand with the "boost hand" and then use the normal swing. A simple initial transition from a one-handed stroke can be done the same way. The big advantage of this particular method is that it involves very little change in timing or technique from that used with the current grips.

CHOICE OF "DOUBLE-FORCE" APPLICATION POINTS

The "DOUBLE-FORCE" strokes allow for a great deal of variation in the "grip" and the "application point" as needed for the shot and the circumstances. The means of applying the "boost force" should be chosen on the basis of convenience and effectiveness. The location can vary from <u>on or near the hand</u> to <u>up toward the armpit</u>. The "grips" and "application points" eventually get to be selected automatically as appropriate for each situation. But it is necessary to make an initial evaluation of the suitability of all of the methods given in "APPENDIX A", otherwise an unwise choice might become permanent habit.

The term "grip" is not an entirely accurate description of the means of transmitting the "boost force" to the racquet arm. In most cases the second hand does not hold on to the racquet arm but is merely in contact with it to exert a pull or push as needed. The area on the racquet arm where the "boost force" is applied should preferably be nearly flat, firm, and vertical during contact. Since such conditions can seldom be met exactly, the player must learn to compensate for any resultant torque, as will be explained later on.

The suitability of the position of the "grip" along the arm is usually of more importance than the characteristics of the arm at the selected point. A point low on the arm is effective in reinforcing it against a very fast oncoming ball. It would also be a good choice when a cramped or short swing has to be used.

A point further up on the arm extends the reach, frees the swing, lengthens the hitting zone, and gives priority to racquet velocity over racquet firmness. However the effectiveness of the "boost force" is diminished, which in some cases is not a advantageous tradeoff. If the "application point" is at the elbow or higher a very natural arm flex can be added to the always available wrist action.

Ordinarily the "boost hand" is placed on the racquet arm

early in the forward swing, or just before the start it. Both the grip and the location can change during the swing, especially in emergencies. The hand should disengage <u>right after contact</u>, leaving the racquet arm free to finish the follow-through on its own. This has the very important advantage of allowing selection of the "application point" as appropriate for the actual hit, not either as suitable mostly for the first part of the stroke or as too much of a compromise to accommodate the entire swing.

BACKSWING FOR "DOUBLE-FORCE" STROKES
The racquet can be taken back by any convenient means, and with one or two hands. If two, the location and "grip" of the "boost hand" for the backswing can be the same or different from that used later on for the forward swing. The length of the backswing can be a little less than for a one-handed stroke because of the extra strength furnished by the "boost" hand. The one-handed strokes generally require a longer backswing than the two-handed. But the converse is not true: the two-handed do not require a shorter backswing. There just is more freedom to choose.

Two-handed strokes generally use a lower end-point of backswing than the one-handed, and therefor can be much more effective in creating topspin, particularly on the back-hand. There is easy conformance to the adage "from low to high". But a low end point should not be regarded as a requirement. Selection and refinement are continuous, and no technique is ever final.

STANCE WITH "DOUBLE-FORCE" STROKES
It is hard to predict what the consensus preferred stance will be for use with the "DOUBLE-FORCE" techniques. Tournament players using conventional styles seem to open the stance very soon during the hit, often apparently unnecessarily or even undesirably, especially on sharply angled or very deep shots close to a line. The major reasons for opening the stance seem to be to look at the target and watch the travel of the ball. But there are advantages. One is that it

eliminates interference of the swing by the body.

The fact that "DOUBLE-FORCE" swings are of a dual nature (two-handed in regard to strength and one-handed in regard to freedom) allows the stance to be selected mainly as suitable for the hit. A fairly closed stance would seem to be appropriate because it makes if easy for the "boost hand" to apply its force during the contact interval.

The extra reinforcement of the racquet arm may encourage some players to adopt or stay with a fairly open stance. But on the forehand most of the suitable "application points" are then somewhat out of the reach of the "boost hand". There also is poor leverage for applying the necessary pulling force to the racquet arm. A strange fact is that most good players use better positioning, arm extension, and form on two-handed strokes than on the one-handed, even though there is extra strength available with the two-handed to make up for a deficient swing.

There also tends to be better conformance to form on volleys than on ground strokes. It would seem that there would be less rather than more because there is not much time to get into position, and the ball is mostly just blocked back. Yet the stance tends to be exceptionally good. The major reasons are that the impact may get unmanageable, and the angle of the racquet and the direction of the return unpredictable, if the positioning is not consistently good. The jolt of impact of a fast ball can be damaging if the arm and body relationships are not right.

There are two main means of applying a "boost force".
    1. Grasping the racquet arm.

2. Just applying pressure against the racquet arm.

A push or a pull can be developed with either the "grasp" or the "pressure" method. Pressure on the inside of the racquet arm delivers a push, which is suitable for a backhand. Pressure on the back of the arm exerts a pull, suitable for a forehand.

The "grasp" generally produces less twist or torque than the "pressure". But most players will probably find the "pressure" types more convenient than the "grasp" on both forehands and backhands. Lists of grips for both strokes are given later on in this chapter. At that point the reader can apply the "grips" while reading the text.

FOREHAND "APPLICATION POINTS" AND "GRIPS"
In general only the fingers should be used for a grasp, not the full hand. For the forehand the "grasp" works better with locations on or near the elbow, or on the lower arm, than with locations on the upper arm. Most people's arms are too thick, soft, or slippery at the higher points to make a workable grip possible. Some kind of loop or handle could be devised for attachment to the racquet arm to make it easier to exert a pull on it. Hopefully such devices will be banned before they can come into common use.

If the "application point" is above the center line of the racquet arm a torque will be generated that will tend to close the racquet face (turn it downward). When the point is below the center line of the racquet arm there will be a torque that will tend to open the racquet face (turn it upward). It is not hard to compensate for and become accustomed to. But it will probably be the cause of most of the initial difficulties during the transition from other styles.

When the hitting point is low the ball has to be directed upward. On the forehand that direction is more easily achieved when the "application point" is below the center line of the racquet arm, opening the racquet face. If the hitting point is very high the ball generally has to be directed downward. So advantage could be taken of the torque generated when the "application point" is above the center line of the racquet arm, closing the racquet face. Some players will prefer to use one of the locations exclusively if they find that consistency suffers by switching.

BACKHAND "GRIPS" AND "APPLICATION POINTS"

On the backhand the "boost force" is <u>always a push</u>. It is much easier to use a push than a pull. The "boost" pressure can be applied at many points and in many ways: with the fingers; tips of the fingers; backs of the fingers, knuckles, fist, palm, back of hand, heel of hand, etc. The bony areas are more efficient than the fleshy in transferring the "boost force" to the racquet. But some locations may produce torque and change in direction, at least initially.

A big benefit from the use of "DF" techniques on the backhand is elimination of the feelings of insecurity about the strength of the racquet arm. So over time the compromises associated with insecurity, such as deficient stance and arm extension, are almost automatically discarded. Eventually a good momentum-powered, extended-arm swing, very similar to the classic one-handed type, is likely to develop.

The text under the following two subheadings contain the lists of the major types of "grips" for the forehand and the backhand. Variations other than those listed can also be used. When reading about a grip it is desirable to place the "boost hand" on the racquet arm in the manner described. The means of actually using the grips is covered in the "DOUBLE-FORCE" drills in "APPENDIX A".

The applicable "grips" for the serve and forehand overhead are forehand grips "A", "B", "E", and "F" and all backhand grips except "E". <u>All backhand "grips" except "E" can be used with the backhand overhead.</u>

LIST OF FOREHAND "BOOST GRIPS"

The "grips" available for use with the forehand are:

**A. Grasp the racquet arm lightly with the "boost hand", thumb ON TOP of the arm. Use just the fingers or the entire hand, as desired.

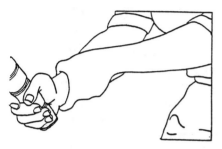

**B. Grasp the racquet arm lightly with the "boost hand", thumb BELOW the arm instead of on top. Use just the fingers or the entire hand, as desired.

C. Position the "boost hand", palm up, UNDER the racquet arm. Bend the fingers up against the BACK OF THE RACQUET ARM to be able to exert a FORWARD PULL on it. Use the entire length of the fingers on the "boost hand" or just a part, as works best. Do not use a grasp in this drill.

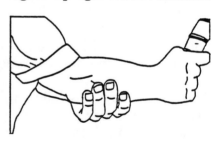

D. Same as grip "C" except use just two or three fingers against the back of the racquet arm instead of all of them.

E Position the "boost hand", palm down, ON TOP of the racquet arm. Bend the fingers down against the BACK OF THE RACQUET ARM so as to be able to exert a FORWARD PULL on it. Use the entire length of the fingers of the "boost hand" or just a part, as works best.

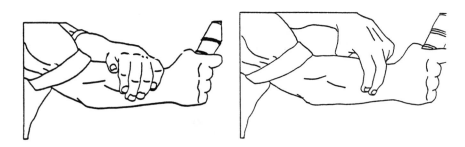

F. Same as grip "E" except use two or three fingers against the the racquet arm instead of all of them.

G. Position the "boost hand", <u>palm down</u>, <u>UNDER</u> the racquet arm. Place the <u>BACK OF THE HAND BEHIND</u> the racquet arm to be able to exert a <u>FORWARD PULL</u> on it. The wrist of the "boost hand" is bent back slightly.

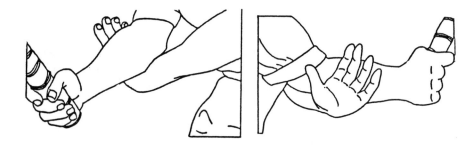

H. Position the "boost" hand <u>UNDER</u> the racquet arm, with the <u>palm down</u>. Extend the fingers and place the <u>BACKS OF THEM BEHIND THE RACQUET ARM</u> so as to be able to exert a <u>FORWARD PULL</u> on it. The wrist is bent back slightly.

19

J. Position the "boost hand" UNDER the racquet arm and place the "V" FORMED BY THE THUMB AND FOREFINGER BEHIND the racquet arm so as to be able to exert a FORWARD PULL on it. The other fingers can be anything from being extended and bent back to being closed in a loose fist. Another variation is to place just the thumb behind the arm.

LIST OF BACKHAND "BOOST GRIPS"
The "grips" available for use with the backhand are:

**A. Grasp the racquet arm lightly with the "boost hand", thumb ON TOP of the arm. Use just the fingers or the entire hand, as desired.

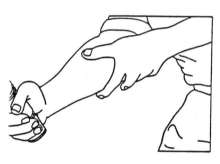

   1. "Grips" "A" and "B" provide easy transition from standard two-handed grips.

**B. Grasp the racquet arm lightly with the "boost hand", thumb BELOW the arm instead of on top. Use just the fingers or the entire hand, as desired.

C. Place the TIPS or the faces of the tips of the fingers against the racquet arm so as to be able to exert a PUSH against it. As many of the fingers as desired can be used.

   1. Experiment with having the palm facing up or down, or anywhere in between.

   2. When the faces of the tips are used the pressure bends the fingers back slightly. This gives a springy action that helps prolong the "boost" through the contact interval. The greatest reach for applying the "boost" is obtained with the fingers extended.

     **   Denotes usability on both forehands and backhands.

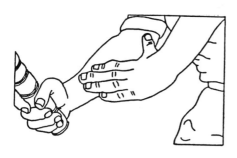
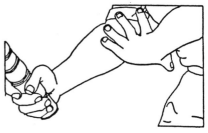

D. Place the <u>BACKS</u> of the fingers against the racquet arm so as to be able to exert a <u>PUSH</u> against it. As many of the fingers and as great a portion as desired can be used.

    1. Experiment with having the palm facing up or down, or anywhere in between.

E. Position the "<u>V</u>" <u>FORMED BY THE THUMB AND THE INDEX FINGER</u> against the racquet arm so as to be able to exert a <u>PUSH</u> against it. The "V" can be along or across the arm depending on which works best at the location.

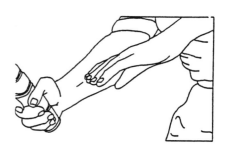

F. Place a closed or loose fist (try both) against the racquet arm to be able to exert a <u>PUSH</u> against it.

    1. Experiment with having the palm facing up, down, or anywhere in between. This "grip" is useful when extra strength or a large application area is needed to counter the force of impact.

    2. Another means of getting resistance against impact is to lower the "application point". Any method used for that purpose tends to reduce

the reach of the "boost hand".

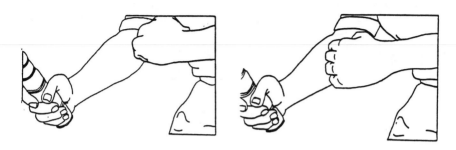

G. Place the palm against the racquet arm so as to exert a PUSH against it. The fingers can be above, below, or along the racquet arm. This grip provides good resistance against impact.

All backhand "grips" except "E" can be used with the backhand overhead.

RACQUET VELOCITY VS FIRMNESS
The velocity of the "boost hand" tends to be somewhat constant. As a consequence the velocity of both the racquet arm and the racquet tend to be determined by the location of the "application point".

RACQUET VELOCITY INCREASES as the "application point" is moved UPWARD toward the shoulder, and DECREASES as the "application point" is moved DOWNWARD toward the hand. At the same time the REINFORCEMENT of the racquet against the force of impact varies oppositely: decreases as the "application point" is moved upward.

The more racquet velocity developed by shifting the "application point" upward the less reinforcement obtained, and vice versa. Ordinarily reinforcement gets preference. Increased racquet velocity alone is not enough. Racquet velocity is wasted if there isn't adequate reinforcement. Here there can be both.

For fast approaching balls the "application point" can be low on the arm to provide sufficient resistance against the force of impact. For slow approaching balls the point can be higher to emphasize racquet velocity. The ease of balancing velocity against reinforcement makes it not only possible but advisable to vary the "grip" and the "application point" as appropriate for the circumstances of each shot. Fortunately, the variations tend to happen automatically as a player becomes familiar with the use of the "DF" options.

The real function of the "boost arm" is just to assist the racquet arm. The latter is not idle but is carrying on with its tasks as usual. So whatever "boost" is given to it improves the results. The "boost arm" cannot get tired because, besides not having to work too hard, it gets a lot of rest between forward swings. Only a fraction of the strength of the "boost arm" gets to be used, and the muscles automatically gauge the amount required for the particular point of application.

SELECTING THE APPROPRIATE RACQUET VELOCITY

A natural urge is to vary racquet velocity DIRECTLY with that of the oncoming ball (which is wrong), as opposed to varying the velocity INVERSELY with that of the oncoming ball (which is correct). Few players at any level succeed in always varying racquet velocity INVERSELY with oncoming ball velocity. The paragraph "PRACTICAL UTILIZATION OF RACQUET VELOCITY" in the chapter on "ELASTICITY" gives some of the reasons why inverse variation of racquet velocity is a necessity.

While one-handed hitting techniques are conducive to the use of the wrong "direct" racquet velocity variation the "DOUBLE-FORCE" techniques (and the standard two-handed) tend to automatically produce the correct "inverse" response. This is because the player finds it unnecessary to use high racquet velocity to compensate for an imagined deficiency of strength in countering the impact of very fast balls.

THE CHANCES FOR WRIST OR ELBOW STRAIN

The racquet arm is strongly reinforced when "DOUBLE-FORCE" techniques are used. While the task of the "racquet" arm is eased considerably thereby the task of the "racquet" wrist is not, and in fact is considerably increased. The wrist has to transmit the force of two arms instead of one to the racquet, and so can be easily overloaded, particularly if the timing is not exactly right. Use of a wrist band or brace is advisable as a precaution against injury. The danger is greatest when receiving serve, as could be expected.

When the wrist is sore, or in danger of being so, the "application point" should be near, on, or below the wrist for almost all shots. The "boost hand" can even be placed directly on top of the other. While the reach becomes somewhat limited it is still better even in that respect than with the standard two-handed strokes. If it is the elbow that is hurting the "application point" should be on or below the elbow. So sore elbows are not only not likely to happen but can easily be kept from getting worse. "Tennis elbow" need no longer be a problem, but "tennis wrist" might be.

"DOUBLE-FORCE" AESTHETICS

There are a number of sports that are rightly judged on the basis of conformance to form. Examples are figure skating, diving, dancing, equestrian events, gymnastics, etc. There is a considerable aesthetic element in tennis also, especially in the classic style. That attribute was probably what most attracted people to the sport in the great tennis boom of the 60's and 70's.

The aesthetic element of tennis is still there, but not to the same extent. The main emphasis at all levels is now on results. In addition to the loss in rhythm and aesthetics, the current styles have their own set of drawbacks in terms of reach, feel, satisfactions, strength and energy requirements, etc. This need not be. The "DOUBLE-FORCE" techniques restore the aesthetic element, retain all the advantages of the standard methods, and eliminate the disadvantages.

"DOUBLE-FORCE" ADVANTAGES

The angular velocities of standard two-handed strokes can be faster than those of the one-handed, but racquet velocities may not be. The reason is that the standard two-handed grips limit the reach. This reduces the arc of the swing, which equates to reduced racquet velocity. But the reinforcement provided by the strength of two arms is the great equalizer. It enables most people to obtain great pace and/or topspin instead of just a gifted few, and with no more than ordinary strength and effort.

The "DOUBLE-FORCE" techniques eliminate the two-handed limitations on the reach and freedom of the swing. They even improve on the reach available with the one-handed because the extra strength permits greater arm extension. Ball velocities can be both greater and more easily controlled than with other methods.

All of the main factors that can enhance pace are available:

1. Abundance of reserve strength.

2. Two-handed reinforcement against impact.

3. Involvement of the body.

4. Free shoulder and body rotation.

5. Large arc of swing and great reach produced by an extended arm.

6. Great racquet velocity because of the enhanced arm extension and strength.

7. Momentum of two arms behind the shot instead of one.

8. Easy racquet acceleration through contact.

9. Better wrist and arm flex than with standard two-

handed shots.

10. Swing instead of muscular push.

11. Forward direction of racquet travel at the hit.

12. Free follow-through.

13. Involvement of the "boost hand" only when needed.

14. Smooth instead of jerky effort.

15. Appropriate racquet velocity relative to ball velocity.

16. Ease of moving the racquet upward for topspin.

17. Strength and effectiveness at all heights.

18. Lessening of feelings of insecurity and the use of desperation techniques.

Anyone who has trouble developing good pace can use the above list to search for previously unknown or neglected areas to work on. The heretofore commonly used "correction" for poor pace, just hitting like hell, is obviously likely to cause more problems and deterioration than enhancement in the above factors.

THE BUSINESS PART OF THE STROKE

It is obvious that the only part of a swing that has any direct effect on the ball is the interval of contact of racquet and ball. Standard formal instruction covers such other elements as grip, footwork, stance, preparation, swing, and follow-through in rather extensive detail. This is all very desirable because those items help determine what can and can not be accomplished with the racquet during contact.

Whether or not they are as good as possible is measured not by their conformance to style but by whether or not the best attainable results were achieved. Workable concepts of the nature of the hit and of the contact interval must be developed before it is possible to optimize the processes and the timing that together make up a swing. It is therefor very desirable to know a little about the intricacies of that very minuscule but very significant slice of time.

MINUSCULE BUT IMPORTANT

It might be said: "Who cares? It all occurs in a flash. You can't do anything about that thousandth or whatever part of a second anyway." But a hit involves more than just the instantaneous reversal of the course of the ball. The interval of contact of racquet and ball covers a FINITE AND EXTENDIBLE slice of time during which an all important sequence of actions and reactions take place. Though the period of contact is seemingly insignificant in duration the events within are nevertheless paramount in importance.

The rules governing the events therein hold the keys to

pace, accuracy, spin, touch, efficient use of energy, shock to the arm, and the means of improvement. Even a person's intentions, expectations, and style are basically dependent on the understandings (conscious or intuitive), misunderstandings, or just ignorance of the processes that operate during contact. So if the net results of a hit are good the explanations are to be found within that period. If they are bad it had better be possible to make changes therein.

The pattern of a stroke in the case of an ineffective player and that of an expert may sometimes look quite similar. But the differences that are present during contact determine who is who. This should become very apparent as the elastic processes are analyzed in the following paragraphs, and as the practical applications are developed in the succeeding chapters.

The processes that will be discussed are not just idle theory, but are the determining factors of the effectiveness of the hit, the satisfactions obtained, and ultimately of who wins and who loses. Knowing the principles of hitting helps both to hit expertly and to decide correctly where to make changes. Understanding the mechanics of a hit is also useful in insuring that any changes will be directed toward improvement, otherwise there are apt to be changes in the other direction.

INITIAL ASSUMPTIONS

In order to simplify the analysis it will be assumed that a "flat" shot (without spin) is used. Also assumed is that the preparation, path of the swing, hitting point, follow-through, attitude of the racquet during contact, and all other such details will be perfect unless specifically indicated otherwise. Elasticities themselves are also considered to be perfect, and air resistance to be zero.

The reason for making these assumptions is to allow concentration on the characteristics of elasticity in an ideal sense, and to postpone qualifications until later. Some of the statements are generalized. Though accurate enough for the present purpose they should not be considered as furnishing a technically complete picture of all the actions and reactions.

Each of two colliding objects LOSES EXACTLY THE SAME AMOUNT OF MOMENTUM. MOMENTUM IS DEFINED AS "MASS TIMES VELOCITY". "Weight" is just a property of mass". So a more rigorous analysis would be based on the momentum of the racquet rather than on its velocity. In effect, **the arm can add "mass"** to the racquet. That fact explains why a racquet propelled at a certain speed by a heavy arm can send the ball away with much greater pace than can the same racquet propelled at the same speed by a lighter arm. And the effective mass of a particular arm is also not an independent constant. It varies importantly with the reinforcement. The "DOUBLE-FORCE" methods tend to optimize technique as well as both mass and reinforcement.

WHEN THE RACQUET MEETS A STATIONARY BALL
We will first consider the effects of ball elasticity alone, as if those of the racquet and strings were not involved. In the first example of a hit to be discussed the ball is assumed to have zero initial velocity, as in a serve or as when the ball hits the ground in such a way as to bounce vertically.

When the racquet just begins to touch a stationary ball, say at 20 miles per hour (20 mph), the ball at first hardly moves because of having INERTIA. In this case the inertia amounts to RESISTANCE TO CHANGE IN MOTION FROM A STATE OF REST. At the instant of contact THE COVER ON THE SIDE THAT IS BEING HIT BEGINS TO FLATTEN. THE AREAS TO THE SIDES AND FRONT BEGIN TO BULGE OUT. The flattening and bulging processes continue while the ball gathers speed UNTIL IT BEGINS TO BE CARRIED ALONG AT RACQUET VELOCITY, 20 mph in this case. So far so simple. But then some strange processes begin to operate.

Due to the assumed perfect elasticity the ENERGY STORED IN THE ELASTICITIES is equivalent to THE FULL IMPACT VELOCITY, 20 mph. This represents a POTENTIALLY RECOVERABLE VELOCITY. But there is an existing ball velocity of the same magnitude due to the BALL BEING CARRIED ALONG AT RACQUET SPEED. Since the ball had zero initial velocity the stored energy was actually all derived from racquet velocity. But for technical reasons the stored energy will be discussed in terms of ball mass and velocity, not racquet.

With the racquet and ball moving forward together at 20 mph the COVER BEGINS TO RESTORE from being flattened on one side and bulged out elsewhere to becoming round again. In snapping back into its original shape THE BACK COVER PUSHES OFF AGAINST THE RACQUET. Therefore THE REST OF THE BALL PICKS UP SPEED and actually begins to MOVE FASTER THAN EITHER THE FRAME OF THE RACQUET OR THE BACK COVER OF THE BALL. The velocity generated by the rounding out of the ball IS ADDED TO THE EXISTING 20 MPH, which was derived simply from the ball being carried along at racquet speed.

If the cover is perfectly elastic all the energy taken up in the storage process is converted into ball velocity as the ball regains its original round shape. Since in fact we assumed that ideal type of elasticity, as well as the benefits of a perfectly executed hit whatever that entails, we can say that ALL OF THE IMPACT VELOCITY (20 MPH) GETS TO BE RECOVERED AND IS ADDED TO THE CARRYING VELOCITY (also 20 mph). Therefor after the recovery the ball would be MOVING FORWARD AT 40 MPH even though the racquet continued along at the original rate of only 20 mph.

Looking at the same type of situation in another way: If you are riding in a van moving at 20 mph as it strikes a station-ary ball you will see, if you have good enough eyesight, the ball first deform and then recover in shape as it bounces away from the van at a speed of 20 mph. But since you are observing the ball move away at 20 mph with respect to the van while the van itself is moving in the same direction at 20 mph with respect to the ground, the total velocity of the ball with respect to the ground is the sum of the two, or 40 mph.

But only in the never never land of perfect elasticity.

WHEN MOVING BALL MEETS STATIONARY RACQUET
In the above example we assumed initial velocities of zero for the ball and 20 mph for the racquet. If the roles are reversed, with a ball having a speed of 20 mph meeting a racquet that is held stationary, the ball would still bounce off at the full 20 mph with respect to the racquet, the same as before. Adding the ball velocity to that of the racquet, which in this case is zero, RESULTS IN A FINAL BALL VELOCITY OF 20 MPH with respect to the ground RATHER THAN THE 40 MPH obtained in the previous example, which involved a moving racquet.

WHEN A MOVING RACQUET MEETS A MOVING BALL
If the ball and racquet are approaching each other and are both moving at 20 mph with respect to the ground, the velocity relative to each other is the SUM OF THE TWO GROUND SPEEDS. The IMPACT VELOCITY IS THUS 40 MPH. It results in an equivalent amount of energy being stored in the elasticities.

When the flattening of the ball reaches its maximum the ball is again carried along at racquet speed, which is 20 mph, the same as in the first two cases. Adding the velocity derived from the stored energy (40 mph) gives a ball velocity of 60 mph with respect to the ground.

THE BALL VELOCITY FORMULA
To simplify: "FINAL BALL VELOCITY with respect to the ground equals BALL VELOCITY PLUS TWO TIMES RACQUET VELOCITY", but in the realm of perfect elasticity only. The conversion of a moderate and easily developed speed in the racquet into premium grade pace for the ball is a very fortunate and phenomenal circumstance. But the extra velocity is not free since it is supplied by the player in moving the racquet.

In the real world the velocity will not be increased as efficiently as described, and the amount of enhancement will vary from about sixty percent of the total input energy to twenty percent or less.   The determining factors will be explained in more detail in this and other chapters.

While the formula seems to indicate that racquet velocity is of more importance than oncoming ball velocity, *let it not be assumed that racquet motion must be raised to the maximum,* and that other requirements can be correspondingly compromised. *As will be developed, the optimum use of the elastic processes involves conditions and results not at all in keeping with the seemingly simple implications of the formula.*

The gains predicted by the formula also signify that there is that much to be lost in *unrealized enhancement* in the speed of the ball *if there is inadequate accommodation to the characteristics of elasticity.* Therein can be found both the explanations for disappointing results and the means for advancement to higher levels.   In the real world the potential gain would not be as much as given by the formula and therefor neither would the potential loss.

The figure below shows what happens with a racquet speed of 25 mph and an oncoming ball speed of 35 mph.

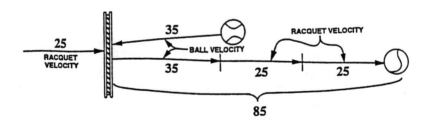

MAXIMIZING THE RECOVERY OF ENERGY

The phrase *"inadequate accommodation"* in the above paragraph is meant to imply that *other factors besides racquet speed are involved in recovering energy from the elasticities.* Not satisfying these other conditions will result in the failure to obtain the benefits specified by the formula. Even the selection of a perfectly appropriate average racquet velocity for a particular shot is still far from enough to insure a proper hit.

In the previously discussed imaginary world of perfect elasticity the cover of the ball would have to be weightless. And it would have to be able to change from being flat on one side to becoming perfectly round again without overshooting that state. In the real world the cover has weight, in fact almost all the weight of the ball. Consequently, when the flattened cover rebounds to its original round shape it doesn't stop there but is carried a little farther because, like any moving mass, it has momentum.

The momentum causes the cover to overshoot its normal position, reverse, overshoot again, and CONTINUE IN DIMINISHING OSCILLATIONS until the stored energy is used up, mostly in internal friction. Unless the player uses appropriate techniques to dampen at least some of the initial overshoot there will be a big waste of energy. With it goes the enhancement of pace predicted by the formula. The partial solution, and that is all that can be hoped for, is to keep the racquet pressed against the ball. But that is quite difficult to do.

NEED FOR CONTINUOUS RACQUET ACCELERATION
The interval of contact and the recovery of energy can be maximized by continuously accelerating the racquet to compensate for the ball picking up speed relative to the racquet. There should not be a constant racquet velocity, or a hurrying of the racquet either, but rather a smooth, controlled, continuous acceleration. One of the biggest mistakes, as always, is to overdo things.

Maintaining acceleration enhances recovery by improving the ability of the racquet to **keep up with the ball**, and thus **extending the contact interval**. Maximum racquet velocity should not be reached until just after contact has ended, which means that the acceleration has to carry into

the follow-through.

It thus turns out that energies are recovered at higher racquet velocities than those at which the energies were stored. ENERGY IS BEING STORED IF THE RACQUET IS MOVING FASTER THAN THE BALL. Otherwise energy is being RECOVERED AS LONG AS CONTACT IS MAINTAINED. After that any remaining stored energy is lost. **Contact will be broken too soon if the racquet velocity is constant or is slowing down.**

But the enhancement in pace CAN BE MORE THAN OFFSET IF THERE IS INSUFFICIENT RESERVE STRENGTH TO COUNTER IMPACT. Other penalties for the lack of reserve strength are variation in timing and technique, and an increase in the error rate.

WHAT CAN BE DONE IN A MINUSCULE INTERVAL?
At this point there ought to be a well-justified doubt about the validity of the above reasoning in the light of the minute amount of acceleration possible in a very minuscule slice of time. *But it is quite long event-wise*, as was proved above. The complicated processes involved in the storage and recovery of energy also occur in that same seemingly inconsequential slice of time. If any acceleration at all is present a proportionate amount of it occurs in every interval, no matter how small. Contact will be extended thereby, and not insignificantly compared to the duration of the events that occur within the interval.

It is obvious that the cover of the ball goes through the two distinct stages of flattening and recovery during the seemingly insignificant contact interval. The AMOUNT OF STORED ENERGY THAT GETS CONVERTED INTO BALL VELOCITY IS BASED ON THE SUCCESS OF KEEPING THE RACQUET PRESSED AGAINST THE BALL so as to maximize the period of contact. The LENGTHENING OF THAT INTERVAL ADDS TO BOTH THE STORAGE PERIOD AND THE RECOVERY PERIOD. So the method of developing racquet momentum determines how much is stored and how much is recovered.

The operations of the elasticities are not restricted to a fixed amount of time. The processes do not have to be squeezed into a preset interval because *they themselves determine the length of that interval*. If the elasticities required more time than is available during contact to both store energy and reconvert a good part of it into ball velocity then that interval would simply be longer.

ADDITIVE PACE WITH CONSTANT RACQUET VELOCITY

An interesting application of the velocity formula is as follows. Assume that ball and racquet both move at 20 mph with respect to the ground as they approach each other. Per the reasoning developed previously, THIS CAUSES THE BALL TO DEPART AT 60 MPH. Then if the OPPONENT'S RACQUET IS AGAIN MOVING AT 20 MPH when it again meets the ball the RESULTING SPEED OF THE BALL WOULD BE 100 MPH (ball velocity of 60 plus two times racquet velocity of 20). In the theoretical world of perfect elasticity THIS INCREMENT OF 40 MPH WOULD CONTINUE TO OCCUR ON EACH HIT if each player just maintained a racquet speed of 20 mph.

Although the theory promises this really marvelous bonus from the elasticities there are other factors in the real world that put sudden and severe limits on attainability. The limits are due to friction, the physical limitations of the body, imperfections in the techniques, and the elastic limits of the materials in the racquet and the ball.

The percentage of energy recovered in the case of a fast-traveling oncoming ball would be less than for a slow, mainly because of increased frictional losses and the waste of momentum in a greater backward jolt of the racquet. Another reason is that as ball velocities increase the acceleration of the racquet becomes proportionately less significant than ball velocity. Contact will generally end earlier in the recovery process than for a slower moving ball.

The inefficiencies cause the predicted progressive increases in speed to terminate so very soon that players simply do not become aware of the described phenomena. By not knowing about the theory they may fail to understand the implications and derive the advantages. But it can now begin to be understood how a relaxed and seemingly rather moderately paced swing can produce explosive ball speeds.

RELATIONSHIP BETWEEN RACQUET & BALL VELOCITIES
The more pace an approaching ball has the less velocity can be given to the racquet before there is NOT ENOUGH RESERVE STRENGTH LEFT TO BOTH COUNTER THE IMPACT AND MAINTAIN A CONTINUOUS ACCELERATION. THE STORAGE PROCESS IS THEN INEFFI-CIENT AND THE RECOVERY PROCESS INCOMPLETE. There are problems in other areas as well, such as in maintaining accuracy and control, reinforcing the arm with the body, minimizing shock and effort, etc.

The way to handle fast balls is not "hit like hell". You don't have to hit harder and harder the faster and faster the ball comes. Just the opposite. Untalented players may just freeze the arm defensively and jerk the racquet around in an ever more convulsive, unprofitable, and unreasonable manner in spite of thousands of previous unhappy experiences.

One side lesson that can be learned is that it is a great mistake to let annoyance at the tactics of an opponent, or an excessive urge to win a point, trigger an attempt to blast the ball back with the use of all the strength that a person is capable of mustering.

THE ROLE OF ELASTICITY IN REPAIRING A GAME
THE ONLY AVAILABLE MEANS TO OPTIMIZE A HIT IS TO UTILIZE THE PROPERTIES OF ELASTICITY IN THE MOST ADVANTAGEOUS WAY. It follows that learning to hit properly and getting rid of bad habits can proceed on a sounder basis through a knowledge of the characteristics of elasticity than through aimless variation, recourse to patterns, unevaluated hits, etc.

When a game needs improvement, at any level of play, a common procedure is to analyze the strokes for VIOLATIONS OF

ACCEPTED PATTERNS. Since this is not the same as examining a stroke with respect to the PRINCIPLES OF HITTING, developed above, it can be expected that even with apparent improvement in form there may nevertheless be adverse effects on results.

If nothing else the strokes could become more artificial, and the processes for the storage and recovery of energy could be harmfully affected in subtle ways. It must be remembered that even the games of many of the most successful pros differ markedly from the norms, and that they have their own ways of extracting as much as they can from the elasticities, some with considerably more success than others.

It ought now to be apparent that technical knowledge can help a tennis game, and that a player, especially one having difficulties, should be very concerned about the *techniques that maximize the contact interval.* Even patterns themselves can be refined and made more effective by being based on the principles of elasticity rather than on traditions.

The dismal rewards of improper execution need not be dismissed as lack of talent. They can begin to be related to the techniques used, and to the violations of the laws of elasticity that are bound to occur to some extent. As the understandings are improved so are the results and satisfactions.

Corrective measures intended to enhance recovery of energy, accuracy, feel, fun, etc, will not only work but will stand a good chance of gaining acceptance in the player's way of thinking. Not insignificantly, false remedies and illusions will no longer find similar acceptance. The mind is involved in the execution of a stroke, the subconscious apparently much more so than the conscious. Concepts, but not commands, can influence the inner mind. Therefor false assumptions about the hit MUST BE REMOVED FROM THE TWO MINDS: CONSCIOUS AND INNER. AND THE CONSCIOUS SHOULD NOT BE

UNDER THE ILLUSION THAT IT HAS THE POWER TO TELL THE INNER MIND WHAT TO DO.

Understanding the physical processes that occur during contact is the essential element in the ability to evaluate results, relate consequences to causes, determine what is missing, what needs correction, what will work and what will not, and what will succeed in replacing illusions with reality in the inner mind. But the rules and recommendations given thus far should not be taken as restrictions under all conditions. There has to be freedom to use for the needs of the moment what under ideal circumstances would be considered undesirable.

chapter four other elasticities

Thus far the only elasticity that has been discussed has been that of the ball. It is admittedly very important as anyone discovers when hitting a ball that has lost some of its pressure, or even when using a brand that is either bouncier or the reverse of what a person happens to be accustomed to. The elasticity of the ball stores an important part of the energy of a hit. But there are other elasticities that store appreciable amounts of energy and ought to be looked into as well. They are the elasticities of the strings and of the frame of the racquet.

FAST RECOVERY OF THE STRINGS

While the strings do not absorb and store as much energy as the ball they have special importance because of having very little weight and internal friction. They also have a very fast recovery, much more so than the ball. So the strings are both the first to return to their original shape and the best at giving back a major part of the energy that they store. When they snap back they <u>increase ball speed</u> above the <u>carrying velocity</u> of the racquet, independent of, but in the same manner as the rounding out of the ball.

The early recovery of the strings causes an enhancement of the pace of the ball that tends to SEND IT OUT OF CONTACT with the racquet before the energy stored in other elements has also been reconverted into ball velocity. Since the elasticities of the ball and racquet store more than half of the total energy it is important to maximize recovery of their stored energies by ACCELERATING THE RACQUET THROUGH THE CONTACT INTERVAL. If there is no strength held in reserve to counter the impact and to maintain the forward acceleration, the recovery processes can become very inefficient.

The partially sequential operation of the elasticities (string, ball, and racquet) does not change the nature of the recovery process. It also does not change the formula that has been previously described for the enhancement of the pace of the ball. That formula refers to the cumulative overall effect and not separately to each individual elasticity. The maximum theoretical departing ball velocity is still oncoming ball velocity plus two times racquet velocity.

But the imperfect efficiencies of the equipment and of the techniques limit the recovery of energy to at best about sixty percent of what is theoretically available, and to much less than that if the principles of hitting are not observed or if the ball is hit very hard.

THE EFFECTS OF STRING TENSION

The tighter or shorter the strings the faster do they recover, but the less energy gets stored in them, the less is available for conversion into ball velocity, and the sooner is the limit of the string's elasticity reached. The effect of the elastic limit in this case is not inelastic stretching but mostly just a reduction in the amount of energy that the strings are able to store.

Conversely, the looser or longer the strings the greater is the percentage of the total amount of energy that can be stored in them and the longer will it take for the strings to recover (although still extremely quickly). There is another advantage to a longer recovery time for the strings: the recovery is more nearly simultaneous with that of the ball. However the strings are not elastic at all degrees of looseness. They have to be tight enough to be slightly stretched. Otherwise there is a great loss of energy in merely bringing the strings to a slightly stretched condition.

The fact that short or very tight strings store less energy than long or moderately tensioned strings, does not mean that the energy not taken up in the strings is lost. Most of the remainder is merely absorbed by the other less efficient elasticities: bending of the racquet and flattening of the ball.

There is more energy loss in these two because of the presence of more weight and internal friction than there is in the strings. Thus they convert a lower percentage of the stored energy into ball velocity than do the strings, but not to a degree that constitutes a serious problem. Jay Monroe, a scientist who wrote fine articles explaining the physics behind tennis phenomena, measured the loss in the strings at "..only 6% compared to the 45% for a tennis ball"**

Two other effects that go with various string tensions are changes in the degree of control and, very importantly, in the feel. These may or may not suit the player's preferences or style of play. Contrary to popular belief, the best control is not achieved at high tensions. That is because very tight strings reflect errors fairly accurately, somewhat as a mirror reflects light, whereas moderately tensioned strings tend to be more "forgiving". The chapter on "RACQUET ATTITUDE" contains an analysis of the rebound angle.

Strings at low or moderate tension have a cupping effect, putting more surface in contact with the ball and extending the contact interval. Both of these factors tend to improve control. According to a fine experimental study by the Davis Racquet Company,* strings at the moderately tight tension of a little above 60 pounds produced better accuracy than strings at higher or lower tensions.* The test was made in the small racquet era. The large types used today work best at somewhat tighter string tensions. It is a matter of response time: the longer the strings the greater the response time unless tension is increased proportionately.

An undesirable consequence of looseness is a corresponding increase in the amount of slippage between the horizontal

* *Victor Sports 1965*
**World Tennis*   *41*

and vertical strings. Slippage is the major factor of wear since the strings tend to cut through each other as they move back and forth in the stretching process during each hit. Recreational players often choose a tension that is tight enough so that the slippage is not excessive even after a normal slight loosening of the strings. Tournament players have strings replaced before they have loosened, and so can restring at the exact tension that works best for them.

Plastic inserts are available for placement at the cross points to minimize slippage. There is some loss in response due to the frictional losses that occur as the strings slide through the grooves of the devices. Strings slide over each over with much less friction and loss of energy than they do through the grooves of the inserts. The effect on the response of the strings is not appreciable unless more that about a half dozen inserts are used.

They can be cemented in place to eliminate frictional loss. But in that case it is probably better to omit the inserts and just cement the cross points. FAST SETTING CEMENTS SHOULD BE USED ONLY WITH EXTREME CAUTION IN A SUITABLE WORK PLACE (NOT ON AN UNPROTECTED PIECE OF FURNITURE). THERE SHOULD BE VERY GOOD VENTILATION. EYE PROTECTION AND THIN DISPOSABLE GLOVES ARE ADVISABLE. VISION CAN BE DAMAGED JUST AS EASILY BY A LITTLE CEMENT AS BY A HARD HIT TENNIS BALL.

ENERGY STORED IN RACQUET ELASTICITY

The racquet stores energy by becoming bent. The recovery of energy occurs as the frame snaps forward out of its bent back condition. The velocity of the forward rebound of the racquet head is additional to the overall forward movement of the frame. It thus adds to the velocity of the ball in the same manner as discussed for the rounding of the ball and the snapping back of the strings.

Although racquets of different sizes or materials may have the same elasticity they can differ in internal friction, affecting the efficiency, quickness of response, and damping characteristics. The preferences as to the material, stiffness, balance, and design of the racquet depend mostly on a person's game, likes, and dislikes. For instance, a person with a quick swing may like a stiff racquet with quick recovery, but then again may find the shock to the arm to be more unpleasant than with a flexible frame.

Large racquets and long strings store more energy but have more air resistance than do the lesser. And large frames have a large rotational inertia. This is also true of racquets that have extra weights at the edges of the frame. Rotational inertia is useful in countering torque on off center hits, but requires expenditure of extra strength and energy for any manipulation of the attitude of the racquet.

THE RECOVERY SEQUENCE

Since all the elasticities behave the same in terms of enhancing ball velocity above the overall velocity of the racquet it doesn't really matter which recovers first. One major preference is to recover energy first from the elasticity having the least loss. This does happen since the strings recover first and are also by far the most efficient.

Another preference is to recover as completely as possible from the elasticity that stores the most energy, which is the ball. But there is no way to exert any influence on the sequence of the processes other than to use the type of ball, racquet, strings, tension of strings, and manner of hitting that seem to give the best results.

PRACTICAL APPLICATIONS OF THEORY

The above discussions show that a knowledge of the behavior of elasticities can help a player refine techniques and optimize results. Other benefits include helping to identify, interpret, and correct flaws; understand the requirements for timing, acceleration of the racquet, follow-through, etc; and to recognize and avoid false cures. The knowledge can also help in interpreting the feel of the strokes, a very useful indicator as will become apparent in

succeeding chapters.

Many people assume, not unreasonably, that in an interval as small as that of contact it is not possible to have a sequence of discrete events such as the storage and return of energy by each of the three types of elasticities. Yet those events are there, and not only in tennis but in all other hitting sports as well. In golf and baseball the elasticities of the equipment are so slight that the storage and recovery of energy occur in a fraction of the time that it takes in tennis.

In baseball the wood fibers of the bat deflect very minutely and quickly. Nevertheless they function in the exact same manner in the storage and recovery processes as the strings of a racquet. The bending of the bat, of course, operates in the same way as the bending of the racquet. Note when bat meets ball the much greater velocity of the ball than that of the bat, and how the ball is well on its way before the bat has gone more than a little past contact in the forward swing.

THE MYSTERY OF THE DIFFICULTY OF LEARNING

Most recreational players have read or heard of most of even the fine points that coaches discuss when giving lessons. But incorporating those ideas into their games is an entirely different matter. Even a thorough knowledge of the nature of expert level strokes is not enough to enable a person to become or remain an accomplished tennis player.

Therefor, before going on in the following chapters to consider how a knowledge of the characteristics of elasticity can be used to refine current techniques it is well to study the impact of several important influences, and how they can either inhibit or promote improvement.

In the first chapter the anomaly was mentioned that bad tennis habits creep in very easily while desired corrections are made with great difficulty if at all. This would suggest that there is a special importance to understanding the means by which bad habits are generated and perpetuated.

COLD FACTS VS WISHFUL THINKING

A common source of many player's problems are visions of hits beyond athletic capabilities and physical realities, what is defined here for the purposes of this book as "ILLUSIONS". One typical illusion would have the ball disappear across the court as fast as thought. This might seem to evidence a disordered mind, but such desires not only control just about every shot of some otherwise very rational and intelligent recreational players but an occasional shot by the experts as well.

For people whose play is controlled at least in part by such notions, which includes most of us, results judged to be first rate by rational standards do not come close to measuring up to the much more compelling mental fancies. Understandably, the practical reality is considered to be an unacceptable substitute, not consciously but through the influence of subconscious motives.

Unless the illusions can be thoroughly understood and discredited the unrealistic expectations will continue to trigger the personal set of idiosyncrasies. This does not mean that coaches must then act as psychologists, but that players must become fully aware of the consequences of their impractical intentions, urges, and emotions.

Reality must come to be appreciated more than fantasy. Beyond that it is necessary to know which characteristics of stroke production are really synonymous with the best results. Thus the basis for change has to be a reasonably accurate intuitive or factual understanding of the principles (not patterns) of hitting, and the ability to recognize violations of the same.

INABILITY TO FACE THE FACTS

There seems to be more numerous wrong ways to do things in tennis than in any other sport. Some of the methods are so spectacular that there would be a great incentive for change if the player could merely accurately picture what the self and the swing looked like on each shot. But the inner eyes are not often educated eyes.

Another incentive for change would be to be able to assess and admit the extent by which the real results failed to meet the wild expectations. Unfortunately the reality of what actually happens is often far different from what the player believes happens.

The same can be said for what is physically possible and what many players mistakenly believe to be possible, or play

as if they seem to believe it were so. In light of some of inappropriate techniques one sees, and to an alarming extent uses, it is apparent that what is commonly expected of a stroke often amounts to illusions.

That remark is not intended to be derogatory of recreational tennis, but merely a necessary recognition of the fact that substantial numbers of people are blind to the complete irrationality of some of their techniques. They apparently lack, or pay no attention to, the feedback mechanisms by which the feel of their shots should exert their appropriate influence on subsequent execution.

Even the most inept players are likely to entertain hopes of acquiring the better shots some fine day. But giving up their unrealistic objectives is not part of their plans, however poor the current results and unpleasant the feel. When they realize that there is no prospect of achieving major improvement, no matter what means are tried, the inevitable result is withdrawal from tennis.

MENTAL PICTURES

Most players who have not seen themselves on video have serious misconceptions about how they actually play. They are apt to overestimate their degree of conformance to good style and to be only vaguely aware, if at all, of conspicuous deviations. And even seeing a replay on video seldom seems to equate to realistic evaluation, and almost never to eventual success in switching to preferable alternatives.

At the other end of the scale, if there isn't a fairly accurate awareness of how an exceptionally fine shot was just made there is little possibility of being able to make that fortunate event happen again, except accidentally. If there is an inaccurate idea of what the strokes and flaws look like, or insufficient feedback through monitoring the feel of the hit, or a lack of knowledge of what constitutes a good hit, it follows that there is little chance of making corrections. The awareness of the feel is an important factor in evaluating

a previous shot, controlling the intents for a coming shot, or developing the images for an improved technique.

In order to be able to identify and correct flaws, or to understand what it was that produced an exceptionally fine result, it is desirable to be able to visualize and re-enact the complete action in the last stroke as if having watched it as an observer or experienced it as the player. This calls for reconstruction of what the shot looked like from remembrances of what it felt like. The term to be used here to cover the reconstruction in the mind of a good or bad action, or to picture a coming action either as it should occur or is intended to occur, will be "VISUALIZATION".

This invoking of an image of the past or of the future can be very useful, but it is not as easy to accomplish as one may think. It is in a way only a substitute for the use of video recordings. But it has special advantages:

    1. Can be used at any time.

    2. Can be more complete because the mental picture covers every detail, and in three dimensional form.

    3. Introduces a fourth dimension in that there is a mental equivalent of the feel.

    4. Can be projected for a coming stroke instead of being limited to recalling the past.

One way to practice visualizations is to once in a while try to mimic the entire sequence of a stroke just exactly as it happened, not sparing a single trivial or unpleasant detail, but not exaggerating them either. On each re-enactment or visualization consider in the background of the mind whether it would be pleasant or unpleasant to re-experience that shot done the same way. Disregarding the feel and its causes, and letting subconscious impulses control every shot, is exactly what happens over and over without awareness or intent.

Visualizing a replay of those situations in which a shot was flubbed can be especially useful. It can be very revealing as to errors of both commission and omission. In some cases the most valuable outcome of such a mental review is a downward re-evaluation of the satisfactions derived from an apparently effective hit. Results alone will not suffice to compensate for the perpetuation of techniques that do not also have satisfying feel, or that compare poorly with what is really possible.

Correctly visualizing how a stroke should look equates to success in installing the mental controls required to hit that way. A piecemeal approach to the building of a more desirable style may then not be necessary. In applying this method the procedure amounts to something like getting the body to adopt the intents and techniques used in the mental picture. But correct visualization is not easy, as covered under the next sub-heading, "VISUALIZATION DIFFICULTIES".

Preparatory visualizations put the intentions under the control of more ambitious yet more rational expectations than those conjured up by habits, urges, fears, illusions, unsound ideas, unnecessary doubts, and irrational expectations. Taking control away from these all-powerful influences is an essential prerequisite to change.

As the skills at evaluating the last hit improve there will be automatic refinement of the concepts and intentions for the next. This is extremely important since a stroke cannot be better than the idea of it. The process of progressive refinement of the concepts has the additional advantage that it continues to operate in raising the level of a game even as the person advances to successively higher levels of play. Unfortunately for self-satisfaction, but fortunately for continued progress, there is also a simultaneous heightened awareness of the remaining shortcomings.

THE DIFFICULTIES OF VISUALIZATION

It might be expected that it would be easy to execute flawless strokes mentally even if the real strokes are far from being so. But that is not the case. Strangely, visualized normal speed strokes contain the same flaws as the real. Getting the racquet to do the right things mentally is as difficult as getting it to do so actually. Conversely, straightening out the visualized strokes will simultaneously do the same for the physical, but only if the diagnosis of the affliction and the prescription for the cure are both correct.

So a principle task is to straighten out the concepts, intentions, and satisfactions. They must be made both valid and compatible. The fact that these items all have a mental or emotional basis is one explanation for the ineffectiveness of the mechanical "how-to" drills   in changing established games. Making the correct changes in the mental factors is what this book is really about.

The fact that visualized strokes tend to have the same characteristics and inflexibility as the real is more helpful than not. It makes it possible to work on problems mentally. A new type of visualization can be introduced to make the task easier: "SLOW MOTION VISUALIZATION", abbreviated "SMV". Some of the reasons why it can be of help are as follows:

(1) A slow paced swing is the antithesis of emotional and muscled shots.

(2) The smooth relaxed flow is what is found in really fine strokes.

(3) Most importantly, many compensations and idiosyncrasies are somehow automatically excluded. This is exactly what one hopes to be able to do but finds next to impossible to accomplish otherwise, either mentally or actually. If such corrections can be made to the mental images then the barriers to improvement to the real swing may also be removed.

It is advisable to use mental practice to reset the automatic controls, whatever they are and wherever centered, instead of wasting a lot of time and energy in a futile attempt to drill new habits into unknowing and unwilling muscles. With "SMV" it is possible to visualize making a stroke without the eccentricities that invariably seem to accompany full speed performance, either in actuality or via regular speed visualization. Initially the SLOW MOTION VISUALIZATIONS will take some time. Ultimately they may take almost no time at all.

One cure for "illusions" is progressively better visualizations. In a sense a stroke is merely the set of images and intentions that dictate a set of mechanical responses. Important factors in the nature of mental control are the images that are missing, as well as those that are not but ought to be.

MENTAL PRACTICE OF SEQUENCES

A further extension of the process of visualization is to practice a sequence of strokes mentally: imagining moving into position, getting body and racquet ready, swinging freely but not wildly without the slightest bit of push, evaluating the swing for the need for adjustments, repeating the stroke to iron out difficulties, etc. This could be followed by imagining a return from the opponent in a way that is difficult to handle, forming the intentions and visualizations for the required swing, and so on.

ANTICIPATIONS AND PREPARATIONS

Some of the most damaging differences between what did and what should happen will very often be in the preparation for the shot. The plain fact is that the inadequate extent to which the mind, feet, body, arm, and racquet are made ready often precludes a genuinely good stroke before the forward swing has even started.

Much lack of talent is merely inadequate or inappropriate preparation. The first and most important phase of preparation is mental. But most players are too busy agonizing

51

over the results of past events, or allowing illusions to float through the mind about the results expected from the next, to do any anticipating of the manner of getting ready to accomplish a satisfactory hit.

Examples of the consequences of inadequate preparation are the use of improvisations in the grip, swing, hitting point, etc, to compensate for a happenstance initial position and a compromised readiness for the shot. If a player is unaware of inadequate readiness, not just ostensibly in terms of having the racquet back but also in terms of getting the body involved and intending to make a good hit, a lot of time can be wasted in looking for remedies for nonexistent flaws while failing to see those that are real.

chapter six

circumventions, coercions, expedients, compensations, deprivations

Ideally each element of a stroke should have value in one of four ways:

1. By being a directly useful function.

2 By fulfilling or helping to fulfill a directly useful function.

2. By being a part of the preparation for a directly useful function.

3. By being a natural ending for a useful function.

Any particular action if not actually justifiable in any of the above ways should at least be neutral in the sense of not detracting from or interfering with elements that are useful. In reality no stroke can be executed that well, but even with an allowance for a large degree of imperfection it is still hard to explain the strange antics and flourishes that dominate the strokes of many players. In order to find the means to deal with these personal eccentricities it is necessary to analyze the rationale behind their origin and use.

INSTINCTIVE CORRECTIONS

Unexpectedly enough though, there can be useful aspects to apparently purposeless habits. When a useful element of a stroke is omitted or is not executed properly the natural result would be a miss-hit unless something not normal to a good stroke is inserted as a remedy, usually in the form of

easy-way-out expedients. The term "compensations" will be used here for these automatic adjustments or manipulations introduced mainly to avoid the harmful results of real or perceived deficiencies in techniques or capabilities.

Such makeshift remedies are just by the nature of their origin created not consciously and wisely but automatically and unwittingly. They will therefore often be something that is a far cry from what the coach would recommend, or even what the player would voluntarily select. An unfortunate corollary is that such adjustments are in effect merely crutches that make it possible to live with the underlying problems instead of having to get rid of them.

THE WORKINGS OF COMPENSATIONS

It is obvious, for example, that if a player is in a wrong position but swings as if from a proper position the ball will have to go wrong. If the basic problem, the position, is not recognized and remedied then some of the correctness must be taken out of the swing. Suitable modifications to the stroke are introduced which, though perhaps bizarre in themselves, make it possible to get by with being in an improper position.

But if a hit is made under conditions that are not compatible with a decent swing then the player is developing and reinforcing compromised techniques. It is by this type of circumstance that idiosyncrasies become permanent and prominent characteristics of players' games. There are enough problems in getting the most out of a particular style without saddling it with compromises which it make possible to retain harmful or at least unproductive peculiarities.

As a corollary, seemingly extraneous manipulations may in reality be easy-way-out compensations for flaws that the player may not even be aware of. Therefor the recognition of an extraneous manipulation as being a compensation could be of use in identifying an underlying fault. At any

rate compensations usually cannot be ignored. They almost always have harmful effects of their own on the stroke, as well as the potential to generate additional compensations. No swing is perfect, and each imperfect item may require corresponding accommodations in the stroke.

SUPPRESSING COMPENSATIONS

It is generally of no avail to merely tell a student to get rid of a seemingly meaningless manipulation of the racquet, or elbow, or feet, etc. If the action is in fact of the nature of a compensation, then the more rational approach would be to try to make the mannerism unnecessary by eliminating the responsible basic flaws. Otherwise the player will be compelled to retain the compensations, not because of stupidity or stubbornness but out of necessity.

If the basic flaw cannot be identified it may be possible to discover it by the following means. Consciously repress the seemingly meaningless eccentricity. Do not make any other changes and do not worry about the consequences. Let the ball go wrong if it will. Then search back to try to find the one or more basic problems in the execution that caused the ball to go astray, and for which result the now suppressed compensation had provided corrections. This may not be easy because flaws usually exist in layers.

An additional task is to also determine whether the ostensible flaw is a desirable feature that ought to be retained or a defect that ought to be eliminated. One of the most notable examples of this type of dilemma pertained to the Western forehand grip, which at one time was thought to be an anomaly that anybody taking lessons should be compelled to discontinue. And now it is one of the popular standards.

GENERATING COMPROMISES IN THE STROKE

The usual reasons why players find themselves compelled to compromise their strokes are a desire for an unattainable result, an inner awareness of incompatibilities between elements, or the feeling of a need to make up for a personal athletic inadequacy. The modifications are automatic, not pre-planned, and are therefor little affected by attempts to impose conscious mental controls.

As an example, an incompatibility can occur when a server turns the body around to face the net too much or too soon. The grip may then have to be shifted in mid-swing so as to be compatible with the effectively open stance. The compensation may not be known to the player or be apparent to an observer. But if some such adjustment is not made the racquet will be faced in the wrong direction. So an accommodation is necessary to compensate for the wrong racquet attitude arising out of the basic defect: the swivel of the body. Thus one defect is converted into at least two.

When corrective manipulations are introduced on a one-time basis in emergencies those actions are expedients rather than compensations. Both the compensations and the expedients can be considered to have a useful function, even though merely that of diminishing the penalties for violations of the basic principles behind stroke production.

Occasionally a perceived problem will be just a misconception as to the technique required to produce a certain result. Or it may be an imagined defect. An example is the feeling of not being physically strong enough to hit with good pace, and of the need to resort to enhanced efforts and special manipulations to obtain a ball velocity that in reality should not be a problem even for people with frail physiques.

Justified or not, the "I can't" attitude automatically causes the introduction of the same compensations as for the real deficiency. However, the majority of problems are real enough, although not exactly easy to identify. Henry Ford is quoted as having said "Whether you think you can or think you can't, you're right"

A SENSE OF DEPRIVATION
Players develop a sense of dependence on habits, even those

that are bad. So to remove one basic flaw and just one related compensation requires not only the suppression of those two largely automatic actions but then putting up with a feeling of deprivation of each of them.

So even in the case of a simple flaw and one associated compensation, and with no interactions with other elements of the stroke, there are multiple forces prejudicing the player against any change. Notice, for instance, how hard it seems to be for players to get rid of the useless habit of dipping slightly at the knees just before the toss for the serve.

The difficulties are further compounded by the fact that the faults, compensations, and deprivations interact with each other to create timing problems. Added to this are the difficulties of learning the desired new habits and suppressing rejection responses. It is obvious that when players allow a faulty technique to become habit they thereby create an almost insurmountable chain of obstacles to advancement.

By the above reasoning the total number of forces opposing the removal of a single flaw and one associated compensation is at least ten, and could be much more:

Remove (unlearn) the flaw as well as the associated compensation. (2)

Overcome two feelings of deprivation. (2)

Learn two replacement techniques. (2)

Overcome at least four timing complications caused by the two removals and two replacements. (4)

When a new technique creates feelings of deprivation or rejection there will be a strong urge to get rid of them by retreating to the comfort of the old habits. Unfortunately it is not likely that many players will become aware on their own that the cure does not come about through merely refusing to kowtow to the demands of habit. Players must

progress in a positive sense by developing and recognizing satisfactions in the feel and manner of execution of really good hits.

CIRCUMVENTIONS

Problems and bad habits never seem to fade away but just come back in new disguise. So although urges, flaws, or compensations may at times appear to have been conquered they often return in modified form, and the players are right back where they started from, out in the cold again. While reversion to the exact previous techniques may not actually take place it might just as well occur because the old habits and results are there as if they had never been gone.

What happens is that the player may succeed in using an improved technique but is nevertheless very uncomfortable in living with it, largely because of the many feelings of deprivation and rejection, as discussed above. It therefor seems necessary to revert to the old ways without being very open about it. In other words, the new methods are ostensibly retained but means are found to circumvent them and bring back the old habits in disguised form. This helps explain why initial progress is often quickly followed by a sudden letdown.

An example of a circumvention is when a person with an inappropriate grip successfully switches to a new, but then may have control problems because the attitude of the racquet has been changed too. In this case the change of grip may be quite proper, but it is not compatible with the old flaws and compensations. Ordinarily a means will be invented to sort of regress, not to the former grip but to the former attitude. This could possibly be done by a simple turn of the wrist. Compatibility with the old habits is restored. So the old problems are likely to remain even though the grip stays as corrected. A by-product of such difficulties is a loss of confidence in the worth of legitimate remedies.

A CARD-HOUSE OF COMPENSATIONS

Consider a more complicated possible set of compensations. Conjecture that the real initial flaw on a forehand consists of an eagerness to demolish the ball, and that it results in an extra quick swing. The fast swing in turn causes an early hit, which puts the contact point too far out in front.

The arm has little remaining forward extension in the forward area and must begin to travel prematurely in the roundhouse or sideways direction. The body may interfere with the sideward movement of the arm in the latter stages of the swing. So the player may then unconsciously pull the "net" foot away from the path of the ball to eliminate interference by the body. But this rotates the body away from the hit, further opening the stance and aggravating the roundhouse and its effects.

If the grip used is for a swing from a sideways stance the attitude of the racquet would now be wrong. A new compensation would be required for this factor, and it could take the form of rotating the wrist upward to give the racquet a proper attitude. The wrist may also have to be bent backward to face the racquet in the desired forward direction. At the end of the swing the wrist might then be returned to normal by being rolled forward quickly, possibly accompanied with a simultaneous lifting of the elbow.

The most visible faults in this case would be the sideward movements of the racquet and the front foot, and the lift of the elbow. However the basic causes would be the quick swing and early hit, and these in turn would have a psychological origin in the emotional urge to demolish the ball.

While the above sequence is only conjectural it is entirely realistic in respect to how problems and compensations are built up, and in how they can cause a game to fall apart. A coach looking at the described stroke would probably not be able to deduce the relationships as just conjectured, and of course they would differ considerably from individual to

individual. But it can be seen that piecemeal attention to the visible faults would not do much good.

It is easy to see that a person who develops just a very few basic faults can soon end up with a game consisting mostly of compensations. Granted that the use of a patterned swing would temporarily eliminate the major physical flaws all at once, but it would not address the basic causes and the feelings of deprivation and rejection. Reversion could be practically guaranteed.

NON-STANDARD NEED NOT BE NOT GOOD

Sometimes a seeming flaw is actually a refinement. An example is the habit of some top level players of stopping the swing on the serve a little more than half way down in front of the body, in other words cutting down on the follow-through. But it may also be noticed that during the actual hit the expert will probably be bearing down as if fully intending a free follow-through.

The usual main purpose of the deviation from good technique is to get ready as soon as possible for the return. By stopping the swing short there is some loss in power. At times it may be advisable to sacrifice speed in order to ensure readiness for a possible sizzling reply from the opponent, but at the risk of even more sizzle.

CHAIN OF GOOD CONSEQUENCES

The same instincts that introduce compensations for wrong body position, swing of arm, etc, will also work to introduce accommodations for corrected body position, swing of arm, etc. However this is likely to happen only if the changes are based on the combination of educated concepts, attitudes, intentions, and satisfactions. It is not enough to rely on the traditional approaches such as repetitive drill, emulation of patterns, or piecemeal correction of mannerisms. Strokes are built from the ground up, not from the top down.

Some flourishes are just that and nothing more, neither adding to nor subtracting from the effectiveness of the

stroke, but merely satisfying a habit, image, or emotion. If the aesthetic effect is not too bad, and if no great amount of energy is wasted, timing affected, or strains created, then such flourishes can be allowed to remain so that more attention can be given to higher priority problems.

"COERCIONS" AFTER CONTACT

A different type of attempted correction has neither effectiveness nor a real function since it occurs after contact has ended, when the ball is no longer under the control of the racquet and may be well on its way toward its destination. This type of behavior can be called "post-contact coercion". It is not necessarily harmless.

Examples of such actions in another sport, bowling, are the agonized contortions that many bowlers go through as the ball rolls steadily on, completely unaffected by the telepathic attempts to influence its path and destination. This particular type of physical agonizing is usually called "body English". In the case of the bowler the "body English" has no beneficial or harmful effect other than providing a little extra exercise. Basically similar maneuvers are sometimes seen in tennis on both serves and ground strokes, but are usually less visible because of the fast pace of the action.

HARMFUL EFFECTS OF COERCION

A post-contact coercion that seems harmless in itself may nevertheless not be tolerable, if only because it is unwise to be telegraphing remonstrances toward the last shot when there is a need to be getting ready for the next. More importantly, the coercive motion will probably not be entirely harmless if it was started or perhaps merely prepared for before contact was broken. In that case there will be interaction with the timing of other elements. An additional possibility is that a coercion may be used as a substitute for a needed real remedy. A post-contact coercion can therefor be much worse than just a useless gesture.

In citing specific examples of such attempted coercions only

the type that might affect contact need be brought up. One common instance is holding back on the racquet at the end of the swing, as if to influence the ball similarly and keep it from sailing out. But this action has to commence earlier in the swing, and will therefor result in the slowing down of the racquet before and during contact. Spin and pace are reduced, and even if the ball lands in court the bounce is likely to be rather nice for the opponent to hit off of.

Another example is the turning of the racquet face over or under at the end of a swing, usually with the intention of instructing the ball how to behave in the vicinity of the net. However this type of manipulation is not always post-contact coercion. It could also be the natural ending of a compensation initiated during contact, or a part of some special technique needed for a specific purpose.

An action that may occur after contact, although it often occurs during, is a downward pull on the racquet at the end of the serve to persuade the ball to drop similarly downward as it passes the net. The results of stopping the racquet short or pulling it down are usually counter to the intent. They tend to preclude the topspin that does help to bring the ball down in court.

While there are some post-contact gestures that are no more than personal idiosyncrasies, most of them arise out of a desire to make after-the-deed corrections for something perceived to be undesirable in either the execution or the impending unpalatable and unavoidable result. Consequently the real cure for post-contact manipulations is to try to eliminate the cause of the perceived need.

Once a coercion is discovered, and if it seems to have harmful consequences, then the task is to identify and eliminate the cause rather than the resultant problem. Correction via the typical emulation-of-patterns type of approach will not stick because it is based on appearances, not causes.

Chapter seven — follow-through

One of the elements of a stroke most intimately related to the contact interval is the follow-through. The close relationship comes about because the acceleration of the racquet necessary to maximize the length of the contact interval is a major factor in determining the nature of the follow-through.

But it must seem strange to the reader that we already turn to the tag end of a stroke, by which time the business part has ended, without first having discussed all of the components of a swing in a more logical sequence. The explanation is that it is not the purpose of this book to develop or recommend particular patterns or techniques. The goal is to create the understandings that can be used to improve the existing techniques via better use of the characteristics of elasticity and the principles of hitting.

An arrangement of topics that provides for an orderly discussion of factors involved with the nature of the hit seems to be the most efficient way to develop the understandings needed to begin the progress toward higher levels of play. The concepts are general in nature and are not restricted to specific styles. It is not necessary, for instance, to employ a certain stance or grip before it becomes possible to apply the already discussed concepts of elasticity, visualizations, illusions, and compensations to whatever techniques the reader happens to be using.

FOLLOW-THROUGH JUST HAPPENS

The interval of contact was previously discussed in some detail, and was described as the only part of the stroke that had any direct effect on the behavior of the ball. However this should not be taken to mean that a person can feel free to do anything at all in either the preparation or the follow-through. What happens before contact should produce or lead up to what should happen during. What happens after is the natural consequence of both. The hit, whether done rightly or wrongly, thus depends on the preparation, and both largely determine the follow-through.

The ball is constantly gaining velocity during contact and hence is moving fastest just after contact ends. Accelerating the racquet to try to have it keep up with the ball increases the tendency of the racquet to overshoot the mark, extending the follow-through.

Conversely, if there is no acceleration into the follow-through the racquet is slowing down during contact. This creates serious inefficiencies in both the storage and recovery of energy. Even a constant forward momentum of the racquet diminished by the momentum of the ball at impact translates into a slowing down of the racquet.

The real follow-through cannot affect the ball directly because it doesn't begin until contact is broken. It is therefor not an end in itself, but is significant only in so far as an improper ending of the stroke starts before the ball leaves the racquet or is the result of improper execution during the hit. A follow-through that is made to conform to a pattern is highly likely to cause troubles in the business part of the stroke. Trying to straighten out the swing by means of the follow-through is a "tail-wagging-the-dog" approach. The main concern should be the hit. The follow-through can take care of itself.

Whatever beneficial activities occur during contact cannot start or end in that very short period of time, and neither can the undesirable. So an idiosyncrasy during the follow-through, when it doesn't matter, may very well have existed, been started, or at least been prepared for before or during contact, when it most certainly does matter.

Follow-through is good, but only to the extent that it is the product of proper racquet acceleration, momentum, and reinforcement. It has the passive function of providing an easy and natural finish to the swing, hopefully well executed, and that is all. It is neither a means to an end nor a path to a cure.

However it can have significance as a symptom of good or bad execution, or of various types of problems such as stopping or slowing the swing, improper timing, stance, footwork, hitting point, etc. Forcing the racquet to finish at a prescribed end point, will not automatically optimize the previous elements of a stroke.

THE SWING END POINT CANNOT BE DEFINED
The classic ending of a ground stroke has frequently been defined as having the racquet head, or the front edge of it, point in the direction of the hit. But that rule is too restrictive and unnatural for those players who do not need to observe exaggerated requirements in the follow-through

to control harmful tendencies in the swing.

The preoccupation with an intended ending has the adverse effect of focusing attention on a nonfunctional detail that does not deserve any direct attention in itself. As long as the hit is proper the player ought to be free to have the racquet end up as occurs naturally and takes the least effort, attention, and time. It is unfair to ask novices to subscribe to theories concerning a stylized ending that the pros themselves do not use and would find burdensome and counterproductive.

However the player should also be aware of the dangers inherent in not keeping the racquet moving in a consistently forward direction during contact. Any changes in the heading or speed of the racquet (except as needed for spin) may result in those changes being actually initiated during contact, with undesirable effects on the processes that are proceeding therein.

THE SHORT FOLLOW-THROUGH VS THE LONG
Many people with deficient follow-through think that they understand how long it should be, and that they fully observe the requirements. But the execution is almost always less extensive than the intentions. Unfortunately the intentions themselves are usually based on an incomplete knowledge of the principles involved. To inexpert players carrying the racquet forward to anything approaching the adequate is likely to feel highly exaggerated, something to be tolerated in practice under the eye of the coach but not to be risked in actual play with a point at stake.

A common motive for stopping the racquet short is that a quick termination of the swing equates in the mind to a quick flight of the ball to its destination, an idea quite at odds with reality. Another reason is a subconscious fear that the extra pace obtained with a long follow-through will increase the probability that the ball will be misdirected, and to a greater degree. But stopping the racquet short has adverse effects on the direction, depth, and spin of the ball, and on the storage and recovery of energy. Although the ball will not then have the speed to go very far astray there will be an increased probability that it will go astray.

There is greater harm in cutting contact short than in continuing the follow-through too long. In view of this danger some overemphasis on follow-through, as is fairly common when coaches demonstrate the standard patterns, probably amounts to being in error on the safe side. However extending the follow-through too far can be a disadvantage too, as will be shown.

A means of making some use of the fear of hitting out freely is to consider the fear as an indication that the subconscious mind may have recognized a flaw whose consequences would be magnified by a normal follow-through. This sets up the situation, as discussed in the chapter on "compensations", where there is a double chance of improvement: find and replace the flaw and then the related compromises may be made to disappear also.

THE PROBLEM OF THE POSE
Some players, particularly those with "schooled" strokes, compound the problem of prematurely curtailing the swing by then paradoxically holding the end position too long. This is discrimination against what is useful in favor of mere display. There is then the double penalty of both compromising the contact interval and also delaying the start of the preparation for the next shot.

Although some people hold the end position too long most do the opposite: start to get ready for the next shot before sufficiently satisfying the requirements for the present. It is therefor risky policy to advise players who already do not carry the swing far enough that an extended follow-through is a luxury in which it may be unwise to indulge.

But if more time than advisable is spent on the termination of the current stroke then the ball had better be put away. Otherwise the opponent is given lot of extra time to do the same. There may not then be a need to worry about a next swing. It is therefor sometimes advisable to compromise by taking a little off both the follow-through of the present shot and the preparation for the next.

Either choice may weaken a player's strokes, and the opponent may then be able to come on all the more strong. At the expert level any weakness is likely to be taken advantage of, and any slight unpreparedness for a return apt to be noticed and exploited. A player must not only be ready but must be ready for any type of return. The one for which there is the least readiness is the one most likely to come along. Therefor, the compromises to the follow-through that have to be made as expedients should not be continued when the pressure is less severe and there is time to use more optimum preparation and execution.

THE EXAMPLE OF THE PROS

A common misconception is that the pros cut their follow-through short too. Quite often they do, but careful observation will reveal that an adequate acceleration of the racquet through contact is usually observed. Only then does the direction of racquet travel change, perhaps with some abruptness. The momentum of the racquet is not particularly easy to overcome, and the experts do not waste much energy trying to stop it. On ground strokes they tend to accomplish the purpose by changing the racquet's direction. This can be done with less effort than is required to stop the motion entirely.

Casual viewers, while perhaps noting that the end of a stroke did not resemble a traditional follow-through, are generally not similarly observant of the behavior of the racquet during contact. They may thus mistakenly attribute to the business part of the stroke the characteristics that pertain mostly to what happened after contact had ended.

Observation of just the forward motion of the racquet will usually reveal that even when the expert players show some signs of stopping or diverting it too quickly they have by that time carried it through much farther than do the players at lower levels.

While the pros cannot allow more than minor compromises in the functional elements of a stroke they are under intense pressure to be ready for the next shot. They are therefor at least as careful to avoid using any excess of style in the follow-through as to get a good recovery of energy during contact. This is evidenced by their ability to hit with heavy pace and still move comparatively unhurriedly to an ideal spot to get properly ready for the return.

In spite of the emphasis that has been placed on an adequate follow-through obtained by continuing the acceleration of the racquet through contact, one standard precaution is in order: not to overdo it. Forcing the racquet to continue the follow-through farther than necessary will provide diminishing returns in the amount of additional pace on the ball, may introduce unnaturalness, cause a loss of balance and a lack of readiness for the next shot, and require excess effort. Doing whatever is needed for an optimum hit will ensure that too much emphasis will not be placed on a nonfunctional element such as follow-through.

Chapter eight roundhouse

The slowing or even stopping of the forward movement of the racquet have already been mentioned as habits that make for an inefficient contact interval. Another common flaw that slows the forward movement is roundhouse: swinging the racquet in a curved path around the body rather than forward in the direction of the hit. If it occurs only after contact it has no influence on the results.

Top players are often guilty of roundhouse also, but they generally do not allow a curved termination of the swing to intrude on the contact interval to any significant degree, except when they too succumb to emotions or pressure, or are not playing very well. Even in properly executed strokes the forward component of the swing usually diminishes rapidly, and the sideward becomes correspondingly larger, very soon after the racquet gets past the hitting point.

GOING IN TWO DIRECTIONS AT THE SAME TIME
The horizontal motion of a racquet can be described as being made up of two components at right angles to each other: forward and sideward. When the racquet is moving straight forward the sideward component is zero. But when the motion is roundhouse the sideward component can be larger than the forward, and the latter may even drop to zero.

If roundhouse intrudes on the contact interval it reduces forward racquet motion and resultant ball velocity just as effectively as if the swing were simply slowed down or stopped. The racquet is then less and less able to keep up

❖❖❖❖❖❖❖❖❖❖❖❖❖❖❖❖❖❖❖❖❖❖❖❖❖❖❖❖❖❖

with the accelerating ball. So contact and the storage and recovery of energy are terminated prematurely.

When roundhouse is present the horizontal travel and the horizontal attitude of the racquet are continuously changing, and so can become somewhat indeterminate. The racquet tends to roll over as the racquet travels around the body. So the vertical attitude is also affected. Control can be very erratic and the path of the ball uncertain. It can be seen that roundhouse is likely to result in a powerless, unreliable hit.

The normal reaction of a player plagued with the disappointing speed and unpredictable direction of the ball is to hit ever more compulsively, which in turn will further accentuate the roundhouse and its effects. Violent exertions seldom solve problems or confer benefits, but are pretty sure to aggravate old troubles and create some that are new.

THE MANY ORIGINS OF ROUNDHOUSE
Roundhouse is one of the most prevalent of faults. It can be a serious problem even in strokes where it would seem that there would be little likelihood of it occurring, such as in the serve and even the volley. The effects there will be discussed more completely in the chapter on the "SERVE".

The flaw is difficult to cure because it has a multitude of origins, and usually in combination: jumping in a circular manner, not shifting the body forward into the shot, pulling the body backward, holding the arm stiff and swinging the racquet by rotating the body, trying to move the racquet with a greater speed than the strength of the arm is capable of achieving, swinging in a tired or lazy manner, pulling the elbow in, swinging the "net" foot back or the "fence" foot

❖❖❖❖❖❖❖❖❖❖❖❖❖❖❖❖❖❖❖❖❖❖❖❖❖❖❖❖❖❖

forward during the stroke, not understanding the nature of a hit or the requirements of the contact interval, turning too much or too soon to get ready for the next shot or to watch the other side of the court and the path of the ball, etc. (The "net" foot is the one nearest to the net, "fence" nearest to the back fence.)

When a swing is made at maximum reach the racquet can not go forward easily, and therefor has to go around. The roundhouse gets to be even more pronounced if the hit is also made forward of the body (toward the net). So pace and control suffer badly. Yet, when players have to chase down a very wide ball, and therefor have to hit with a very extended arm, the hitting point is usually too far forward of the body. If the hitting point is moved back to the proper location on such shots the time available for the swing is increased, the reach is maximized, and the quality of the hit is likely to be much improved.

The problems on wide balls are almost always compounded by a very short backswing, a hurried forward swing, and a premature turn to face the net. This partially explains the high percentage of errors and weak returns. To get good results the backswing must be early, the stroke almost leisurely, and the hit made a little later, if anything, than on a normal shot. The turn to face the net should not occur until after the hit.

At the other extreme, when the racquet is held in too close to the body, it travels in a tight circle and <u>veers rapidly</u>

❖❖❖❖❖❖❖❖❖❖❖❖❖❖❖❖❖❖❖❖❖❖❖❖❖❖❖❖❖❖❖❖❖❖

toward the side after the midpoint of the swing. The side-ward component of the swing in the vicinity of the hitting zone is then high and the forward component deficient.

Roundhouse can also be caused by swinging too soon for such reasons as poor timing, emotional execution, and making up for lost time due to late preparation or a late start of the forward swing. The consequent changes in racquet velocity, attitude, and direction can each have serious effects on pace and control.

There can even be situations where some types of round-house occur because they are mistakenly assumed to be embellishments. For instance, an apparently harmless or even decorative upward and sideward flourish of the racquet at the end of the swing may actually amount to roundhouse during contact. In such cases the player probably doesn't have a remote inkling that the cherished pleasant flourish at the end of the swing, instead of being a stylish and rhythmic enhancement, is roundhouse in disguise.

It is easier to fall into the habit of hitting roundhouse from an open stance than from a closed. But quite a number of expert players at the tournament level hit forehands from a fairly open stance and yet do not generally hit with excessive roundhouse. The hitting point, timing, development of racquet momentum, etc., have to be just about optimum to hit well from that position. Some extra strength of the arm is also required. For the latter reason women players tend not to hit from a true open stance as much as men. On the backhand roundhouse is very difficult to avoid if the stance is at all open.

ROUNDHOUSE IN BASEBALL
In baseball, as could be expected with the much heavier bat used and the suddenness of the swing, the players are even less likely to succeed than in tennis in having the bat travel almost entirely in the direction of the hit during contact. A roundhouse swing is therefor very much more common in

❖❖❖❖❖❖❖❖❖❖❖❖❖❖❖❖❖❖❖❖❖❖❖❖❖❖❖❖❖

baseball than in tennis, even at the professional level.

Occasionally the bat is swung around with all the violent effort that the player can muster, sometimes to the extent that the body is noticeably retreating backward as the bat goes forward. This is a violation of the principles of hitting, and unfortunately not only are the elastic processes the same as in tennis but so also are the penalties that go with improper execution.

FIX THE CAUSE TO GET RID OF THE EFFECT

The task of curing roundhouse is formidable. It is first necessary to learn to feel whether or not it is present. This is not at all easy because most players have not learned to visualize or interpret the feel of their hits, and because roundhouse often occurs for only a brief instant late in the stroke when the attention can have been switched to the other court. Although it may not be easy to detect if it occurs late in the swing it will probably still have grossly detrimental effects on the shot.

For a cure it is particularly useful to think in terms of getting ready for a solid hit, since if roundhouse is present the body is almost certainly being prepared for roundhouse, not for a proper forward swing. So committing the body early will reduce the chances of a switch to roundhouse later on. In fact, getting completely prepared for a good hit will help in suppressing many other types of bad habits as well. A good place to start the cure is to re-establish the "hitting plane", "swing distance", and hitting point with the drills in "APPENDIX B".

The progress can be enhanced if the player has a working knowledge of what constitutes a good hit, is aware of the

◆◆◆◆◆◆◆◆◆◆◆◆◆◆◆◆◆◆◆◆◆◆◆◆◆◆◆◆◆◆◆◆

nature of roundhouse, and can therefor identify probable causes. It should be noted that in the list of suggestions above it is not being recommended that the player should merely be told to straighten out the swing. People seldom deliberately use a circular swing so they can't deliberately discontinue it. Roundhouse is a result, not a cause, and it is always the cause that has to be eliminated before it is possible to get rid of the result. Once it is there, however, it causes other consequences.

Although rotation of the body can deteriorate into round-house some rotation has to be present to allow for a free movement of the arm, assist in the acceleration of the racquet, and promote naturalness. Body rotation is in fact needed toward the end of the swing on the forehand to move the body and shoulder out of the way of the arm. Hitting with no participation rotation-wise by the body can be just as bad as hitting with too much.

Although there are widely different styles of stroke production all have the common requirement of good timing. The standard concept of it as consisting of just meeting the ball at the most appropriate hitting point is wrong. The job is much more complicated than that. All of the many internal elements of a stroke must also be sequenced and optimized with great precision within the overall pattern. The actual hit will be adversely affected if any element is not readied, started, interleaved, developed, and ended satisfactorily at precisely the right times.

If any action is mistimed, even a quirk or an expedient, the essential initial conditions for succeeding elements may not be set up properly, initiating a ripple effect. The elements that come later may not be able to fulfill their functions because of being squeezed out of their normal sequence, thereby interfering with the timing of still other elements. This is evident in the uncoordinated appearance of the strokes of unskilled players, even when the racquet arrives at the exactly correct hitting point at the right time.

TIMING INVOLVES MORE THAN THE HITTING POINT
There are two types of timing, internal and external. Internal timing is involved with the mechanics of the swing and the hit. External timing consists of coordinating the internal operation with the arrival of the ball.

In an ideal sense external timing should not be permitted to influence the nature of the stroke or the internal timing, but should just allow them to happen unhindered in any way.

In other words, the player should anticipate and allow for the external circumstances so well that internal timing can proceed as if unrelated to anything except the mechanics of the swing. Such complete separation is not possible since nobody is capable of perfect internal or external timing. The internal timing must therefor often get involved with adjustments for deficiencies in the external, and vice versa.

The various elements that must be timed in proper sequence are as diverse as the start of the backswing, turn of the shoulders, flex of the wrist, development of racquet momentum, and transfer of weight. And internal timing adjustments are particularly difficult because it is not possible to directly observe and isolate bad timing of individual internal elements. The process is complicated by the need to reconcile any changes with all interacting elements, and with external timing.

Timing difficulties vary with the circumstances. The ball could be close in, wide, high, low, or whatever, and the stroke could be cramped, extended, hurried, etc. No matter what the stroke, or the location of the ball, it should be possible to time the internal elements as if the swing were entirely independent of external conditions.

The major cause of errors at the recreational level is faulty internal timing. At the professional level it is faulty external timing. In neither is failure to "watch-the-ball" the usual cause. And if it "ain't wrong don't fix it", or the timing will degenerate. Although internal timing may qualify as the most important factor in stroke production it apparently has not been specifically discussed in the literature.

SWING-CONTROLLED "EXTERNAL" TIMING

There is an old adage that says that in a correct serve there is a "toss at the swing" rather than a "swing at the toss". In other words, the server should feel free to use an ideal swing since the ball should appear in front of the racquet at the right point and time with unfailing accuracy and certainty.

If the ball is not normally at the correct point when the racquet gets there then the <u>swing should not be compromised to meet the ball wherever else it may be</u>. The timing of the toss, the toss itself, or both should be modified until the ball does appear as expected. This is discussed more fully in the chapter on the "SERVE".

"Tossing at the swing" for strokes other than the serve is a little difficult because the "toss" is made by the opponent. However the point of impact is controlled by the receiver through the external timing of the swing. The receiver must carry out the preparation and the external timing well enough so that the swing and internal timing can proceed as if entirely independent of the arrival of the ball.

There should be no resort to push, paw, poke, pull, jerk, slap, swipe, roundhouse, slowing, stopping, hurrying, leaning, cramping, reaching, or other expedients and compensations. If such flaws are allowed to occur then the timing that has to be used will not be compatible with anything other than the individual collection of bad habits, and specifically not with a proper "swing-controlled" stroke. The bad timing and bad swing each needs and deserves the other. Neither can be discarded independently because each depends on the presence of the other.

For many players a paradoxical but rather common obstacle to improvement is that they often interpret the unpleasant and jarring sensations associated with improper timing as indicative of a very hard hit. Even top players are apt to succumb to this misconception, and sometimes allow an urge to hit hard cause regression to habits relating back to their amateurish days.

THE COMPLEXITIES OF TIMING INTERACTIONS
When a change is made in the pattern of a stroke the

assimilation problems, rather than the techniques, are the major difficulty. This is due to the complexity of the interactions in and between the two types of timing, internal and external. There are also likely to be problems arising out of incompatibilities between the timing of the new features and of those that are retained, especially since some of the retained no longer belong. Both the timing and the execution of each retained element tend to remain unchanged in spite of the need to adjust to the new elements. With such interaction of factors no wonder that good timing may seem to be mostly a natural endowment rather than an acquired skill.

TIMING THE VARIATION OF RACQUET ATTITUDE

Ground strokes have often been claimed to require an exactly perpendicular attitude of the racquet face during at least the latter part of the forward swing. If this were true there would then be the substantial advantage of not having to time variations in racquet attitude. But the trend away from the strictly classical style, and the rise in popularity of the topspin shot with Western forehand grips, make variation in the attitude of the racquet not just permissible but necessary in many strokes.

It will be proved in the chapter titled "RACQUET ATTITUDE" that perpendicularity does not necessarily exist at any point in the stroke, and is generally inappropriate at the hitting point. Change in racquet attitude does exist, and the timing of it has to fit in with the timing of everything else.

TIMING THE BACKSWING

A very significant but highly unnecessary problem is the timing of the backswing. A common mistake is to keep the racquet pointing forward until the ball has approached so close as not to allow getting the racquet back soon enough for a normal forward swing. This delay amounts to timing the backswing, instead of the forward swing, with the bounce of the ball. The resultant problems are bound to plague the remainder of the stroke.

A late backswing can affect the whole character of a swing, including the development of momentum, the extent of reinforcement, the amount of reserve strength, the degree of extension of the arm, etc. But instead of trying to avoid the lateness by thinking in terms of the familiar phrase "racquet back" it is better to visualize getting the whole body involved and prepared for a "swing-controlled" hit. The detail of "racquet back" will then take care of itself.

A specific means of improving the timing of the backswing is to think about being ready to begin the development of forward racquet momentum by about the time the ball bounces. If it is necessary to consciously focus on a single aspect of timing it might best be the timing of the development of racquet momentum. The backswing must not be allowed to interfere with that development.

CAN'T BE PERFECT

"Perfect" timing of all elements is not even theoretically attainable because there is some incompatibility between the needs of the various elements, between racquet velocity and hitting point for instance. If the racquet is continually accelerated during contact, as it should be, maximum racquet velocity is obtained not at the hitting point but a moment after contact has ended.

A lack of understanding of this particular concept triggers an intent to maximize the racquet velocity just at the beginning of contact, or even a little before, instead of a little after. This habit is responsible for many fundamentally wrong strokes. The impact then tends to be an anticlimax, resembling a slap rather than a solid hit. Another factor that becomes optimized in an area farther out in front than the hitting point is reinforcement. That subject is covered in the next chapter.

Optimum overall timing is merely the best possible compromise of the timing needs of all the individual elements of a stroke. The correct balance is determined by the feel in the context of the best use of momentum and the most solid hit that can be obtained with a sustainable amount of effort. Among the real experts there is relatively little violation of the basic principles, so the amount of possible improvement may not be very much. But at the top levels each small increment of improvement gets to be of disproportionate importance.

WHEN THE EXTERNAL TIMING IS LATE

If the swing is late (ball approaches too close) there will be a feeling of the arm getting caught in a position where it has insufficient strength, of the racquet not having developed enough momentum, and of the ball creating a heavy and perhaps painful shock at impact.

The player becomes increasingly aware of the lack of time as the ball approaches closer, prompting an attempt to hurry the racquet by pulling the elbow in toward the body. This is an instinctive reaction intended to shorten the swing interval by shortening the length of the radius. It is also intended to substitute strength for momentum. Bringing the elbow in very close may thus be a symptom of lateness in the preparation, or at least in the start of the forward swing.

WHEN THE EXTERNAL TIMING IS EARLY

If a player is too early with the swing (the ball hasn't approached close enough) the problem becomes one of a lack of forward reach instead of time, and a different collection of compensations is in order. One of them is to push the racquet through the too-far-out-in-front hitting point, rather than swinging it through a more comfortably reachable location. Since the racquet is getting to be at the extremity of its travel, where it begins to slow down and go roundhouse, the push is introduced to continue to move the racquet in the desired forward direction.

There are at least four interacting problems to overcome in that case: the too early completion of the swing, a too far out in front hitting point, the push, and the intrusion of roundhouse. It can be seen that merely trying to change any one by itself, even if correctly identified, has little chance of success. One possible approach to a solution would be to determine the rationale for the quick or just early swing. Another approach would be to try to improve the hit and the feel per the now educated concepts.

Since the push will not provide adequate pace the player is likely to try the remedy of swinging even faster than before. But the extra effort will bring the racquet around sooner than previously, further aggravating the problem of the too early arrival of the racquet at the location of the optimum hitting point. With the instinctive remedies tending to

83

aggravate the situation, people who are in the habit of hitting early may get to believe that correct timing and a satisfactory pace are skills that are not within their capabilities for reasons beyond comprehension and control.

Some players may use a slap instead of a push for similar reasons and with similar effect. The push and the slap are deficient in pace because of inadequate racquet momentum, lack of the necessary acceleration through contact, and a reduction in the contact interval. The slap has the additional drawback of being an arm alone swing with a considerable amount of roundhouse. And the weight of the body is isolated from participation in the hit.

THE CHOICE BETWEEN EARLY AND LATE

The choices available to a player as to the location of the hitting point are not just in terms of negatives since hitting either early or late has its positive side. In order to be able to make intelligent decisions about the matter a player should have some knowledge of the advantages of each.

The major advantages of hitting a ball late (ball approaches closer than normal) are:

> There is considerable remaining room for forward racquet travel available at contact. For that reason the acceleration and follow-through can proceed without restraint.

> There is a large leeway in the hitting zone. This eases the timing problems compared with the situation when hitting early.

> The racquet path is more easily kept to a rather straight line through and past contact.

> On forehands the body has less of a tendency to be in the way of the arm near the end of the swing.

> The stance is not apt to be opened too soon.

84

The movement of the body and the shoulder into the shot is not almost all used up before the hit occurs.

The wrist does not have to be bent back at the hit to face the racquet in the desired forward direction.

On backhands it is easier to hit topspin if the hitting point is not too far forward.

The major advantages of hitting early (the ball not yet having arrived at the normal hitting point) are:
A long swing is available in which to develop racquet momentum.

The arm is far enough forward so that it is angled slightly toward the line of flight of the ball, giving good reinforcement with the body.

A ball out in front appears to have less than its actual speed, making it easier to follow and judge.

It is easy to keep the ball and the opponent in the field of vision.

In reaching out at the end of the swing the body is pulled around to face the net, making it easy to get into position for the opponent's return.

NARROW VIEWS OF TIMING
To associate timing with just one element of a stroke is overemphasis of that one item at the expense of the many others that also have timing requirements. Therefor the act of paying increased attention to a single detail, like the ball, is more likely to result in deterioration than in improvement. There is more discussion of this topic in the chapter "WATCHING THE BALL".

Merely knowing during a match that the timing is off is

gratuitous information, providing more in the way of worry than hope in the way of improvement. Even subsequent heavy drill on a specific faulty element, such as the start of the forward swing, is more apt to be a source of confusion than of help. For one thing, taking the attention away from the stroke as a whole will result in the improper execution of some of the elements. Thus are bad habits born.

The simplest concept in correcting internal and external timing may be the idea of using an uncompromised "swing-controlled" stroke, and letting the hitting point, aim, pace, etc, take care of themselves. Another technique that may be effective in correcting external timing is introduced under "VERIFYING THE HITTING POINT" in "APPENDIX B". It amounts to shifting the attention to the "hitting plane" an instant before the ball arrives there.

ORIGINS AND RESULTS OF TIMING VARIATIONS
The most common causes of mis-hits lie in timing, internal as well as external. Therefor in the rest of this chapter a further examination is made into the generally overlooked intricacies where many timing problems really lie. In most cases it may not be possible to correct for the specific minuscule timing variations involved, but the mere awareness of their existence tends, over a period of time, to introduce the corrections needed. The well-known description of tennis as a game of inches could more correctly be in reference to ten-thousandths of a second.

An episode regularly seen even in tournaments is a player mis-hitting the ball and then expressing frustration by action or attitude as if to suggest that the equipment is guilty of behavior so perverse as to be beyond understanding or tolerance. But the equipment is hardly capable of momentary lapses in performance, and of a magnitude to affect the results, to say nothing of accounting for a grossly misdirected ball.

HOLDING BACK

At very critical moments in a match it is quite natural to hold back on the follow-through. Unfortunately this action will almost always commence before contact. The slowing down of the racquet has a secondary consequence, besides a decreased pace, of which the player is not likely to be aware: the hit will be a little late (the ball approaches a little closer than usual). The lateness in the external timing is made more severe by the fact that the racquet should normally be accelerating through contact rather than slowing down.

The opposite condition is also a source of variations in the hitting point: external timing being advanced too much. The most obvious way of advancing timing is by simply swinging faster than usual. This is typically made to occur by bringing the elbow in so as to swing the racquet through a smaller than usual arc, and with a vicious application of energy. A more subtle cause of advanced timing is moving or swaying away from the ball. This is discussed under a following heading: "HITTING ON THE MOVE".

When a timing variation occurs in either the late or early direction, and the errors begin to mount, there is then further excuse to get more cautious in the one case and to swing more intemperately in the other, merely aggravating the respective timing problems.

So at critical times there often is both a frustrating loss of pace and also a seemingly mysterious surge of timing errors. In such situations it is incorrect to say "my timing was off". What should be said is something like "I got chicken (or reckless) and changed the length and speed of my strokes, but didn't realize that this made a difference in the timing".

INTERNAL AND EXTERNAL TIMING INTRICACIES

Although most people associate bad timing with the location of the hitting point an equally important form of bad timing is a lack of coordination of the movements of the arm and body. There can be various combinations of early, late, or correct internal timing interacting with early, late, or correct external timing. Yet, instead of making an effort to discover and correct the intricate real causes of poor results, unsuitable hitting points, or mis-hits, even top tournament players are apt to exclaim "WATCH-THE-BALL!!!"

Complicating the picture is the fact that some variations in stroke production can affect timing in ways that may seem to be the reverse of what should happen. For instance, taking a larger than usual forward step into a shot equates to retarded external timing (hitting late) rather than advanced. This comes about because the enlarged step brings the racquet into contact with the ball sooner than without the large step. So the swing is not as complete, and the hitting point is not as far forward of the body, as usual. This phenomenon is discussed in more detail under the heading "INVOLVEMENT OF THE BODY" in the chapter on "BLASTING".

Increased rotation of the body can cause either advanced or retarded external timing. If the rotation brings the racquet around faster than usual the timing is advanced thereby. However, if the body rotates ahead and drags the arm along then the external timing is likely to be retarded (the ball arrives before the racquet). While such lines of reasoning may seem obvious to some people, few take them into consideration when things are not going well during play, especially on critical points when there are more compelling demands on the attention.

The real timing complications will almost always be even more complicated than as discussed above, and will involve many other factors: flex of the arm and wrist, tightness of grip, attitude of racquet, slowing or stopping of the racquet, shift of weight, etc. If an accurate enough analysis, or effective experimentation, cannot be made then about the only safe recourse for the time being is to avoid an action that causes a difficulty. That is much better than repeatedly using a technique that repeatedly causes the same error,

perhaps affecting other elements also, and ultimately causing the player's game to fall apart.

DECEPTIVE SPEED OF THE BALL

An oncoming ball appears to move faster as it approaches closer, and therefor becomes progressively harder to follow as it nears the hitting zone. There is not apt to be conscious recognition of this factor as such. However the effect is experienced often enough so that over a period of time most players begin to adjust by moving the hitting point forward from the optimum. Although there may then be a sense of security in terms of seeing the ball more clearly there is likely to be a deterioration in respect to the effectiveness and accuracy of the hit.

A similar accommodation often occurs when taking a ball that lands short. It is quite common for players of all levels to hit early at a low ball by reaching out with the racquet way ahead of the standard hitting point. One justification, of course, is to try to hit the ball before it touches ground again.

It so happens in the case of low balls that hitting a little early is not at all wrong, since for low bounces the body can and should be leaning more forward than usual, and this moves the shoulder forward a similar amount. Generally speaking, the correct hitting point is determined relative to the racquet shoulder, not the "net" foot (closest to the net when in a sideways stance). But for most strokes that foot happens to be a convenient reference point for purposes of instruction.

HITTING ON THE MOVE

A disadvantage associated with moving up for a hit is that the ball is hard to see for a player in motion. The problem is aggravated by the fact that <u>running toward the net</u> in effect <u>increases the speed of the ball</u>. So if a <u>normal swing</u> is used while running in then <u>the hit will be a little late</u>, ball approaches too close (retarded external timing). The ball will then go wide on the same side as the racquet except where the player anticipates and compensates, or panics and overcompensates.

The standard and unnecessary advice is not to hit on the run, but to first stop and then hit. For many players this may be a reasonable precaution. But the same purpose can be accomplished by adjusting the timing. If it is necessary to take the ball while running in, as is quite common, the swing must either be a little faster or be started a minuscule moment earlier than usual because the time available to get the racquet around will have been reduced. An advantage is that the forward movement adds to the velocity of the racquet and to the pace on the ball.

The reverse of the above reasoning is applicable to hits that have to be made while retreating from the oncoming ball. In this situation the pace of the ball is effectively slowed. With a normal swing the racquet has more than the usual amount of time to complete its journey. So it arrives at the best hitting point before the ball gets there (advanced external timing). A cure is to swing a little slower or start the forward swing a little later. Another solution is to try to always get back soon enough so as to be able to stop and step into the hit normally.

When making a desperate run toward either side it is usually best not to change the timing from that used for a normal, easy swing. But here an overcompensation with a quick swing seems to be the rule, and the ball is usually hit too early, even in those cases where preparation is

late, which is also usual. This makes for an unpredictable, ineffective hit when such consequences are least tolerable.

As all tennis players know, it is very difficult to maintain optimum techniques and timing when under pressure. But some of this is due to abandonment of the regular way of hitting in favor of previously eliminated but still trusted old habits. For instance, when making a shot on the run there often is an ordinarily unnoticed flaw of not making a preparatory body turn. This in itself is enough to ruin a shot. If there is no awareness of the respects in which the techniques and timing are off, and of the types of adjustments that can be of help, there is small chance of recovery of composure and return to the normal game.

TIMING PROBLEMS WITH THE BOUNCE
Inexpert players often neglect to adjust the timing to the nature of the bounce. Besides the factor of the height there is also the matter of the rebound angle off the court. The angle of the bounce tends to be equal to the angle of the impact except as influenced by spin, wind, and the amount of friction between the ball and the court surface.

On a high bounce the forward component of ball speed is low, and this requires the receiver to introduce a corresponding timing delay in the forward swing. The receiver has to generate most of the pace on such bounces, and this takes a good swing with plenty of acceleration, reinforcement of the arm, and follow-through. This shortens the interval of the swing, creating a need for an additional delay in the timing. Many errors can result from not changing the timing to suit the requirements of the situation. So bad hits off easy bounces are very common for good reason.

THE BACKHAND TIMING IS DIFFERENT
It is not generally realized that the external timing for the backhand is somewhat different from that for the forehand, mainly because the backhand involves a bigger arc and a slightly more forward hitting point. This timing variance

accounts for some of the extraordinary difficulty that many players have with that shot. The matter is discussed in greater length in the chapter on the "BACKHAND".

DIFFICULTY OF ISOLATING TIMING PROBLEMS
Timing has to be applied to many supplementary actions. Maybe the rotation or movement of the body occurred too soon, wrist or elbow flex occurred too late, etc, rather than that the swing was mistimed. It is impractical to analyze and discuss each of the many possible problems separately. In general they will be automatically corrected and refined as the concepts and the feel of the hit are improved.

At this point in the book the reader should have acquired a sufficient knowledge of the principles involved in stroke production so that special individual problems can be investigated with some success. A useful device is to re-enact a faulty technique several times in all its poor form. The repeated unpleasant experience may help to both pinpoint the source and motivate a reform. Slow motion visualization (SMV) can be very useful. As mentioned several times, the ability to learn is a skill to be mastered the same as any other tennis skill.

TIMING AS A TACTIC
Although timing can be used as a standard element of strategy by varying the behavior of the ball to cause the opponent to mistime and mis-hit, this should only be done during play and not during the pre-game warm-up. The latter is a cooperative effort by the players to get their timing under control before the match begins.

During the warm-up it is strictly unethical for either player to run the other around, create poor bounces, or try in other ways to unsettle the opponent's timing or composure. Even during play the techniques for tricking an opponent to mistime a shot should be confined to variation in speed, bounce, depth, spin, etc, without resort to behavior designed to upset timing, composure, and concentration.

chapter ten

involving the body

It is very difficult to describe the involvement of the body in the preparation and execution of just one type of stroke in just one style: the movements of the feet, knees, hips, shoulders, wrist; the coordination with the arrival of the ball; which muscles to tense and relax, how, when, and why; etc. And such explanations would not do much good since execution varies with the circumstance, objective, and player. However it is both possible and desirable to become acquainted with a few of the important roles of the body.

NOT BY ARM ALONE
Even when all problems with the preparation, timing, acceleration, and hitting point have been eliminated, that still does not guarantee strong tennis strokes. An important yet very common problem is allowing the arm to do the work alone without help and reinforcement from the body. The jolt of the ball can then counter enough racquet momentum to seriously impair the storage and recovery of energy. A pain in the wrist or arm caused by a mistimed hit can be convincing evidence of the power stored in the momentum of a fast oncoming ball.

When two objects collide head on <u>each loses exactly the same amount of momentum</u> regardless of the relative size (the ball, the racquet, the body, or the earth). The <u>change in momentum</u> is defined as <u>mass times the change in speed</u>. That means that for a given loss of momentum the greater the mass of an object the less the change in its own velocity and the greater the change for the other colliding object.

93

Reinforcement of the arm and racquet by the body
effectively increases the mass of the racquet, and therefor
reduces loss of racquet velocity and increases the pace of the
ball.

As the racquet reaches near final speed on the approach to
the hitting point no great amount of effort is needed to
maintain acceleration. The reserve strength can be used to
minimize the "give" of the racquet at impact and the
consequent loss in ball velocity. But a too firm arm and
wrist also has disadvantages. This is discussed in the
chapter "WRIST FLEX AND THE GRIP".

STYLE VS EFFECTIVENESS

The failure of the body to take part in the swing is
frequently a distinguishing characteristic between a
"schooled" stroke and one that is unorthodox but gets
results. It may have been self-taught, but it can
nevertheless have great effectiveness and naturalness
because of having active participation by the body.
Otherwise the real essence of a stroke is simply not there, no
matter that there may be considerable resemblance to the
classic or other excellent form.

In most cases the lack of involvement of the body will be
easily detectable in itself, but in its more subtle forms the
flaw may make its presence known only through such symp-
toms as an unpleasant feel and a lack of pace on the ball.

PSEUDO INVOLVEMENT OF THE BODY

Even when the body gets properly prepared there may not
be a good use of it due to the player switching from a good
preparation to a bad execution with little participation by
the body. A veneer of style is superimposed over the preparation and backswing, but a clumsily executed stroke then
follows.

Humorous examples can be seen in the serves of quite a few
recreational players. The start is made with strong purpose

and an impressive buildup. But this is followed by a swivel of the body toward the net and a gentle tap with the racquet to send a pop shot in the direction of the service court. A more complete discussion of this particular problem is given in the chapter on the "SERVE".

Without trying to be funny, it is useful to note that mothers quickly learn without instruction how to deliver a meaningful whack to the underside of a misbehaving child. There are no mothers who are not proficient with the stroke. Yet many of the same mothers manage to acquire only a very diffident "arm-alone" forehand, even though having had extensive experience with children as well as tennis lessons from the best instructors around.

The difference is largely due to intent. In applying a not very gentle means of persuasion to a child the very whole-hearted intent is to deliver a properly weighty message. With a forehand the intent is often just to act out what is usually an inaccurate interpretation of a highly sketchy outline of a very complicated sequence of events. The body must get into the act of swinging the racquet so that the ball will also get a properly weighty message.

SANS PREPARATION, SANS RESULTS

To a considerable extent a good or bad shot is the result of the corresponding preparation. Knowingly or not, players make the choice as to the results fairly early. The arm-alone swing is generally the inevitable result of a preparation inadvertently designed for that specific purpose. The preparation of the body that occurs before a bad shot is as appropriate for that result as the preparation before a good shot is equally as appropriate for that outcome. Hence, getting the body suitably ready for a weighty shot is a very important part of developing significant momentum in the ball. It is not an add-on feature.

The commonly heard advice relating to preparation such as "turn", "step", and "racquet back do work well for the initial lessons for beginners. But those instructions have been proved to be ineffective.when used in attempts to straighten out established games   For one thing, they amount to a switch from automatic hitting, however poorly done, to sequential execution of details. Some elements are then executed in isolation rather than in combination for a common purpose. In order to get the same results as the experts the student must supplant sequential execution of details with the carrying out of a correct set of intents with the full cooperation and involvement of the body.

TIMING THE REINFORCEMENT

The coordination of body action with the swing of the arm is difficult but most critical. Either motion may start too soon or too late relative to the other. The motions may start at the right times but proceed at rates inconsistent with each other. They may be in step with each other but out of sync with the ball. Or there may be the more usual situation of a combination of several of these problems.

The racquet can be back without the body being back, often to the extent that the body is in the end of stroke position even before the start of the forward swing. Excessive rotation can also occur, causing a continual change in racquet direction rather than a consistent heading in the desired direction.

Reinforcement is an action rather than a static condition. It includes a preparatory turn of the body, cooperation from the body in helping the arm get ahead, development of adequate but not maximum racquet momentum, and the timing necessary to maintain acceleration through the actual hit. Contact should occur at a point where the arm is relatively strong, has room to move forward easily, and is reinforced by the strength and weight of the arm and body.

Two of the most important words in the above sentence are "should occur". In other words, the conditions cannot be achieved by attention to details. But it is nevertheless necessary to be aware of details whenever there is something either especially good or not quite right about them.

By "reinforced" it is meant that the arm is going forward freely on its own and at the same time is being hurried along by the helping but not overpowering force of the shoulder. The impact of the ball is thus met with a more than matching force, and is channeled in a somewhat direct line through the arm into the shoulder, where it is countered by the weight of the body.

However it must be recognized that the workable level of direct reinforcement cannot coincide with the maximum. That maximum would occur at a point where the arm is held straight out in the direction of the ball. The achievable reinforcement during a hit occurs at some point before the maximum, and yet where it can be said that the arm has made a transition from trying to catch up with the shoulder to riding along ahead of it. The correct amount of reinforcement is best developed by forming the proper intents for a hit, not by making specific provisions for reinforcement.

If a player is caught out of position the more controlled racquet momentum attained the less direct reinforcement required. Momentum is not a property of the racquet alone. The arm is effectively a part of the racquet and has momentum too. It is very important because of the great weight of the arm compared with that of the racquet.

THE BODY AND ARM AT ODDS

Some players move the body backwards as they swing and don't realize that they are doing so. The forward racquet motion is decreased thereby. The amount of energy stored and recovered suffers accordingly. In order to make up for the losses there has to be as much extra forward movement and reinforcement furnished via arm motion and strength as was subtracted by the backward move of the body.

The loss of velocity due to energy not stored or recovered

constitutes a severe handicap. At the expert level, where a player cannot expect to be gifted many cheap points, the amount of energy being expended unnecessarily is often the determining factor as to who loses.

OVERDOING REINFORCEMENT
Although reinforcement is necessary there ordinarily is too much use of it rather than too little. The sense of security is greater when blocking the ball back with the use of strength than when using the momentum of the racquet to do the job. There is also a natural tendency to shift the hitting point forward because the resultant direct reinforcement is reassuring, and the ball is easy to see and follow up front.

But the racquet momentum is decreasing there instead of increasing, the racquet direction and attitude are changing, and the reach is becoming limited. In the light of the discussions in previous chapters about timing complications and inefficient recovery of energy caused by inappropriate direction, acceleration, and hitting point it can be understood how a search for security can result in the opposite.

THE PROBLEMS OF COORDINATION
Satisfying the requirement that the arm not remain behind the body but get at least slightly ahead at impact, and yet have the shoulder moving into the shot at that time, is a very involved accomplishment. The arm has to travel a much greater distance than both the body and the shoulder to come from way behind to slightly ahead.

If the arm is behind and is being pulled rather than pushed forward, then the shoulder is getting into the act ahead of its time. Conversely, if the arm gets too far ahead its motion and reach begin to be restricted by the body. By continually monitoring the feel of the hit the player can learn to avoid the extremes of letting the shoulder get too far ahead of the arm, or of having the arm lead while the shoulder provides more of a drag than a boost.

If the rotation of the body is increased while the arm is still trying to catch up there will be an unmanageable additional burden placed on the arm. It then begins to fall behind at an increased rate since there is no unutilized strength left to match the added strain.

In that event reinforcement is either not achieved or is broken if it has been achieved. So it is inevitable that the racquet will be jolted backward with respect to the arm. The error rate will rise because the hitting point, timing, racquet angle, etc, become somewhat indeterminate. The arm should not have to compete with the body, and the body must not exert a strong forward force on the arm before the arm is allowed to get ahead.

Another eventuality is that the available forward movement of the body, which is not very great distance-wise, will tend to be used up before the time when it is needed most and is most productive: at contact. Enough remaining body motion, through a combination of forward movement and rotation, must be available at contact so as to be able to contribute to the steady acceleration of the racquet. This helps extend the contact interval and improve on the storage and recovery of energies.

It is just as important that the body not stay behind and do nothing either. Yet even the best players are not without blame in that respect. Careful observation and analysis will show that even for experts the strength of the body is often either under or over utilized on all types of strokes. The task for both dubs and pros is to keep the excesses at the minimum level.

The ideal relationship between the use of the body and the swing of the arm varies with the situation, style, stance, strength, etc, and thus cannot be exactly defined. The criteria to be used are a comfortable feel and the absence of any harmful compensations such as hurrying, roundhouse, freezing the arm, etc. Fortunately, mastery of the individual elements is achieved by just improving on the intents, satisfactions, and the now enlarged concepts of the hit, rather than by a one by one mastery of the many individual details.

GRUNTING

The loud grunts so often heard may merely mean that the arm is being used to its extreme. Not the body, because only a small percentage of the strength of the body is needed to fulfill all of its functions in a stroke. The heavy loading of the arm does not guarantee that the body is also doing its share of the task, and the grunts may even mean that the arm is assuming some of the duties of the body.

Real grunting is not produced by the exertion, but usually by holding the breath and then releasing it with added sound as the effort ends. Thus the noise may be a symbol instead of a result, and is therefor not really useful or necessary. If it is not produced in that way it may not be a normal grunt. It then amounts to vocalizing rather than grunting.

There are an increasing number of cases where sound seems to be produced and prolonged for its own sake, not in relation to the amount of effort, and not as the unavoidable consequence of holding the breath. It seems to be a type of behavior that one commentator described as "a good psychological move". The viewpoint is quite contrary to that of most fans. It is a huge annoyance to the many people who spend a day or a week at a tournament, and to the much greater TV audience.

Footwork is a subordinate item in that it is a means instead of an end. But it is a controlling item in that it occurs first, and in that neither a good swing nor the desired end results are possible if the footwork does not provide for appropriate and timely positioning of the body.

Since the final step or adjustment should be a part of the sequence that combines a forward motion of the body and the actual hit, getting into position can be almost as important as being in position. Being statically ready before the hit is not as good as moving into position at the hit. The final adjustments tend to improve accuracy by optimizing the initial conditions, and to enhance power by adding to racquet velocity and reinforcement.

A RELUCTANCE TO MOVE

The energy required to move the feet is at least partially recovered in a more effortless and effective swing. However the body does not automatically calculate how to economize on the total use of energy but tends to favor the action that occurs first. This is where the feet get preferential consideration. Consequently when a person gets tired the feet may be disinclined to move into proper position. So the body and the arm are then required to work harder for less than normal results. There will almost certainly be an increase in the total amount of energy expended.

If the feet are uncooperative, or have a talent for starting out or ending up in unsuitable positions, then difficulties may be created for other elements of a stroke such as the preparation, stance, type of grip, swing, racquet attitude, shoulder turn, involvement of the body, hitting point, aim, and follow-through. A small deviation in any one of these will normally require compensations elsewhere. Such added complications can go a long way toward lowering the level of a person's game.

MIND VS FEET

As mentioned in the chapter on timing, the ball appears to move faster and is harder to follow as it comes closer. So to obtain the advantage of having the ball appear to move more slowly than at its actual speed, as well as to improve the view of the other court and satisfy the mindless urge to watch where the ball is intended to go, there is an inclination to open the stance more than advisable when one's confidence becomes shaky in critical situations.

Any variations in the stance not completely reconciled with all the other elements of a stroke will cause a rise in errors. And the feet are then often blamed for not wanting to move. But it is an exercise in futility to give directions to the feet to put the body into a stance that is not what the mind and the emotions really want. If the mind and the inner controls really want the proper stance, above feelings of security, saving on footwork, and watching the other side of the court, the feet will obediently make it happen.

There are advantages and disadvantages to each of the different types of stances, so it is not easy to choose one as most suitable even for just a single individual. And of course it is not possible to specify any particular type as the right one for everybody. A shot may be good or bad despite the footwork rather than because of it. Although some players with the poorest shots use notably individualistic footwork so too do some of those with the most effective shots.

Observation of good players in a tough match may show the feet engaged in a sort of stuttering activity during the wait in the ready position, especially during rapid exchanges at the net. These are not a planned activity but automatic reactions to signals that may be evident in the opponent's moves. The footwork usually becomes quite calm again almost as soon as the opponent has made the hit. The receiver then seems to move with planned ease to the proper spot for the return.

Inexpert players tend to do the opposite, hold a fixed stance too long in the ready position and then, when the ball is well on its way, have to scramble frantically and ineffectively to make the return. In other words, the mind and the body are doing very little during the wait instead of being actively engaged in anticipation and preparation. The feet of players with too much of a "schooled" technique are possibly waiting to be told to "step out with the near foot" or "cross over with the far foot".

FOOTWORK PATTERNS
There probably is more emphasis by teachers on the pattern for moving the feet than there should be, and not enough emphasis on the primary aim of just getting the body ready for the shot. This latter objective lets the feet take care of whatever they have to do to get to wherever they have to be for the particular circumstances.

An often cited objective of particular footwork patterns is to try to obtain the furthest reach with the least number of steps. But this does not necessarily equate to the most important consideration: the least amount of time and effort needed to move the necessary distance. The feet usually have adequate training to make the appropriate decisions, or quickly learn.

The number one obligation of the feet is to provide mobility in the shortest time and most effective manner in all situations. The mind has the authority to decide that the body has to move somewhere, but it is the prerogative of the feet to decide how to make it happen with neither instruction nor interference.

MENTAL OVERRULE OF EDUCATED FEET

Of course clumsy movements should be noted and gradually eliminated, but otherwise the automatic responses of the feet ought not be subject to fixed rules and conscious attention, especially during the exigencies of actual play. Intellectualizing the activities of the feet at times when it is necessary that they use their own good judgment and ability to react and improvise is hardly progress. The feet learn a lot from everyday experience, and a tennis game is not the occasion to let that education go to waste in favor of predetermined patterns, oversimplified assumptions, and questionable, time-consuming decisions.

What the feet can do when called on very suddenly depends quite a bit on what they happen to be doing at the moment. Just about anybody's feet can find a number of good ways to do whatever is called for, but it is not evident that minds have the ability to devise similarly varied and appropriate solutions for the feet on the spur of the moment.

There may be considerable variation in the footwork as appropriate for such factors as the type of shot received, position in the court, footwork required to get there, momentum of the body, power attempted, height of ball, point being aimed at, need for disguise, etc. There is a tradeoff here in that the adjustments appropriate for specific purposes may come at the cost of providing tip-offs to the opponent if the footwork has an observable relationship to the outcome.

FOOTWORK FOR SPECIAL SITUATIONS

When a ball is taken at some other height than is most convenient there is a tendency not to move the feet. The basic reason for the neglect is that the player doesn't know how to hit the ball at inconvenient heights. So the feet aren't told how the body wants to be positioned and don't get trained in where to move and how to participate. They cooperate as dutifully with indecision and wrong decision as with sound intents.

Lack of effective footwork when the ball cannot be taken at a preferred height is most unfortunate. In such situations getting into position, using as decent a swing as possible, and meeting the ball within the available hitting zone have even more than their normal importance. It is therefor wise to get a lot of practice in hitting at uncomfortable bounces. An added reason is that the hitting zone tends to narrow as the height departs from what is most convenient. A match is not the place to start finding answers to such problems.

If there is a loss in effectiveness when the ball is at an inconvenient height it is best to drift forward or back so as to be able to use a customary, normal height swing. Inexpert players tend to stand in the vicinity of the baseline and take the ball at whatever height it happens to have when it gets there. As a rule they are not too willing to move up from the baseline and have an even greater reluctance to move back. There is no overall saving of energy here, and the penalty in terms of results can be very consequential.

THE WAGES OF JUMPING

Even after getting properly into position many people will decrease the effectiveness of the shot by jumping and turning to face the net during the hit, perhaps even before. Some of this is due to the intent to watch where the ball is going, or the desire to get ready for the next shot.

For many people it is instigated by a desire to batter every ball for an untouchable winner. But jumping with that purpose involves a misconception as to how to use the body to obtain maximum power. It is doubtful that any extra pace can be obtained by lifting both feet off the ground. There is some loss of forward shift of the body, and of bracing between arm, body, and the ground unless the jump is in the direction of the hit. The jump is often conducive to roundhouse, which is not a good means of developing pace. The body is more than strong enough to turn or move into the hit on its own without the extra flourish of a jump.

It is not wrong per se to jump, or to turn while doing so. The actions do facilitate swinging freely, viewing the ball and the other side of the court, getting ready for the next shot, and getting a quick start for an advance to the net. Just as the force of the swing can vary with emotions and intents, so can the jump. This added source of variation can have unfortunate consequences on the execution and direction of the hit.

Once the jump starts there is little possibility of any last instant adjustment of the position of the body to compensate for any quirky behavior of the oncoming ball. On the other side of the coin, most tournament players do jump during the hit. Trying to eliminate the habit directly is not wise because the jump may provide advantages in some styles. If jumping is bad for a particular stroke or player it should be made to disappear as a consequence of finding ways to improve the hit.

THE CENTER LINE THEORY

A very common but oversimplified bit of advice is to always return as quickly as possible to the central area behind the baseline after every shot. This involves a sizable effort if the player has been drawn wide to either side. Furthermore, when a player is arriving at that central point the momentum is still pulling heavily on the body to keep it going in the same direction at the same speed. To reverse course completely at that time and run back the full half-width of the court presents a real problem. The opponent can easily take advantage of the difficulty by hitting back to the same side.

There is another often-taught strategy that works better in such situations. If a player merely heads for the central area but slows down so as not to get all the way back before the opponent hits the ball, it is still just as easy to cover the far side of the court because of already being in motion in that direction. When in motion it is possible to cover a much greater distance than when a start has to be made from a dead stop, or when a reversal of direction is required.

If the opponent hits back to the same side this may also not present a particular problem because, although a stop and reversal of direction are required, the receiver will not yet have reached the center line and will be less than half the width of the court from the sideline from which the retreat was being made.

ADVANCING TO THE NET

A similar delay in the case of advancing toward the net is not valid because it is not advisable to be caught in "no-man's-land". A ball hit low into this area by the opponent is difficult to handle, especially if hit hard or with heavy spin. So when advancing to the net it is necessary to get up to approximate volleying position as quickly as possible.

But instead of coming to a dead stop with the feet in a straddle position it is better to retain a little forward momentum. It can be easily redirected toward either side with faster court coverage and less effort than when having to start with no initial momentum at all. Although coming to a stop with the feet spread gives great balance it is not conducive to easy sideways movement. A wide spread decreases the available length of the push and presents too much weight located too far out to allow for a quick start in either sideward direction.

THE OPEN STANCE

The stance used by a top player is likely to be a a free version of a more formal pattern learned initially. This is fine as long as the changes were based on improvements to the stroke and results. But they often come about because of expediency, economy of footwork, and the urge to watch the the ball's progress to the exclusion of all else. A little analysis is therefore necessary to alert players to the need to evaluate the stance in the light of its effects on the stroke.

The following discussion of the open stance refers basically to the forehand since a sideways stance is almost mandatory on the backhand A player does not have to choose between open or closed since any degree of in-between can be used. In this book the terms "open stance" and "facing the net" refer mainly to shots that are made with the chest largely parallel to the net, regardless of how the feet are planted.

A serious problem with hitting while facing the net is that the arm is not free to go very far in either the backward or forward directions. Hence both the backswing and follow-through are not as long as they could be as when facing sideways. Therefor the timing with the shortened swing has to be exceptionally accurate in order to have the racquet meet the ball at the best point within the narrow available hitting zone.

Since the use of the open stance involves a compression of the time and space available to develop the required racquet momentum there may be sudden and large demands on the arm and shoulder muscles. The open stance is therefor somewhat unsuitable for most women. They generally tend to favor a more closed stance, or at least a decided preparatory turn of the torso.

Either of these options allows use of the relatively long swing needed to develop racquet momentum without putting potentially damaging strain on the arm and shoulder. An alternative that is commonly used by recreational players, an evasion rather than a solution, is the defensive slice. It can confuse players in the lower levels but is easy pickings for expert power hitters.

Added problems with the open stance are that it is not conducive to good reinforcement of the shot with the body, and does not permit easy enhancement of the pace by moving the body into the hit. A very important disadvantage is that when the arm is at good extension it is very weak in the forward direction compared to when the stance is closed. So players who use the open stance tend to prefer the bent-elbow over the extended-arm swing. When two-handed strokes are used there is no problem with strength. So the arms are automatically extended. Paradoxically, the stance is usually closed.

Positive aspects of the open stance include minimizing the time and effort required to get into position and allowing easy movement or change of movement toward either side. The open stance stroke is relatively short, which economizes on the time required to finish, and so eases the problem of getting ready for the next shot. It allows unrestricted view of the ball and the other side of the court. It permits easy camouflage of the direction of the hit. It is compatible with the Western forehand grip, which is widely used to get heavy topspin to deal with high bounces. When the player gets tired there tends to be less degeneration in the positioning of the feet and the body than with a sideways stance.

THE CLOSED STANCE
The closed stance maximizes the available length of the swing. This makes it easy to develop racquet momentum, accelerate through contact, vary the hitting point within a

deep hitting zone, have freedom of arm in the back and forward swings (except for the final part of a forehand), and hit down the line or cross court to either side. It provides good arm strength yet also reduces the need for a large amount of strength in the arm. It moderates damage to the arm, provides good reinforcement of the arm with the body at the hit, and allows the body and the shoulder to be moved or rotated into the hit. It works especially well with the Eastern grip and variations.

On the negative side, the view of the other court is somewhat restricted with the sideways stance. Added effort by the feet is required to get the body into position. For that reason a tired player has more of a tendency to neglect getting into position when using the closed stance than when using the open. Getting back into the face-the-net ready position between strokes takes effort, and if that move is late it may throw the timing of the stroke off. While the timing is simplified because of the deep hitting zone, it is at the same time made somewhat difficult in another respect: a long stroke requires that the timing be started earlier and be continued over a greater interval than for a short stroke.

A SEMI-OPEN STANCE
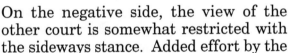

The "net" foot (closest to the net) need not be the "front" or "near" foot (closest to the path of the ball). The "fence" foot (farthest from the net) can be the "front" or "near" foot even though the stance remains partially or even totally sideways in terms of the attitude of the chest. The positioning of the feet is open in this case, but the direction in which they point and the attitude of the body can be partially or totally sideways.

This stance can be approximated from the ready position by

just turning the feet partly toward the side and rotating the hips and torso to assume a closed attitude. The hit is made from a truly sideways position, and is not the same as the other previously described similar shot hit from a more completely open stance. The body gets wound up something like a spring, and body strength and movement augment those of the arm for possibly impressive power.

In this in-between posture the balance is naturally and suitably forward into the hit. It is apt to be used quite frequently on the forehand just because of the minimum time and effort needed to shift between the ready and hitting positions. And, as in the open stance, the body is not in the way of the arm as the racquet goes into the follow-through. However the above advantages are not being cited as a recommendation of the stance over the other options.

t has been said that a person's knowledge of a particular subject disappears at the rate of ninety percent per year as soon as the study of it is discontinued. So a person is either advancing in an intellectual sense or declining at a precipitous rate. There is no such thing as staying on a plateau if a good level and amount of activity is not maintained. It takes real effort just to stay in place.

Somewhat the same may be true of tennis skills, but here the decline can set in even without any drop in activity. One reason is that as a person's game gets better the rate of improvement necessarily tapers off, so it is eventually exceeded by the rate of deterioration. Another reason is that once a high level of play is achieved there is a false expectation that it can be maintained in spite of less than the required effort.

Some of the major avenues to deterioration are: failing to form a proper set of intentions for the hit, economizing on the preparation, succumbing to emotional urges and impulses, seeking impossible results through the use of unworkable techniques, failing to be aware of both the satisfactions and the unpleasantnesses of each experience, making wrong changes, and, importantly, allocating attention to details instead of main purposes.

PAYING ATTENTION TO DETAILS
When a person's game begins to fall apart the usual remedy

of paying increased attention to a single detail is not really useful or wise, especially if it is not known for sure whether or not the requirements for that element are already being met, or whether there is any connection to the problems being experienced.

Conscious attention and decision are probably best reserved for strategy, analysis, anticipation, visualization of the hit, the timing of the development of racquet momentum, evaluation of the last shot, observing the opponent, etc. Attention should not be wasted on a minor or even major detail of execution.

If there is deliberate control or just specific observation of any element of the stroke, such as the stance, hitting point, racquet attitude, movement of the feet, tightening of the grip, or follow-through, it may be possible to obtain improvement by merely letting the body make those provisions on its own.

THE BALANCE OF ATTENTION

In most circumstances preoccupation with a detail amounts to upsetting the balance of attention being paid to the many things that are happening largely automatically. For that reason conscious observation of one item may induce overall deterioration. That may help explain why in many cases the harder one tries the worse things get. In tennis there may only be time to do it, not first think about it. Nevertheless the player must not be completely unaware of details either, even though they should not be subjected to specific observation.

It is as unrealistic to believe that watching the ball will automatically cure whatever internal or external timing difficulty is being experienced as it is to believe that timing involves nothing more than having the racquet meet the ball at a proper hitting point. Just reflecting on the complexities of the timing processes, as discussed in the chapter on that subject, should be enough to convince anyone that it takes much more than watching the ball to obtain a solution for difficulties with timing.

An unfortunate effect of trying to watch the ball is that the eye may gradually begin to concentrate on the departure instead of the approach, a natural development in itself. When that happens the watching becomes self-defeating by transferring attention to the wrong event. Concern with where the ball is going is assigning priority to what can no longer be helped, and at the cost of detracting attention from where it can do the most good: the swing and the hit.

If the intents and preparation are good, and the results and feel of the hit are satisfying then the ball is being watched neither too little nor too much. And, as the saying goes, "if it isn't wrong don't fix it".

When top tournament players have an inexplicable loss of form and then go into rigorous remedial practice to try to make a comeback, it seems that they never fully succeed, in spite of the help of top coaches. One reason could be that the first thing they do is go back to some of the basic rules, such as "watch-the-ball". Since few stare fixedly at the ball when they are playing confidently and well the "remedy" will merely aggravate the problems.

Most people do not really neglect to observe the ball enough. They rather do not pay sufficient attention to the hit as a whole. To "keep your eye on the ball" is neither a directly useful process nor an end in itself. Nevertheless it has come to be considered somewhat of a cure-all.

PRIMARY VS SUBSIDIARY

The detail of watching the ball is subsidiary to that of timing in the same way that the detail of timing is subsidiary to the concepts of the swing and the hit. Watching the ball is thus at least three levels removed from the primary consideration, the hit. It should be a subordinate activity since it is important only to the extent that it can affect the quality of the elements that are themselves directly useful.

Paying special attention to a lower level detail may result in neglect of others at a higher level. So the latter may be correspondingly degraded, even in the rare case when there is improvement in the watched item. This kind of attention is harmful because of blocking awareness of the more important aspects of the strokes, or of the game. It is unwise to diminish awareness of directly useful items, or that provide some evaluation of the quality of the hit.

It is not wrong to observe the ball to some extent, since whatever is sufficient in that way is also indispensable to the achievement of a good hit. A better way is to just "be aware" without doing any conscious watching. A person can be aware of many details but can watch only one, or at best several.

EVALUATION OF QUALITY
Awareness of the overall quality of a stroke, from early preparation through contact, should be present on every shot. The habit of evaluating the quality of a shot promotes paying attention for brief moments in nonspecific ways on details that count as they occur. It may also automatically create an awareness of compromises and deficiencies as they intrude into the functional elements. There is very brief peripheral attention to many details instead of conscious and extended concentration on just a few, or only one.

BEING AWARE OF INTERNAL EVENTS
When a person's strokes are not working and evaluation of the quality of the hit does not seem to provide any leads as to the source of the problems, then it may be time to investigate the more specific details of execution. But instead of watching the ball, which is an external item, it is far better to reflect on some of the internal events and actions involved in the stroke.

If direct observation seems necessary a suitable item might

be described as something that provides an appraisal of the level of excellence of the stroke as a whole. It should involve a precise moment and should be transitory so that it cannot be watched before or after that moment. Even this type of directed observation should generally be used only as a temporary expedient. Specific details are normally not worthy of individual attention, and all other details do not deserve to be correspondingly neglected.

Some suggestions for items that might be suitable for post-mortem analysis and evaluation, or for monitoring if need be, are: the degree of readiness just before the start of the forward swing, the appropriateness of the positioning and stance, the length of the forward swing, the location of the hit with respect to the "hitting plane", and the feel of the ball landing on or off the sweet spot.

Other items are the participation of the body, smoothness or compulsiveness of the swing, direction of the swing going forward or roundhouse, condition of the arm in the way of being cramped inward or extended comfortably outward, the development of racquet momentum, swing-controlled or ball-controlled stroke, intrusion of push, presence of compensations, the arm getting and staying ahead of the body or being dragged along behind, the arm moving freely at impact or nearing the end of its reach, etc.

AWARENESS VS OBSERVATION
All of these items involve a fleeting awareness of several characteristics of the stroke, not just a detail. Observing the ball is automatically included to some extent. There is no intent to change a technique or force a result. Instead of the actions being just automatic reflexes, unmonitored and unevaluated, a little awareness of the mechanics and the quality of the stroke is obtained. But even then there is always a danger of a loss of naturalness, or even workability, when an action that normally occurs automatically becomes the object of conscious monitoring or control.

It is not being suggested in the above discussion to try to see the ball meet the strings since that, if possible at all, is beyond the capabilities of most players. It is also not very useful. The occasionally heard advice to "follow the ball into the racquet with the eyes" is also not being suggested. It is not that easy to define when to commence and when to end following the ball, and there doesn't seem to be much possibility of obtaining an evaluation of the quality of the elements of a stroke, or of improving them, by that means.

It is possible that no solutions can be found by the type of evaluation being suggested, and that there may even be a consequent worsening of the problems. But occasionally an investigation may turn up something of value, and in the meantime the continual use and refinement of the techniques of evaluation will have a growth of efficiency and validity in themselves.

PERSONAL STANDARDS
Another beneficial fallout from such self-evaluation is that it may help to define and perfect the personal requirements for specific techniques. These standards may have use as sort of benchmarks when problems develop and one's game begins to falter. It may be useful to discover the events or actions that are related to either a consistent personal problem or exceptional success. It is unwise to wait to investigate such relationships until when the answers are urgently needed in a match, or have resort at that time only to "watch the ball".

The proper degree of attention paid to an item is best obtained by subordinating the detail to the accomplishment of the task. If a player has the right natural instincts it may not be necessary to be concerned with the details of execution. It may even be a mistake to do so. But when wrong intentions, urges, understandings, etc, creep in it is necessary to have some idea of what is normal so that the wrong tendencies can be identified and redirected.

It is extremely difficult to specify exactly what should be happening at impact. For that reason no definition is being attempted for such things as the exact attitude of the racquet, the point of impact, or any other characteristic of any particular item one chooses to evaluate. If the feel is good, and the sense of what is good is being continually refined, that is what counts regardless of the possible presence of supposedly inappropriate elements. It may be useful to know what is happening but it is dangerous to assume that it is firmly known what amounts to perfection and should be happening.

The above discussions are partly designed to prevent overemphasis on what is one of the most sacred dogmas of tennis instruction: "watch-the-ball". Attention must be paid to the ball to try to accurately judge its speed, distance, direction, spin, and bounce. Even expert players tend to become more interested in watching the other side of the court than in paying the required amount of attention to what is happening on their own.

Many inexpert players are so careless in that respect that errant hits are a frequent consequence. For them it may in fact be desirable to put emphasis on "watch-the-ball". But perhaps even there it may be better to just reflect on some of the other mentioned circumstances or actions to realize the additional advantages obtained from evaluation of quality.

The people who are most likely to go to unnecessary extremes in trying to watch the ball are those who do not learn easily from experience, or do not have good athletic ability, and therefor may take instruction so literally as to defeat the objectives of what in moderation could be perfectly good advice.

RESPONSES IN DIFFICULT SITUATION

A particular situation where there usually is insufficient attention paid to both the internal and external details of a stroke is in the case when it is barely possible to get to the ball and make any kind of return at all. The three most common errors of execution are:

(1) not making timely preparation and yet

(2) reaching out and hitting too far out in front because

(3) the fear of being late causes excessive hurrying of the swing.

Note that merely "watching the ball" does not make any provision to address any of these three items. In fact in this case it is conducive to neglect of not only the above items but the major factor that is conspicuously missing: formulating the intentions for the normal or special preparations required for the hit. That preliminary must always be accomplished, although only in a subconscious manner, and especially in those situations where making any kind of return at all is an achievement.

NEGATIVES AND POSITIVES OF AWARENESS
Ordinarily the best consul about paying attention to details is to just be aware of the quality of execution and to notice a detail only when something unusual occurs, terrible or

terrific. Harmless mannerisms can be ignored, but there must be awareness of any compensations being used as this may be a tip-off that something is being done that does not fit into the pattern of the swing.

It is wise to pay attention to the positive side also, appreciating the items that were good in the stroke just as much as bemoaning what was bad. Anything particularly good or particularly bad should trigger a slight suggestion in the mind as to the nature of the goodness or the badness. Know and feel when something is exceptional in how you prepare, move, stand, swing, make contact, end up, etc. Do not "watch the ball", "bend the knees", and "follow-through" but intend to achieve a quality, "swing-controlled" hit.

There is a still prevalent theory that the face of the racquet should be perpendicular to the ground in the latter part of the forward swing, at least during contact. The idea probably grew out of the elementary techniques taught to novices, with the student hitting straight out off waist high bounces. However the theory is not consistent with such other commonly heard advice as "hit up on the ball", "roll the racquet over the ball", and "the ball should clear the net by at least two feet". It is also not consistent with the facts of physics. If the advice is followed the ball will almost never clear the net.

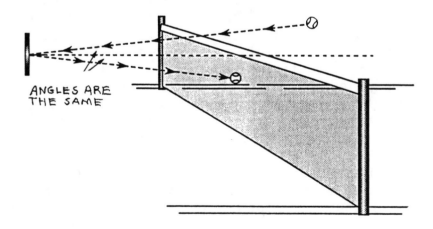

ANGLES ARE THE SAME

OLD THEORIES SELDOM FADE AWAY

There are at least three reasons why the idea of keeping the racquet face perpendicular to the ground should have been

abandoned long ago:

(1) Details do not deserve conscious attention but should be executed automatically.

(2) No justifications or benefits have been cited or proved.

(3) It is simply not true that the racquet face must necessarily be perpendicular during any part of the swing in any style of stroke.

It should again be pointed out that talented players learn to do whatever works well without regard to conformance to patterns. But it seems that when these people become instructors they recite the age-old rules that had been taught them when novices. They generally neglect recommending or explaining the modifications that they themselves adopted at an early stage.

THE RACQUET ATTITUDE IS WHAT IT HAS TO BE

The fact that the face of the racquet is generally not at right angles with the ground, even at the actual hit, can be very easily proved. If a player's shots are landing short the automatic correction will be to adjust the racquet attitude slightly upward to raise the trajectory of the ball. And if the ball is carrying too far the racquet attitude will be automatically adjusted downward, all mostly under the intent to change the trajectory and destination of the ball rather than to adjust the racquet angle. So even if the face would be perpendicular in one case it would not be so in the other.

If anybody is thinking that the up or down adjustment needed to achieve the correct racquet attitude would be the one that would place the face of the racquet in a vertical position then consider the following. If the pace is to be changed on similar hits but the target is intended to remain the same (say a point one foot inside the baseline), the attitude of the racquet must be altered to lift the trajectory or bring it down, as the case may be, to compensate for the

changed carrying power of the ball. Conversely, if the <u>pace</u> <u>is to remain the same but the depth is to be changed</u> on otherwise similar hits then the job is again best done with an adjustment of the racquet attitude.

Of course some people expect to have the ball land short or deep as desired without making any associated changes. An example is a person trying to vary the depth while intending <u>both to hit as hard as possible and to have the ball just</u> <u>barely clear the net on every shot</u>. Some adjustment has to be made someplace.

A similar problem is that players tend to increase the pace as the size of the target decreases. The urge probably relates to the idea that a hard hit ball travels in a nearly straight line. But that advantage is more than offset by the variation in carrying power, techniques, control, and internal and external timing. The most likely explanation of the often sad result <u>is not</u> that "he took his eyes off the ball, at the last instant".

Swinging the racquet upward as well as forward is an alternative means of raising the trajectory of the ball. However if the upward move is strong enough to create heavy topspin the ball may drop so fast that it has to be directed up in a high loop to compensate. The racquet may then have to be tilted up a little more than for a flat shot.

The nature of the bounce off the type of surface being used also has an effect on how the racquet has to be faced. Taking a ball that is rising at some specific rate and angle requires a different racquet attitude than when taking a ball that is rising more slowly, or at a different angle, or is not rising at all, or is actually on the way down. Other reasons for variation in racquet attitude include the height at which the ball is hit, the position in the court, the choice of straight or looping trajectories, the compensations required for wind conditions, the amount and type of spin received or returned, etc.

THE CONSEQUENCES OF HITTING STRAIGHT OUT

If the bottom of a ball is exactly three feet above the ground and the hit is directed straight out with a perpendicular racquet face there is absolutely no way that the ball can clear the net. There will always be gravitational drop, and the lowest point of the net is also at three feet. In fact, if that type of hit is made from the baseline and the ball has a speed of sixty or less miles per hour it will not even reach the net.

So even at this approximately ideal hitting height the ball has to be directed upward by one means or another. Consequently most ground strokes that are not hit with at least some upward move of the racquet, and are also not hit while the ball is on the rise, require that the racquet face be tilted slightly upward to compensate for the effects of gravity. How much is a matter of feel and art rather than calculation.

THE WHY OF MANIPULATIONS

Any player who has learned to hit with consistency has learned to select whatever racquet attitude is required for the particular hit being made. There is nevertheless the possibility that even an expert player's strokes will contain unnecessary flourishes of the racquet, a few that are of no consequence but most being at least slightly detrimental.

Some of these extra flourishes may really be compensations made necessary by other less visible flaws. Others may just be due to a futile effort to influence the ball after contact has ended. If any seemingly unnecessary alteration of the attitude of the racquet does not interfere with the hit, and is also not a compensation for another problem, then there is no great reason to be concerned even if it has no discernible purpose.

But during impact there should be little in the way of sudden changes of attitude except as required by the particular technique, or for special effects, or as a means of

126

adjustment for unanticipated problems. If sudden changes are constantly being used then there is a fair chance that they are compensations for flaws in technique. As an example, a perpendicular racquet attitude on the approach to the hitting point may make it necessary to turn the wrist upward rather quickly at the hit.

A continuous variation in the racquet attitude may be a functional part of some styles of hitting, as for instance in the case of the roll of the racquet associated with the Western forehand grip. Depending on the style or type of grips used, the racquet may start forward very open or very closed or anywhere in between. So there may have to be be a continuous change in attitude throughout most of the stroke, including during contact.

TIMING A CHANGING RACQUET ATTITUDE

A change in racquet attitude during a swing requires a timing of that change, and that entails coordination with the timing of everything else. Conversely, if it is one of the other elements that is changed or mistimed then it is the timing of the racquet attitude changes that has to be adjusted to suit. For an illustration: if the hitting point occurs elsewhere than at the usual point then the location where a particular slant of the racquet would ordinarily occur must be shifted forward or backward so as to have the

racquet end up with the correct attitude at impact.

A large part of the very complicated timing process has to shift along with the hitting point. As a corollary, it is usually very difficult to incorporate a single new element because the subconscious mind and the muscles will resist making the necessary changes to the timing of the many associated elements.

REASONS VS RULES

The cited problems with racquet attitude provide additional arguments for not imposing conscious control over details. This is the type of situation where adults pay attention, follow the advice, and pay the penalty. Children may or may not listen, but in any case choose not to accept or even hear.

The body must be allowed to do whatever seems necessary because there is no way the mind can control a myriad of details. It is obvious that a player who takes the perpendicularity rule as faith, and who makes a special attempt to observe that restriction when problems occur, is merely heading for bigger troubles. This is especially true if a simultaneous effort is made to follow other rules of similar validity. As the saying goes: "a little knowledge is a dangerous thing". And particularly if it is wrong.

WHEN THE BALL TILTS
THE RACQUET

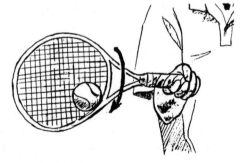

Sometimes the tilting of the racquet is accidental, as when a hit is off center toward either edge. There always is a momentary change in the attitude of the racquet, and an unwanted effect on the rebound angle of the ball. The change happens so quickly as to be almost imperceptible. But it is there and nobody is strong enough to stop it completely.

The degree of the tilt depends on such things as the impact

velocity, the size and characteristics of the racquet, its momentum, the distance of the hit off center, and the strength of the player's grip. The tilt and the effect on the rebound will be upward if the location of the hit is off center toward the top edge of the racquet, and downward if the location is toward the bottom edge.

If off-center hits are the usual circumstance the player is likely to become accustomed to the feel and will probably come to consider it as normal, and thus may have little inkling as to the cause of erratic behavior by the ball. The reader by this time would not be likely to entertain the idea that a cure could be obtained by such means as watching the ball, hitting well out in front, changing the end point of the follow-through, keeping the racquet face perpendicular, or squeezing the grip at impact.

"APPARENT" AND "REAL" IMPACT & REBOUND ANGLES

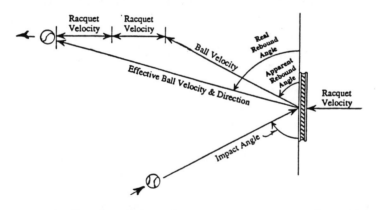

When a ball approaches the racquet at an angle, as is usually true, it will bounce off at an angle that is opposite in direction but approximately the same in magnitude, the way light does off a mirror. The word "approximately" is used because a ball has appreciable weight and therefor does not behave in exactly the same way as light. The rule is valid only if the ball has no spin, and the receiver's racquet is either held stationary or is moving the other way along the

same path as the approaching ball.

The result is different if the path of the racquet is at an angle with the path of the ball. The "apparent" impact angle is then not the same as the "real" angle. The "apparent" angle is what the player sees. It is just an instantaneous snapshot of the path of the ball with respect to the face of the racquet. It amounts to the illusion of a moving ball hitting a stationary racquet.

Suffice it to say here that the "real" impact angle depends on the vector combination of the speeds and directions of both racquet and ball. The eyes have no way of making such calculations and therefor the player has no way of seeing the "real" angle.

The faster the racquet travels the more importance does it have in determining the "real" impact angle. What this means to a player is that the faster the racquet moves the more does it control the direction of the rebound. The ability to correctly anticipate such effects on the rebound angle is part of what is called "racquet feel".

If when a player gets nervous or emotional the hit is made with either the extreme of too much caution or that of too much desire there are apt to be variations from the norm in racquet attitude and velocity. The "real" impact angle of the ball and the angle of rebound may then be affected in unexpected ways because of the complexities discussed above. So here is another situation where unanticipated effects can arise out of physical principles with which many players are not familiar, either intuitively or actually.

SPIN AND THE REBOUND ANGLE
If the ball is hit very hard the spin force is suppressed almost completely. The spin energy stored in deformations of the cover become proportionately unimportant compared with the force and direction of the racquet. There can then also be a relatively inelastic crushing of the ball, in which case

the forces due to spin get largely dissipated by the unproductive crushing action. In such cases the effects of spin on the rebound angle become unimportant.

If an oncoming ball that has heavy spin is met softly a part of the energy of the spin does not get stored but is expended in rolling the ball across the face of the racquet.

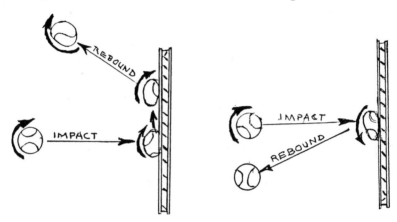

When the ball is hit much harder most of the rolling action is prevented by the flattening of the ball. Some of the energy of the spin then gets to be stored as a deformation of a side of the cover. When that deformation snaps back it tends to send the ball off with spin and direction opposite to what happens in a soft hit (when the ball just rolls across the strings).

Still another variable influence on the rebound angle is the bite of the strings on the ball cover. It varies with the impact velocity.

VARYING EFFECTS OF SPIN FORCES

When only a part of the energy of the spin is stored then the part that is not stored tries to roll the ball across the face of the racquet in one direction while the stored energy tries to roll the ball in the opposite direction. The combination of the opposing stored and unstored rotational energies can cause the ball to leave in unexpected directions. As a result

the direction of departure of the ball is often a matter of surprise even though always strictly a matter of cause and effect.

Note the complexity of the demands on the reflexes, with the correct attitude of the racquet being dependent on the relative dominance of the direction, momentum, and firmness of the racquet over the direction, momentum, and spin of the ball. The correct adjustment has to be a matter of experience, instinct, and art rather than simple rules and conscious calculation.

An actual or intuitive knowledge of the principles discussed thus far can prevent misconceptions, as well as too easy acceptance of unnecessarily all-inclusive rules. It can reduce the number of errors, or at least the false assignment of blame for errant hits. The majority of talented players hit properly without being specifically aware of these principles, but it is not possible to disobey the rules because the ball doesn't.

In order to describe the principles and problems involved with the backswing, and to evaluate the alternatives, it is necessary to supply brief descriptions of some of the standard techniques. These are generalized outlines for the purposes of discussion, not directions or recommendations for any particular style. A great hit is possible only if the actions preceding contact contribute in a positive way. So one of the important factors in a hit is the adequacy of the backswing, which precedes all else in the swing. To optimize the backswing for the purposes of the hit it is necessary to know something about the intricacies.

THE "STRAIGHT" BACKSWING

While the classic backswing is too rigid and methodical for exclusive use in actual play it is a fairly good way to start learning the essentials of the backswing. And it has the advantage of deterring development of wild and unnecessary manipulations of the racquet. A few tournament players use the general form of the method, but there are many others who use techniques that if not better are at least more fluid.

The classic method of taking the racquet back from a face-the-net waiting position starts with a near quarter turn of the upper body, carrying the racquet arm along also. The upper torso is now in a sideways stance with the racquet pointing toward the side of the court, already about halfway to the end of the backswing. The turn continues as a step is made across the body with the "net" foot (closest to the net

❖❖❖❖❖❖❖❖❖❖❖❖❖❖❖❖❖❖❖❖❖❖❖❖❖❖❖❖❖❖❖❖❖❖❖❖❖

in a sideways stance). At the same time the racquet continues the rest of the way to the end of the backswing, carried
by the existing momentum and the use of a little additional
exertion by the arm and shoulder.

NO EXERTION BY THE ARM??

The claimed benefit of this method is that the first half of
the backswing, the quarter-turn, is accomplished with no
arm effort at all. However a little examination and analysis
reveals that the claim is not as technically sound as may at
first seem. Even if the arm is just carried along and is not
moved independently it has to exert effort in overcoming the
restraining pull created by the inertia of the racquet.

The force needed to overcome that inertia is dependent on
four things:
  (1) The total mass of the racquet.

  (2) The location of its center of gravity.

  (3) The distance at which the racquet is held out from
  the body.

  (4) The rate at which the racquet is accelerated.

It is obvious that the force needed to overcome the inertia is
independent of the source of the motion, whether due to the
turn of the body or the swing of the arm. Holding the arm
fixedly out in front so that the racquet is carried around by
the rotation of the body, as in the simplified classic backswing, encounters just as much resistance to acceleration,
and requires just as much exertion by the arm, as when the
body is held still and the racquet is taken back with the arm
alone.

Rather than that the muscles are relieved of any effort, they
must overcome the inertia of both the arm and the racquet
to get to the end of backswing position in of time for the
forward swing. In the process the arm and shoulder muscles

❖❖❖

may even be strained beyond their limits. This is because the body can turn much more quickly than the muscles can conveniently force the arm and racquet to follow.

THE STOP AND RESTART

As the racquet approaches the end of this classic "straight" backswing the motion must be stopped and then restarted in the opposite direction. If the backswing is late the reversal of motion has to be hurried. The buildup of forward racquet momentum will then have to be on an emergency basis, seriously complicating the timing of all the remaining elements of the stroke. Satisfactions are reduced or eliminated, pace diminished, and the chances of error greatly increased.

A consequence of trying to make up for a tardy backswing is that the impact of the ball occurs during the unpropitious interval when the muscles are already under heavy strain in hurriedly overcoming the combined inertia of the arm and the racquet. That will produce the unpleasant and damaging jolt that is the customary experience of armies of players, not entirely restricted to those of the lower levels.

This does not mean that the "straight" backswing is bad, or that the cure for lateness is simply in taking the arm back earlier. That may amount to an "arm-alone" adjustment. It is necessary to carry out intentions to get fully prepared to make a good hit. The backswing will then take care of itself.

THE "LOOP" BACKSWING

A widely used alternative to the classic "straight" method is the "loop" backswing. In this process, instead of the racquet head being taken straight back, it is rotated to the end position at a level that is usually higher than the level of the forward swing. When the racquet head has looped most of the way back in the upper path it begins to move downward into the forward path. Here the force of gravity gives an assist, minimizing the need to use strength and effort to get the gradual increase in speed that is required at this time.

135

❖❖

Effort is further reduced in that racquet momentum is being continuously redirected via the loop rather than stopped and restarted. Also, moving the racquet back close to the body reduces the "moment of inertia" of the racquet and the consequent burden on the arm compared with when the racquet is held out and away.

This is a very important way to save energy because the "moment of inertia" of each particle of the racquet varies as the **square of the distance** from the center of rotation, in this case the shoulder. So if this factor is taken into account the "straight" backswing requires more effort than the loop instead of less, even without considering the waste of energy involved in the stop and restart that occurs with the "straight" method.

The conservation of momentum, the cooperation of gravity, and the easing of strength and energy requirements can be very helpful in maintaining pace and consistency when tiredness sets in, or in making it possible to get a good measure of extra pace when desired. The same factors tend to prevent the onset of "tennis elbow", or help to minimize the damage of continued play if the elbow is already hurting.

The motion of the "loop" backswing is very fluid. While this is very desirable in itself it has the disadvantage of making it easy to exaggerate the motion. The racquet head should follow a rather compact ellipse, not a huge circle, and not either as close to the body or as far from it as possible. But here again some players manage to exaggerate with great success. Billy Johnson of the Bill Tilden era, and with reputedly one of the greatest forehands of all time, is said to have used a "loop" backswing that often took the racquet back at about the full extension of his arm above his head.

Although the racquet goes back in a curve with the use of the "loop" technique the forward swing should ordinarily be fairly straight, even when the racquet is made to follow an upwardly angled path for the purpose of topspin.

A continuation of the circular motion into the forward swing is not necessarily wrong. But it can introduce timing problems due to the great variations in both the direction and attitude of the racquet. It can also take away from the acceleration and the forward velocity of the racquet, interfere with an adequate follow-through, and require extra arm effort to overcome the force gravity.

THE "ELBOW-FIRST" TECHNIQUE

With either of the two described backswings there are two partially simultaneous actions involved in getting the racquet back:

(1) Moving the upper arm back.

(2) Unfolding the lower arm to place the racquet head in its final ready position poised for the forward swing.

Many players separate these actions on the forehand by using an elbow first technique, really just a variation of the "loop" method. This backswing involves "leading with the elbow", which for many years was considered to be taboo. Instead of the body being rotated to "carry" the arm and the racquet back as in the "straight" backswing, or of the racquet being moved through a vertical arc as in the "loop", in this third method it is the upper arm that is moved back, pulling the racquet and lower arm along also.

As the initial pulling motion decreases the lower arm unfolds backwards, taking the racquet head in a loop to the end position. The backward loop can go either upward or downward. If the motion is downward it can create an inefficiency because a downward loop does not flow as easily into the forward swing as does an upward loop.

137

✦✦

Taking the racquet back with a leading elbow, comfortably close in and sort of parallel to the body, requires less effort on the part of the arm than with the other methods. The "moment of inertia" of the racquet is much less than when it is held out and rotated back with the body in the classic method, or pivoted up and back in the "loop" method. Also, pulling the racquet back with the head lagging just happens to be an easier task for the muscles than taking the racquet back head first.

A subtle and valuable by-product of the "loop" method is that it is conducive to the use of a relaxed arm and wrist. Another side-benefit is that as the arm and racquet are taken back the shoulder and body are pulled along too into what can become a rather exemplary readiness for the hit. Not taking the shoulder back by some means limits the length of racquet travel in the forward direction and the development of arm and racquet momentum.

TIMING ADJUSTMENTS

The racquet head usually gets back just in time instead of ahead of time with the "loop" or "leading elbow" methods, and it is easy to get caught with the racquet being a little late going into the forward swing. However it also happens not to be difficult to compensate for such lateness because the racquet can be easily slowed down or speeded up to adjust the timing. The reasons are that momentum has been maintained, a fair amount of reserve arm strength is available, and the "moment of inertia" of the racquet is small because of the small radius of the loop.

With the classic "straight" backswing the timing can be just as accurate, and the adjustments reasonably easy, if the racquet is taken back early and the forward swing is started in time. But the problem with many players is that the timing tends to be late, or at least marginally so, and lateness is accentuated as tiredness sets in. One means of reducing lateness is by visualizing the backswing as part of the process of developing momentum in the forward swing.

❖❖❖❖❖❖❖❖❖❖❖❖❖❖❖❖❖❖❖❖❖❖❖❖❖❖❖❖❖❖❖❖❖❖❖❖❖❖

A fairly common although not very harmful mistake is to exaggerate the backswing by taking the racquet back too far. This complicates the timing problems just by reason of the extra long intervals required for both the backswing and the forward swing. A more serious problem, which is especially apt to occur on difficult shots such as desperation swings and hits off high bounces, is the opposite and more undesirable expedient of not taking the racquet back far enough. It is probably fair to say that more than half of the difficulties with the forward swing originate in an abbreviated or otherwise faulty backswing.

Lengthening the backswing has use when it is desired to hit the ball very hard. Momentum can be both increased and built up more easily in the forward swing over the longer distance. The decrease in the time resulting from a faster swing is negated by the increase required by the longer swing. This equalization of the timing is described more fully in the chapter on "BLASTING".

RECEIVING FAST BALLS

The backswing used for a particular shot depends not only on preferences but circumstances. Many expert players automatically resort to whatever backswing is appropriate for the type of shot and the demands of the situation. For instance, the first half of the classic method (the quarter turn of the body) is commonly used when receiving very fast serves. It can be safely abbreviated and the racquet can always be kept nearly properly faced for the forward swing.

So when a serve arrives unexpectedly fast the backswing can be cut short and the racquet brought forward with proper attitude, and with whatever momentum has been generated by the time the ball zooms into the hitting zone. Not much racquet velocity is necessary or even desirable in this case. The important items are firmness and reinforcement rather than velocity. Most of the return velocity should be obtained by just reusing the momentum of the oncoming ball via a slow but firm forward swing.

❖❖❖

A slow moving racquet also has the advantage of providing good control, especially when an angled return is desired. Unfortunately the natural (and incorrect) tendency is to increase the speed of the swing as the speed of the oncoming ball increases. That topic is discussed in the chapters on "ELASTICITY" and "INSECURITY".

chapter fifteen — hitting with a bent elbow

Why hit with a bent elbow? Or why not? The elbow is certain to be bent to varying extents before and after contact. But during the actual hit should the elbow be bent or shouldn't it? The classic instruction in this regard is that the elbow should be rather straight but not awkwardly so, and this seems to be rather good advice. However, there is no consensus view on that point and many pros do hit with more of a bent elbow than seems to be of use, not necessarily wisely.

EFFECTS OF A BENT ELBOW ON THE SWING

Some of the effects of a bent elbow are that the radius and arc of the swing are shortened, and the "moment of inertia"

141

of the racquet diminished. Reducing the "moment of inertia" has special importance because its magnitude is related not just to the distance of each particle from the center of rotation but to the square of that distance.

The lowered inertia, and the greater strength of the arm close in compared to when it is more fully extended, make the job of accelerating the arm and racquet easy. Other consequences are that the disguise of the direction of the hit can be accomplished relatively easily, and that the interval of the swing is shortened. The short swing interval creates an advantage somewhat akin to that obtained when taking the ball on the rise. An unobservant receiver may be deceived by the ball coming back not faster but yet a little sooner than may be expected.

ANGULAR VELOCITY VS FORWARD VELOCITY

It is easy to associate the quick rotation obtained with a bent elbow as synonymous with added ball speed. So it is very common to see players, even those at the top levels, pull the elbow in to a greater than normal extent when extra pace is desired. But being able to swing the racquet around quickly in an angular sense doesn't necessarily equate to more racquet velocity, particularly not in the direction of the hit.

Developing a given amount of racquet momentum requires the expenditure of the same amount of work whether the swing has a short or long radius. There is no momentum that comes for free, or at a reduced price. Work is defined as force times distance. Since the radius of the "elbow-in" swing is shorter than with an extended arm, the angular velocity has to be greater to develop the same racquet momentum as with the extended arm swing.

So a large angular velocity with a short radius is not likely to produce a forward speed of the racquet head that is any greater than that obtained with less angular velocity but a longer radius. The advantage, except for the factor of the strength of the arm, is probably with the long radius. The arc of the swing (or of racquet travel) is proportional to six times the radius. However the ability of the arm to maintain a given rate of rotation as the arm is extended decreases at a lesser rate. The net result is that in most cases the best racquet velocity is obtained with an extended arm.

BENT-ELBOW DISADVANTAGES

One of the results of using a bent elbow is a shortening of the follow-through. While this permits quick readiness for the return it can seriously diminish the recovery of energy by compromising the duration of the contact interval, and by introducing roundhouse.

That fact that it requires a sudden exertion, usually taking up all the strength of the arm, means that there is little strength in reserve even though there is more of it available initially than with an extended arm. Consequently the arm is likely to be at a disadvantage in countering the momentum of the ball. This inadequacy is aggravated by the fact that the resistance presented to the impact with a bent arm depends largely on muscular force, not on the more rigid reinforcement obtained through the bone structure of a nearly straight arm angled a little forward against the shock.

TIMING VARIATIONS WITH A BENT ELBOW

One of the considerations in regard to a bent elbow is whether it is to be used on all strokes of a type, say all forehands, or just on some. If only on some there will be variation in the durations of the swings due to the mentioned different angular velocities. Therefor when the elbow is brought closer in than normal the swing should usually be made to start a little later than with a more nearly straight arm. Otherwise the racquet will reach the intended hitting point a little before the ball gets there.

The amount of bend in the elbow is not easily kept constant, and the variations become more pronounced as tiredness

143

sets in and the player fails to get properly into position for every shot. Any variation introduces changes in the length of the arc, the angular velocity, the contact interval, the direction in which the racquet faces, and the internal and external timing.

The associated changes may be small, but a very small error at the racquet can mean a sizable error when the ball gets to the other end of the court. On the positive side, it is much easier to accommodate to bad bounces and to time the exact instant of a hit with a close-in swing than with a long, smooth swing.

Although mere awareness of the effects of the variation on timing and on the other mentioned factors will trigger some automatic adjustment, even then the net result of changes in arm extension can be a propensity toward an erratic game. Naturally it is more likely that inexpert players will neglect to make the appropriate changes in timing than that they will have enough knowledge to make suitable finely tuned adjustments. If the characteristics of the "bent-elbow" swing are very consistent shot to shot then there is little variation in timing to contend with.

Average players often time the forward swing on the basis of the ball's position with not enough account of its speed. When the ball arrives sooner than expected one of the few available last-instant adjustments is to bring the elbow in so as to be able to sweep the racquet around extra quickly, and by that means manage to meet the ball somewhat properly. The "bent-elbow" swing is made to order for such an emergency. But a danger is that repeated use as an expedient may soon fix it as a permanent habit.

THE QUASI "BENT-ELBOW" SWING
If in the process of a swing the elbow is initially bent but is then gradually let out as the racquet approaches the hitting point, the extra strength of the arm with a close in elbow is available initially when it can be useful for a quick start up.

And a longer radius and arc become available later in the swing when needed to optimize racquet momentum, the contact interval, and the storage and recovery of energy.

Properly used this combination of the properties of two types of swings can produce exceptional pace. Thus, although more skills must be mastered with this more complicated technique there are advantages that can be gained. It is much used at all levels, but usually with too much retained elbow bend. Many lower level players tend to do the opposite: hold the arm out initially and then draw the elbow in as the stroke progresses.

TIMING AN EXTENDED-ARM SWING

A long swing is graceful and effective but raises the risk of problems inherent with early commitment. There is an extended period of racquet travel during which the ball can bounce unpredictably, be affected by the wind or spin, etc. It takes skill and confidence to risk the difficult timing associated with an early start and a long swing interval. Nevertheless early commitment is something that ought to be cultivated instead of avoided. It promotes good preparation and development of momentum, close attention to timing, and smooth execution. The result can be minimum strain and increased power.

Inexpert players, or those at any level whose skills are declining, are apt to avoid the challenges inherent in a long swing. They increasingly seek the feeling of security of a late swing with a very short arc obtained with a bent elbow. Even the better players at the top of their game tend to do the same when their confidence begins to waver during a difficult match.

The qualms may be excusable where timing problems arise from such factors as a bad court surface, fading daylight, or windy conditions. But if they occur just because of a loss of confidence, then the trust placed in a quicker swing with a reduced radius usually turns out to be misguided. The timing interactions triggered by changes in the length of the arc of the swing generally cause an increase in errors instead of the desired decrease.

PROBLEMS OF DIRECTION

If the "hitting plane" is a little ahead of the "net" foot (nearest the net), a racquet moving along an arc with a small radius is at a greater horizontal angle to the "hitting plane" than a racquet traveling along an arc with a longer radius. The vertical attitude of the racquet is usually also altered.

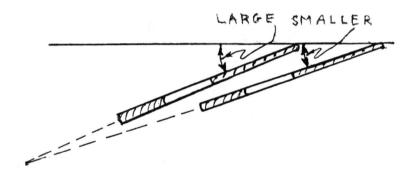

Therefor the use of the small radius may require that the wrist be both bent back and turned up slightly to have the racquet facing in the desired forward direction with the correct attitude at impact. An alternative solution is to move the hitting point back a little. But this is difficult to do. It involves a series of related adjustments, increases the apparent speed of the ball at the hitting point, and brings on feelings of insecurity.

The racquet veers quickly into roundhouse when the radius of the swing is short, even when care is taken to see to it that a correct hitting point is used. Therefor when using a bent elbow it is necessary to make sure that there is an adequate follow-through in the intended direction of the ball. Such refinements to the termination can cause the "bent-elbow" swing to resemble the quasi "bent-elbow" stroke mentioned a little earlier, in which the arm is gradually unbent so as to be almost extended at contact.

CENTRIPETAL EFFORT VS CENTRIFUGAL FORCE

There is a subtle but important problem of a completely different nature with the use of a bent elbow. A swing is basically a section of a circle, or at least partly so, and the body is at the center. Therefor as the racquet and the arm develop momentum some of it is centrifugal, pulling outward on the arm. If the arm is comfortably extended the outward pull is merely taken up by the arm structure, with no need for any significant amount of muscular effort.

However if the elbow is bent then the outward pull of the centrifugal force tries to straighten the elbow. Unfortunately the pull increases as the radius decreases, opposite to what happens with the "moment of inertia." Muscular effort must be exerted to resist the pull and keep the elbow held in toward the body.

Players are probably all too conscious of the resultant unpleasant feel and the tiring effect on the arm, but few are specifically aware of its cause. Such feelings seem to most people to be just the unavoidable attributes of the process of swinging the racquet, rather than the result of the self imposed task of continually restraining the arm and racquet inward.

Allowing the elbow to gradually straighten during the swing transfers the centrifugal tension to the arm structure, reducing the demands on the muscles. It enhances acceleration of the racquet, and extends it into the follow-through. The opposite is true when the elbow is pulled closer in, as many players impulsively do when trying to hit extra hard.

The above theories are not idle conjectures but the type of information that can lead to significant improvement in player's games. They illustrate how unexpected consequences of simple variations in technique remain mysteries if the understandings depend completely on intuitive associations without inclusion of at least a smattering of technical knowledge. While tennis is only a game it cannot repeal or disregard the principles of physics.

For expert players the wrist simply seems to do whatever is appropriate for a particular hit. A description of what actually happens that is simple enough to be put into words runs the risk of being skeletonized enough to border on the ambiguous and misleading. Some wrist action has to be present. Substantial use is a requirement on serves but is more a matter of personal choice on ground strokes. It is another variable to master, but when used properly it has advantages that are ample reward for the trouble of learning the skills.

SQUEEZE THE GRIP??

Tennis books have been quite limited as to descriptions of how to use wrist action. A traditional bit of contrary advice is to squeeze the grip at impact. This is not very compatible with a flexible wrist, if that happens to be what a person wishes to use. An ambiguity about "squeeze the grip" is whether or not there is some definite amount of pressure that is optimum. If so then only people with relatively weak muscles would be candidates for its use. A strong person's "loose" grip is apt to be much more firm than a weak person's "tight".

The grip need only be firm enough to enable application of the increments of force necessary to maintain a gradual acceleration, and to form a path of reinforcement of the racquet against the impact of the ball. A variable that affects the amount of pressure required is the degree of slipperiness of the racquet handle. Slippery handles can introduce awkwardness and unnaturalness by causing uncharacteristic tension in the arm muscles, making the wrist and arm less than normally flexible. This can initiate a ripple of timing interactions, possibly resulting in serious deterioration in a person's game.

There is a greater danger of using too stiff a wrist than too loose. Therefor when a firmer grip than what is being used is desirable a more ambiguous advice than "squeeze the grip" might be in order. This can be done by reference to the task rather than the technique: accelerating the racquet through the hit, intending to hit a "weighty" instead of a slap-type shot, hitting firmly, etc.

Some firmness of grip has to be used to maintain racquet acceleration for reasonable efficiency in the storage and recovery of energy. The combination of forces generated by strength and by the momentum of the arm and racquet has to be greater than that generated by the momentum of the oncoming ball. On a well-executed swing momentum is more important than strength. If the momentum is inadequate then strength will have to be substituted to counter the impact of the ball. In that case it is likely that the grip will have to be very tight.

On a serve the racquet has to contend only with the inertia of the ball, not any initial momentum. So the grip there should be rather loose to make it possible to use wrist flex to increase racquet and ball velocities.

COMPENSATIONS WITH THE GRIP

If a hit is off center toward either edge of the racquet a compensating tightening of the grip will occur as the torque generated by the hit is transmitted to the hand. The tightening of the grip is an automatic response, not a consciously controlled action. For a person to concentrate on that detail will likely amount to overcompensation. It can result in errors by interfering with normal execution, detracting from the required attention to the stroke as a whole, and creating unanticipated timing interactions.

In fact, switching to a looser than normal grip can be of help in such cases. Correcting the real flaw, the off center hit, will then be the only available means to minimize the torque, turning of the racquet, and misdirection of the ball. An exaggeratedly loose grip can also be deliberately used, at least during practice, to begin to eliminate other bad features such as an insufficient backswing, push, bad timing, inappropriate stance, late swing, etc. A loose grip, a "swing-controlled" stroke, and a glance at the intended "hitting plane" are a great combination for use with the very difficult problem of correcting an improper hitting point.

MINIMIZING SHOCK

If the wrist is loose the jolt of impact has no solid path of transmission from racquet to arm. For that reason, and because it doesn't lend itself to the use of strength as a substitute for racquet momentum or as compensation for improper timing and technique, a loose grip can facilitate getting rid of tennis elbow.

In some respects a sore arm or wrist can act as a training aid in learning how to hit with minimal strain and effort. The occurrence of pain will be a persuasive warning of bad execution. Conversely, a less noticeable level of pain will be an indication of a corresponding improvement in the techniques. However it is quite unwise to hit if pain is being experienced. Permanent damage could result.

On the other hand, if a player is going to play a match in spite of some minor pain in the arm then the use of a loose grip may be advisable as a means of minimizing discomfort or added damage. At the same time the loose grip may make it possible to stay competitive in the match by forcing the use of the better techniques. But any shot for which adequate racquet momentum cannot be attained should not be attempted. There can be an increase in the severity of the damage, and the shot will probably result in a setup or an error anyway.

GETTING CONTROL AND POWER WITH THE WRIST

Most players feel more in control of the racquet and the ball with a firm wrist than with the flexible. However, with a firm wrist the entire arm has to become involved when a last instant change has to be made. The same correction can often be achieved more easily with the wrist alone if it is loose. The action is quicker, more flexible, and more precise than that of the entire arm, besides still retaining all the possibilities of moving the arm as required also. "Feel of the racquet" does not come easily with a stiff wrist.

Another potential advantage of wrist flex is power. The velocity obtained in the racquet due to wrist flex adds directly and considerably to the velocity of the racquet due to the swing of the arm and the forward move of the body. Whatever velocity is contributed by the wrist is additive to that produced by the arm, sort of a miniature swing hinged at the wrist added to the larger swings hinged at the elbow and shoulder.

The distance of the wrist to the center of the racquet head is roughly about twenty inches. This constitutes the radius of the arc of racquet head travel created by wrist flex. The distance of the wrist to the center of the hand is only about two or three inches. So the velocity of the racquet head due to wrist flex can be as much as ten times that developed in the hand by the same flex.

A strong person can get decent results with just the use of strength and a stiff arm and wrist in a blocking type hit. The major advantages are in the minimum energy needed to get into a suitable position, in good visibility of the court during the entire shot, and in the feeling of security obtained from a stroke that is not long and complex but short and simple, and that moves in the direction of the hit.

But while a push with the use of strength can be effective in preventing the racquet from being knocked back by the ball, and while a firm racquet obtained with a stiff wrist provides efficient storage of energy, there is a reduction in racquet velocity and acceleration. This results in poor efficiency in the recovery process and in a decrease in the amount of new energy that can be put into the shot.

ARM AND WRIST ROTATION

If the elbow is bent and is held below and about vertically in line with the hand, the arm cam be rotated to give added velocity to the racquet. The elbow acts as the pivot. The hand as pivoted at the wrist can also be rotated. The greater the bend of the elbow the greater can be the rotation of the arm. But the hitting point is then moved closer and closer to the body. So the arc of the swing is very small, as is the reinforce-ment with the body.

There are players at all levels who use wrist and arm flex combined with some wrist and arm rotation, but apparently don't know it. The stroke can be described as a combination of sling and swing. It is more sling with a sharply bent elbow and more swing and flex with a more extended arm.

One on the main problems with many adult novices is that they follow instructions too literally and develop a very plain swing. There is almost no flex, rotation, acceleration, reinforcement, or body involvement.

UNWISE USE OF WRIST FLEX

The caution here, as usual, is that the advantage of extra power should not be the cause of going overboard. If more than enough flex and\or rotation are used the benefits are apt to be canceled by distortions induced in other elements of the stroke. The enhancements should be obtained only as they occur naturally in a good hit, not as exaggerated flourishes in themselves. Strokes cannot evolve as a collection of details.

Trying for more wrist flex than is appropriate also means that the strength of the wrist will be over utilized, with none left to counter the impact of the ball. Although the muscles of the wrist have the advantage of the mentioned multiplication factor in converting flex to racquet velocity, they suffer that same factor as a disadvantage in absorbing the shock created by the impact of the ball.

An additional hazard is that if the ball arrives before the wrist has had a chance to flex forward it can be caught when it is both heavily stressed and is also in a very vulnerable position. Injury can result. Therefor it is advisable to use less than normal wrist flex on balls that approach extra fast, especially since on such balls it is quite easy to misjudge and be tardy in the timing. On the other hand, if the flex happens to be timed exactly correctly the added racquet momentum created by the wrist flex can reduce the normal shock of impact appreciably.

Another example of misuse of wrist flex is the tendency of many inexpert players to swing from the wrist on volleys. Besides being ineffective this happens to be very cruel punishment for the wrist. The shot should normally be hit by blocking the ball back and adding a small amount of shove. The shove is usually referred to as a punch, but that seems to be an exaggerated description of what actually occurs. It is more like moving the hand forward when catching a ball than shooting the hand forward to inflict a blow. While the wrist is not completely locked for the volley only a minor element of flex is normally involved.

The player who tries to swing at the volley is under the

misconception that the ball will not have much pace unless delivered to it by the racquet. On the contrary, just blocking the ball back can provide surprising power since the opponent's passing shots will usually be hit very hard. If the ball is a floater then the use of swing may be justified, and the stroke can be made quite wristy. The use of flex is an ideal method for adding extra pace on balls that sit up.

CONSERVING ENERGY

Older players have other reasons for using wrist flex. As the eyes weaken and the reflexes, coordination, timing, and mobility fade, the long strokes may get to be beyond physical capabilities. The need to minimize the use of strength dictates that the body be placed closer to the path of the ball, and the hitting point be moved more forward than what would be considered optimum.

The change need not mean serious, progressive deterioration. The compactness of the strokes allows a decent level of play when long free swings become impractical. That is probably the reason why the short chop stroke finds so much favor among seniors, and in truth works quite well.

The chop gives good racquet acceleration at the right time; good reinforcement with the shoulder; not much arm motion but all of it directed into the hit (except as used for spin); ease of use with an open stance (which minimizes the amount of movement between the waiting and hitting positions); good visibility of the ball, the hitting point, the court, and the opponent; easy switch from deep hits to drop shots; ease of making last instant adjustments for unexpected bounces; and easing of the "eye-hand" coordination requirements. The last benefit happens because of the short swing and swing interval, and because most of the action is in front in the field of vision.

The demands on the strength are usually further minimized by the racquet moving from high to low as it comes forward. Gravity thus helps in generating enough racquet velocity for a good hit. The elbow is held close to the body, so the "moment of inertia" of the racquet is low. The chop does sacrifice pace, but the flex of the wrist can partially make up. Also, in a realistic sense, the senior game does not depend on heavy pace anyhow.

Underspin is a natural product because of the downward travel of the racquet. The spin is effective in enhancing control because balls with underspin tend not to drop but keep moving in a straight line. On the negative side, the spin tends to make the ball sit up at the bounce and invite an offensive return.

When seniors carry the use of underspin to the extreme of making drop shots against players who cannot move well, then in most cases nobody really wins because there is little likelihood of extended exchanges with solid, satisfying hits. Special rules might well be used for such situations, such as: if a ball doesn't go past the service line on the other side it is "out". Otherwise the players could merely be providing inducements to each other to quit the sport.

There is no one term that is the consensus choice to describe the means used to hit a ball as hard as possible. The subject has not been one of the standard topics of instruction. In this book the process will be called "blasting", not out of any real preference but to avoid the confusion created by the use of a multiplicity of terms for the same thing. Other words that could be used just as easily are "pound", "slam", "slug", "smash", and "wallop". Descriptive terms include "go for a winner", "go for it", "go all out", and "cream the ball". But these are too cumbersome to be used with any frequency.

WHEN NOT TO BLAST

Many tournament players consistently hit the ball very hard, but few go all out for winners more than very occasionally. At that level nobody can afford to make extra errors. Very few coaches would recommend trying to slam the ball on every shot. Some in fact advise that it should never be done.

A well thought out example of the latter type of advice is that the player should approach each and every shot with the idea of winning the point not on that hit but on the one after. This means that even extra hard hits should be intended to be forcing shots, not unreturnable winners. The idea is to keep the opponent under pressure so as to ultimately force either an error or a setup that can be put away easily.

THE LEGITIMATE BLASTING TECHNIQUES

The means for getting maximum pace can be arbitrarily

assigned into five major categories as follows:

(1) Increase racquet velocity, acceleration, and reinforcement.

(2) Conserve racquet momentum.

(3) Improve the length and timing of the swing.

(4) Augment the swing with wrist and arm flex, and body motion.

(5) Lengthen the contact interval.

These categories have been selected just for this discussion as a means of organizing what seem to be important ideas. It is not claimed that the categories are either all inclusive or exclusive, or that other breakdowns would not work just as well. Within them, but often spanning across several of them, are the specific techniques for generating extra power.

One way that the swing can be intensified is through extra effort to increase the firmness of the arm and wrist. This prevents the racquet from being knocked backward by the impact of the oncoming ball. The technique is well suited for balls that approach with a great deal of pace. There are negative aspects to the method in that such firmness inhibits the use of wrist and arm flex, which are important in generating racquet velocity and optimizing control. The application of an extra amount of strength can also cause the stroke to become more like a push than a swing.

Bringing the arm closer to the body is a way of increasing the available strength. Here there is a question of whether that advantage is outweighed by the disadvantages. The arc of the swing and the time interval are decreased, making it necessary to develop the momentum more quickly, and initiating timing interactions. The swing can easily degenerate into roundhouse. Nevertheless the method is used by many of the players who do blast well.

A way to increase racquet velocity and\or acceleration is to use greater force or the same force over a longer arc. The arc can be made longer by using greater arm extension, taking the racquet back farther on the backswing, or increasing the amount of forward body motion and rotation.

A different approach is to preserve the racquet momentum generated in the backswing by carrying it into the forward swing via a looped path. Enlarging the size of the loop, but not to the point of exaggeration, gives added time and space over which to accelerate the racquet. The continuous curved path provides conservation of racquet momentum.

A very important increase in the pace of the ball can be obtained through the use of wrist and arm flex. It was shown in the previous chapter that a flex at the wrist can result in an increase in racquet velocity that can be ten times that developed in the hand by the same flex. Similarly, arm flex obtained via a swing hinged at the elbow can also augment racquet velocity. Both the flex at the wrist and at the elbow add to the velocity generated by the swing of the arm as hinged at the shoulder.

Some players augment arm flex with a rotation of the arm, as discussed in the previous chapter. The Western grip is generally used for this stroke. The elbow is close to the body, points toward the ground, and acts as a pivot. The technique seems to be something that players have picked up on their own since it doesn't seem to be taught, and there has been no mention of it in the literature or discussion.

A forward move of the body in addition to the other techniques is almost always desirable. Racquet velocity is increased thereby, and the reinforcement of the arm by the body is improved. Body rotation during the time when it is carrying the arm forward adds to the forward movement. If the actions are mistimed, typically through uncontrolled effort, the benefits become negative. A certain amount of body rotation is not only unavoidable but useful in all shots. But a danger inherent in a turn of the torso is that the body can easily rotate ahead of the arm, breaking reinforcement.

TIMING INTERACTIONS IN BLASTING

A complication introduced by a swing that is faster than normal is that the racquet may arrive at the optimum hitting point sooner than it should. It can be thought of either as the racquet arriving a little early or the ball arriving a little late. So the racquet will meet the ball at a hitting point a little too far forward of the body, which is advanced external timing.

The rotation of the body when it is carrying the arm forward and not sideward has that same effect. If the timing is not adjusted to suit the increased racquet velocity can become a problem instead of a benefit. The shift of the hitting point forward from the optimum will cause a loss of pace in the ball instead of the enhancement intended by the fast swing. The negative reward may lead the player to use ever more compulsive efforts on succeeding shots instead of making the required corrections to the external timing of the swing.

There is an obscure complicating factor involved in the effort to swing faster. Extra effort is expended to develop more than the normal racquet velocity. But to the extent that this is actually accomplished the time interval available to do the job is correspondingly reduced to less than normal. That factor tends to diminish the rewards for the trouble. A normal interval is largely preserved when the faster swing is obtained with wrist flex,.or with a longer swing. In the case of flex the initially laid back wrist lengthens the racquet travel. The racquet speed is increased but that of the arm is not. So the timing is only slightly affected.

INVOLVEMENT OF THE BODY

Two essentially similar methods of moving the body into the shot are shifting the weight forward and stepping into the hit. This equates to increased ball velocity. So the time

DOUBLE-FORCE TENNIS STROKES

available to complete the swing is reduced. If not compensated for with either a change in arm speed or an earlier start of the swing, the hitting point will be a little too far back with respect to the body, which is <u>retarded external timing</u>. So, as far as the hitting point is concerned,. the effect of moving the body into the shot is opposite to that caused by swinging the racquet faster.

The means of adjustment for <u>retarded</u> external timing caused by a forward move are:

1. Advance the start of the forward swing a tiny amount.

2. Shorten the stroke by shortening the backswing.

3. Bring the elbow in a little to shorten the arc of the swing.

4. Swing faster.

The main means of adjustment for <u>advanced</u> external timing caused by a faster swing are:

1. Delay the start of the forward swing a tiny amount.

2. Lengthen the stroke by lengthening the backswing.

3. Increase the arm extension a little to increase the length of the swing.

4. Swing slower.

If an increased forward movement of the body and a faster swing are both used then the time variations tend to cancel. Which effect will dominate depends on the particular combination of internal and external timing variations. Obviously an improper mix can create unexpected results.

In some cases the techniques being used all add to the same effect. An example is a slow swing, a late start, and a greater than normal forward movement of the body. All cause the hit to be late, resulting in the hitting point being too far back with respect to the body. Conversely a faster stroke, an early start of the forward swing, and a body rotation timed to increase racquet velocity are additive in causing the hit to be early: hitting point too far forward with respect to the body. This combination is very common on attempts to hit with maximum pace.

When the effects of timing variations are additive the results on the hit can be disastrous. And if it does happen it is not likely that the player would know why it happened. These are ideas that should have some control over the intents for the shot, but not conscious control. They could help to explain some types of errors, and could minimize misconceptions or false assignment of errors.

The complications associated with variations in the movement of the body and the swing of the arm illustrate the fact that when something special is attempted then all required changes to subsidiary actions must be taken care of. If they are not it may be of worse than no use to try to do the something special. Little factors not accounted for can equate to big errors.

Some of the best players can be seen making inexcusable errors because of violations of fine points such as those just discussed. Timing complications help to account for the fact that many attempts at blasting end up as points for the opponent.

THE ROLE OF STANCE
Many players take a more sideways position than usual in preparing for an all out effort, or may just turn the torso back an extra degree, or both. The more sideways attitude makes it possible to increase the length of the swing. This will help to develop added racquet momentum and thus

offset the need to slow the timing to compensate for the faster swing. But almost nothing is simple and few rules are fast. As discussed under "THE OPEN STANCE" in the chapter on "FOOTWORK", extra power can be obtained with an open stance by initially placing the torso in tension via a strong twist of the body.

Some very successful pros hit with less of a sideways stance and less movement of the body and shoulder than would seem to be sufficient. The apparent motives, besides the desire to loaf like anybody else, are to optimize the view of the ball and the other side of the court, keep the body out of the way of the arm on the forehand, and make it easy to get into position for the next shot. It must be recognized that there are secondary objectives that could be given priority under some circumstances, not always wisely.

NEGLECT OF THE CONTACT INTERVAL

A most important consideration that may not get the attention required on attempts at blasting is the length of the contact interval. The traditional instructions relating to that subject are to "hold the ball on the racquet as long as possible", and to "follow-through in the direction of the shot".

But, while both ideas are entirely valid, the instructions invite exaggerated application, and they don't take into consideration other factors without which the actions can be rather useless gestures. The principal means of getting increased length in the contact interval are:

(1) Develop adequate racquet momentum.

(2) Accelerate the racquet through contact.

(3) Maintain racquet travel in the direction of the hit during contact.

(4) Reinforce the racquet and the arm with the body.

Disregard of the requirements related to lengthening the contact interval has negative consequences on the storage and recovery of energy. For that reason a player's most impulsive efforts may not produce a particularly fast paced ball, while a long, relaxed swing in the direction of the shot, with enough reserve strength to counter the impact and provide good acceleration during contact, may with seemingly only moderate effort produce a bullet.

The mentioned definitions of the means of getting extra power (increase racquet reinforcement, acceleration, and velocity; conserve momentum; improve the length and timing of the swing; augment the motion of the arm with flex and body motion; and lengthen contact) can be employed either largely individually or in combinations, mostly the latter. There also has to be considerably better preparation for blasting than for a normal hit. But any attempt to augment a means that happens to be already optimally exploited will yield negative results.

Conscious individual application of any of the means of getting increased pace may cause those techniques to be unnatural, exaggerated, and self defeating. And it is not wise to attempt to superimpose selected details onto an existing style. The proper techniques and the proper intensity come out of an intent to hit for effect with a feeling for how to do it, and with the involvement of the body in a full and free expression of that intent.

INDIVIDUALITY IN BLASTING

Any available technique may be given special emphasis at the expense of others. Such imbalance does usually happen and need not be detrimental. For instance, if the elbow is brought in for a swing with a shortened arc, which is usually considered undesirable, there can be benefits such as reduced racquet inertia, better arm flex, and increased arm strength.

Whether or not this really provides an advantage over other

methods is another matter. There is a danger of bringing the elbow in just because of a feeling of weakness, lack of reinforcement, and artificiality when the arm is extended. The short swing and short time interval give the impression of high racquet velocity, but that could be just an illusion. Given the same extra involvement of the body, a long swing with an almost extended arm might do even better.

If the arm is gradually extended as it moves forward the overall result of a close-in, bent-elbow swing can be substantial power. This general type of technique is in fact used by many, but not all, of the top players who blast frequently and well. The particular style and the amount of extension of the arm tend to be very individualistic, and the people who do blast successfully are their own best advisors as to which technique works best for them.

The question may be raised that since the mentioned bent-elbow technique for blasting seems to be quite popular and successful why not use it all the time? The main reasons why not are an increase in the rate of error, a disadvantage in terms of reach, a high expenditure of energy, less pace rather than more if the ball is not set up approximately right for the purpose, and the availability of just as much or more pace with an extended arm.

THE EFFECTS OF THE INTENTIONS
Blasting has a tendency to bring out the worst habits in a player. The methods brought into use quite often involve violent but abbreviated effort, body ahead of arm, muscling rather than stroking, poor reinforcement with the body, a circular rather than forward swing of the racquet, jumping and turning instead of moving the body into the shot, an unpredictable racquet angle at contact, hitting with extravagant initial effort instead of maintaining a sufficient reserve, not adjusting the timing to suit the technique, blasting on every hit, etc.

The quite normal urge of wanting more than is obtainable

with legitimate means triggers the use of the unsuitable. The often misguided intent is as if to discard the proper hitting techniques and create a sort of explosion at contact intended to send a weightless ball instantaneously to the farthest quarter inch of the court. Since these attempts involve a fantasy-land type concept of the nature of the physical processes, and of the chances of hitting that last quarter of an inch, the real world results are likely to be an unsatisfactory pace and an enormously increased rate of error.

Some players are motivated to blast not by a feeling of super competence but by a subconscious feeling of not being capable of really "earning" a point, sustaining a rally, or hitting a small target. They therefor find it necessary to try for a lucky and spectacular winner instead. The fact that there is no rationality in the technique, that the feel of the hit is very unpleasant, the error rate multiplied, energy used at an excessive rate, and the pace of the ball not at all augmented as expected, does not deter the continual use of impractical means.

A disappointing pace is apt to cause a player to choose the irrational solution of trying to do even more than what already proved to be unattainable: untouchable passing shots, impossible angles, line drives intended to pass right through the opponent, balls that barely clear the net and land right on the base line, balls aimed at a point impossibly close behind the net, drop shots intended to reach the net and then slide down the other side, getting set to hit in one direction but then hitting in a completely different direction, etc. One lucky success appears to justify any number of ignominious failures. Unfortunately for such intents, lucky shots occur unpredictably and only occasionally for anybody at any level of play.

THE MISUSE OF ENERGY

A common illusion is the idea that a violent effort guarantees a sensational result, a placing of faith in the savageness of the force instead of the appropriateness of the technique. The association is not entirely irrational since it is logical to believe that if good results can be obtained with moderate effort it should be possible to get fantastic results with extravagant effort. But the energy expended and shock experienced do not in fact correlate to the best utilization of the characteristics of elasticity.

Since effective hitting is not in actuality the consequence of a great amount of strain and shock, the extra exertion is in some ways akin to the attempts of motorists to blow the horn louder by jamming down harder on the horn button. At least the horn behaves the same in any case, no better or no worse, while in tennis the consequence may be counter to the intention.

A frequent motive for the use of all out effort, especially on setups where it is not needed, is the feeling that an extra hard hit is somehow that much more painful to the opponent. But there is no profit in hitting with reckless violence and the substantial possibility of an inexcusable error. The opponent can then enjoy a monopoly on the use of the legitimate methods of winning points. The heavy expenditure of energy is in itself a very high price to pay for an unnecessary display of power. And even if the blast is impressively successful it does not provide any bonus points.

EMOTIONAL EXERTION

Extra emotional effort causes the tensing of a great many muscles that have no useful function in the stroke, and so would ordinarily be idle. Extravagant use of normally uninvolved muscles interferes with the mechanics of the shot. Allowing the emotions to run wild prevents adequate concentration on the intentions, preparation, and execution.

Some players engage in outbursts that arouse resentment in the opponent, goading that person to resort to the above described emotional responses. It is too much to expect that people under heavy stress and exertion will always refrain from engaging in disruptive behavior over real, trivial, imagined, or even fictitious problems. But where it is only the other player who then hits shots in anger the outbursts are at best inconsiderate, and at worst may be deliberate use of unfair tactics.

The best response by the victim of such behavior is to make good use of the free time. Take the opportunity to recuperate, analyze problems, restore a feel of rhythm, review strategy, decide on the means to improve execution, use "Slow Motion Visualization", etc. At the same time the agitator is otherwise engaged and is not similarly benefited. The biggest disappointment for players who attempt to unsettle their opponent could be the realization that the plot did not work, and may even have backfired.

INTELLIGENT BLASTING

In spite of the problems and risks involved with blasting, the probable trend in the future will be toward greater use of attempts to blast the ball past the opponent whenever a suitable bounce occurs, rather than just playing it safe at all times. In the future the question will probably not be who blasts and who doesn't, but who blasts better more often? The "DOUBLE-FORCE" strokes introduced in this book give almost all players the means to blast frequently and well. That ability may lower the importance of the "serve-and-volley" game.

Fortunately the principles outlined as necessary to get the maximum results out of the standard strokes are also those that are the key to getting the same out of blasting. Making the best use of elasticity imparts the best velocity. The pattern for blasting may not look like that of a standard stroke but the principles of elasticity, acceleration, reinforcement, recovery of energy, etc, have to get the same consideration, and even more. The more speed desired the more necessary to obey the basic principles.

The power stroke should still be hit with control, not with

an emotional, wild swing above the capabilities of the body or the responses of the equipment. The objectives of the swing can change but not the basic concepts of a good hit, otherwise the player will abandon most of what is productive to revert back to satisfying emotional urges and paying the inevitable penalties.

BLASTING OFF OF LOW BOUNCES

An interesting phenomenon that can be put to good use in blasting is that a ball can ordinarily be hit harder off a low bounce than a normal bounce. Some of the possible reasons are automatic nearly full extension of the arm, a longer swing, automatic positioning of the arm and body for good reinforcement, involvement of additional sets of muscles because of the need to hit up as well as forward, and the equivalent of added momentum in the approaching ball in the form of the pull of gravity.

However, if a ball is hit from a low position there is a big danger of sending it long because the hit has to have an upward slant. So topspin is advisable. But when energy is diverted into creating spin it takes away from pace. The trick is to optimize spin, not maximize it unless the extra high bounce is desired that comes with high spin. The objective in blasting is usually speed, not bounce, and it doesn't take much spin to bring even a hard hit ball down within bounds. So the spin should usually be moderate.

If a player doesn't happen to understand intuitively the subtle ways to get extra pace, and also is not aware of the physical laws involved, then various brute force expedients, such as a quick, overpowering turn of the body, are often used as substitutes. The urge to use wrong techniques to try to achieve devastating velocity is not restricted to the recreational players. Even in major tournaments it sometimes happens that top players blow very important setup shots by resorting to the most obviously inappropriate ways in the attempt to wallop a winner past the opponent.

The discussions in the previous chapters were generally applicable to any stroke. What digressions did occur were largely restricted to explaining a few special conditions. So part of the remaining task in the following chapters is to examine the special aspects of troublesome strokes. The backhand provides an area of special interest and concern because of the problems it seems to present and the misunderstandings that are often involved.

While a well-executed one-handed backhand is one of the finest and most graceful shots in tennis it is also the major source of frustration. The latter is particularly true for those players who did not get instruction early but picked up both techniques and expedients on their own, consulting neither teachers nor texts for guidance.

The following discussion will pertain mostly to the classic one-handed backhand because it is felt, rightly or wrongly, that it is a particularly fine stroke, is a pattern to which the principal requirements can be conveniently related, and is basic to the "DOUBLE-FORCE" techniques introduced in this book. It should not be assumed, however, that a recommendation is implied as it being the best style, or the one most suitable for all players. The discussion also applies in a general way to the other methods.

THE SIDEWAYS STANCE

The most important way that the one-handed backhand differs from the forehand is that the racquet arm and foot

are on the "net" side of the body rather than on the "fence" side. This makes it advisable to use of a fairly closed stance. By "closed" it is meant that the body faces toward the side even though the feet may not point there. If a face-the-net stance is used the arm is limited to a short backswing and forward swing. The racquet arm then also lacks both strength and extension in the forward direction.

A sideways stance eliminates inter-ference from the body in the back-swing and makes a fuller and freer stroke possible in the forward swing. So whereas the stance on the forehand is often partially open, it is usually closed on the backhand, even to the extent that the player's back can be somewhat turned toward the net.

A MORE FORWARD BACKHAND HITTING POINT
On both the forehand and backhand the hitting point is slightly ahead of the racquet shoulder. This would seem to mean that the hitting point for the backhand should be the width of the body closer to the net than for the forehand, since on the forehand the racquet shoulder is on the "fence" side of the body while on the backhand it is on the "net" side.

However on the forehand the body turns somewhat forward during the stroke, while on the one-handed backhand the body should remain in a mostly sideways position. So although the hitting point for the backhand is somewhat advanced compared with that for the forehand it is not by the full width of the body.

THE BACKHAND REACH
On the classic <u>forehand</u> the arm is progressively <u>restrained</u> <u>inward</u> by the hitting shoulder as the <u>racquet approaches</u>

the hitting zone. The reverse is true on the <u>backhand</u>: the arm is <u>constrained inward at the end of the backswing</u> but becomes <u>remarkably free as it moves through the hitting zone</u>.

Therefor, unlike what commonly happens on the forehand, the arm is almost fully extended at the hit, requiring the player to be <u>positioned farther away from the ball</u> than on the forehand. If this distance requirement is not met the closeness of the body to the path of the ball restricts the free flow of the swing, and the traditional difficulties which many players experience with the backhand begin to develop.

AN INITIAL OUTWARD ARC

On the classic backhand the path of the racquet differs in an important way from the standard concept of it being a rather straight line more or less parallel to the body, and pointing in the direction of the hit. In fact the arm goes from being held close in and parallel to the body at the end of the backswing to being held away from the body through most of the forward swing and the hit. The arm remains at about full extension throughout, again unlike the forehand.

Therefor the first task on the forward swing is to move the arm away from the body. This means that the racquet must initially circle somewhat outward toward the sideline before rounding the corner and moving forward.

The outward arc is not an add-on detail, but is something that will occur naturally if the body position is sideways, the stroke is swing rather than push, the location of the hitting point is proper, and the arm is simply allowed to move out and forward to that point. The swing is free and the arc is big,

so very good racquet velocity can be generated, especially if wrist and elbow flex are also used.

Without that initial outward arc the one-handed backhand tends to deteriorate into a push, deficient in acceleration and momentum, hard on the elbow, and costly in terms of the strength and energy required. Since one of the major advantages of the backhand is the availability of a long, unhindered swing it is undesirable to waste it with a push, or with other degenerate forms such as roundhouse, swipe, and slap.

AN UNCLASSICAL ALTERNATIVE

A one-handed backhand that is preferred by most players nowadays is accomplished by omitting the initial outward arc and using what is basically a forward push or fling of the racquet from a fairly sideways position. While the results can be very good a strong arm is required, as well as considerable exertion. And the higher level of shock and strain can make repeated use a source of damage. The body and shoulder are quite often partially frozen rather than moved and rotated into the hit, thereby limiting the freedom of the swing.

The body is positioned closer to the path of the ball than for the traditional stroke, resulting in the loss of the advantage in the matter of reach and length of arc. The backswing is usually abbreviated and the arm is held quite stiff. The chances of developing tennis elbow are increased because the racquet is muscled into the hit instead of sent with a momentum-powered swing.

Players seem to adapt very easily to this alternative to the classic swing. The arm is much stronger held close in than in the extended position. There is a

sense of security and appropriateness in the direction of motion of the racquet since it travels forward rather than out in the early stages. While the stance is generally sideways it is not quite as closed as for the classic, so the view of the opposite court can remain relatively good throughout.

THE ROLE OF THE IDLE HAND

A common recommendation regarding the one-handed swing is to support the racquet with both hands during the backswing. The second hand is then supposed to help start the racquet forward. The first part of this advice makes sense since the use of two hands can produce a more controlled ending to the backswing and can relieve the hitting arm of the weight and inertia of the racquet.

For the one-handed shot it is best to take the second hand off the handle at the start of the forward swing, or shortly thereafter. Otherwise that hand prevents the racquet from traveling in a natural outward arc to the required near full extension. With the "DOUBLE-FORCE" backhand the second hand is on the racquet arm rather than on the handle, and disengagement need not and ordinarily should not occur until after contact ends.

SIMILARITY TO A BASEBALL SWING

In confirmation of the initial circular motion, the backhand has been compared by Don Budge [*] who is considered to have had one of the greatest classic style backhands of all time, to be similar to the swing of a baseball bat. Because of the relatively great weight of a bat compared with that of a racquet, the final part of a baseball swing continues in more of a circle around the body than can be tolerated in tennis. Also, swinging a heavy bat forward results in a strong counter push created by the sizable inertia of the bat.

It is therefor not uncommon on a very hard swing in baseball to see the body being pushed backward, while in tennis it can and should be moving easily forward. A

forward motion of the body is just as desirable in baseball. Very hard swings that result in a noticeable backward move tend to cause the extra effort to be counterproductive.

The laws of elasticity and recovery of energy apply to baseball as to any act of hitting. This is true even though the contact interval in baseball is much shorter than in tennis due to the comparatively minuscule elastic deflections in both bat and ball. A moderately paced forward swing that allows the body to move into the hit, rather than have it be pushed back, should provide the most power in baseball for the same reasons that it does in tennis.

THE ROUNDHOUSE BACKHAND
A few of the causes of the all too prevalent, wild, unpredictable, and unlovely roundhouse backhand are as follows:
1. The one-handed backhand is started in a correct, naturally-curved outward arc, and the curve just continues rather than gets straightened out.

2. The player may not do enough about either getting the body ready initially, positioning it far enough from the path of the ball, or having it participate in the forward swing and the hit.

3. A turn to face the net may occur too soon.

4. The ball may be hit too early (too far toward the net), resulting in premature use of the available racquet travel in the forward direction.

5. Many players just resort to the expedient of swinging both the body and the arm around as suddenly as possible on the assumption that power is created thereby, or simply because they have not mastered a more proper swing.

6. The player incorrectly assumes that the arm is too weak to continue the swing in the forward direction.

EFFECTS OF AN OPEN STANCE

When a backhand is hit from an open stance the movement of the racquet arm with respect to the body is something like that of the front blade of a pair of scissors. Swinging upward is an action that is not easy with that technique. The arm is just not strong in the upward direction with an open stance.

The backward and forward swings are both limited, and the path on the approach to the hitting point usually becomes either somewhat of a circle or goes mostly sideways. The forward movement at the out-in-front location has to be forced, so a natural tendency is to pull the racquet down and across the front of the body. The pull and the circular motion make control of the direction of the hit rather difficult.

The actions create underspin, but a not very good variety in terms of effort expended, pace, accuracy, and control of spin. The same poor results are obtained even from a closed stance if the body and shoulder are rotated too far forward and around before or during the hit. In that case the upper body in effect operates out of an open stance regardless of where the feet may be.

The above criticisms do not apply to a properly executed underspin shot, and underspin is not undesirable per se. But here it is the inadvertent result of a cramped and deficient swing from an inappropriate position with little body participation, rather than a skillful stroke with its own special advantages.

BACKHAND TIMING DOESN'T MIRROR FOREHAND

Since the arm is relatively weak on the one-handed back-hand and may be slow in gathering speed, and since the length of the forward swing is a little greater (due to the mentioned factors of a rounded and more outward-going initial arc, a more extended arm, and a more forward hitting point) it therefor happens that the elapsed time for the classic backhand is likely to be a little greater than for a forehand.

The increase in time is minuscule to be sure, but it may be enough to cause the racquet to be a little late. This results in such things as a hurried stroke, wrong hitting point, incomplete development of momentum, damaging shock, and erratic control. Therefor the start of the forward swing must begin a little sooner than for a forehand. The timing interactions and complications that can arise out of such variations are covered in the chapters on "TIMING" and "BLASTING".

While timing should be an automatic operation, and while players should seldom make timing compensations deliber-ately, it is useful to know that the timing of the backhand does not exactly parallel the same for the forehand. Without that knowledge a person may subconsciously try to treat the two strokes as if they were mirror images of each other, which it is obvious they are not. The ultimate measure of correctness is the feel of a solid, momentum-powered hit.

A COLLECTION OF BACKHAND DIFFICULTIES

The mentioned timing differential, the unique nature of the arc of the swing, the positioning of the body further from the path of the ball, the lack of confidence in the strength of the arm, and the advanced hitting point are probably the major reasons why players have unnecessary difficulty in becoming comfortable with one-handed backhands.

Feelings of insecurity due to lack of mastery of the more complicated pattern, the timing of a long swing, and the

178

special grip and stance are other factors that are sources of trouble. Nevertheless, the prevalence of problem backhands is probably caused more by bad habits acquired early than by the inherent complexities.

A major cause of degeneration in the backhand is to turn toward the net too soon. On the forehand this is not all bad because the arm is made more free to move in the forward direction. On the backhand, however, the turn pulls the shoulder and the arm away from the hit. A powerless sideways swipe in front of the body can result.

PROBLEMS WITH THE VIEW OF THE BALL

Another difficulty with backhands is the poorer view of the ball due to the closed stance. This creates special difficulties for players who wear glasses because the view of the ball on the backhand tends to be through the outside edge of the lens nearest the net. The head must be turned decidedly forward to make even that possible, particularly if the lenses are small.

Light reflections from the skin onto the back surface of the lens increase in strength toward that same outside edge. The view of the ball can therefor become obscured, and may actually be blocked momentarily but totally by the reflections. Players are ordinarily unaware of the interference with the view of the ball unless told about it, and are usually only subconsciously aware of any difficulty at all. The light from other sources besides the skin, such as from the eye, the surroundings, and the sky may also cause interference. The reflection of the sun can cause total blocking if it happens to be in a critical position.

The cure is to have the glasses made with an anti-reflective coating, as on camera lenses. The coatings on plastic lenses are still easily damaged. Any lenses, glass or plastic and coated or not, should be washed or at least rinsed to remove gritty dust before wiping.

On sunny days some sort of visor is advisable because bright light striking the frosted edges diffuses throughout the lenses, giving the effect of looking through a slight haze. The effect is minimal if the edges are completely enclosed in the frame or if some sort of opaque film is applied over them.

Players who find head wear uncomfortable or unbecoming may have less objection to miniature visors that shield only the glasses. These have the additional advantage of not interfering with the view of the ball on overheads.

TWO HANDS FOR BACKHANDS
In the discussion that follows the limitations associated with two-handed backhands do not apply to the new "DOUBLE-FORCE" strokes.

A few players, even at the top, use a two-handed forehand. Some hit great shots even though, in baseball terms, it is a "cross-handed" hit. It is possible to get around the difficulty by switching hands. In that case the player is really using a two-handed backhand on both sides. Switching can become impractical during fast exchanges at the net.

Two-handed shots provide a means to make up for the

deficiency in strength of an extended arm. The major disadvantage of two-handed shots, <u>except</u> the "DOUBLE-FORCE", is loss of reach. The main advantages are that the combined strength of the two hands makes it easier to maneuver the racquet and counter the impact of the ball. The two-handed swing gives strong acceleration in a short distance and span of time, great resistance to the shock of impact, ease of learning, and ease of execution. These factors can help improve timing, control, manipulation, and disguise. For many players it can also mean improved pace.

But if the greater freedom, extension, and length of swing available on the <u>one-handed shot</u> are properly exploited, then more pace should be obtainable thus than on the standard <u>two-handed</u> stroke (not the "DOUBLE-FORCE"). However the level of proficiency required to hit the ball with heavy pace with the one-handed shot seems not to be easy to master, and particularly not for those people who started out with another style, or who acquired bad habits first.

An interesting fact is that two-handed shots are generally hit with <u>greater arm extension and more of a closed stance</u> than with the one-handed. The arms, in fact, are customarily held just about straight out. It may be something that the players just find appropriate, or something necessary because of the limitations of the reach. But the probable main reason is that players do not feel a need to bring the elbow in for added strength, or to protect the arm against the shock of impact, with the two-handed shots.

THE "DOUBLE-FORCE" BACKHAND
The "DOUBLE-FORCE" techniques eliminate all of the disadvantages of both the two-handed and one-handed strokes, and retain all the advantages. These include the best pace, maximum reach, combined strength of two hands, optimum control, complete freedom in the swing, reduced shock of impact, reduced effort, satisfying feel, good aesthetics, ease of learning, great adaptability to circumstances, effectiveness on difficult shots, and suitability for all physiques.

THE POSSIBILITIES OF IMPROVEMENT

Initially learned techniques have been almost invulnerable to change, especially in the case of the backhand. It is not possible to throw an old backhand away and just start using a new. Among the biggest reasons is the tremendous sense of insecurity that comes with attempts to use any other than an already insecure technique. One of the least recognized of reasons is the feeling of deprivation when any element is removed. There is also the frustration that develops out of the inability to make changes with "how-to" methods.

This book teaches principles, not patterns. After reading it a player will not have the same viewpoint of the backhand, be content with the same satisfactions, or search for remedies in the same unprofitable way as before. The ideas help the player to identify problems accurately and make proper decisions about standards and goals. Standards are not defined but discovered by experimentation. So, knowingly or not, the ideas get to be applied.

Stroke production tends to be more attitude and habit limited than task or talent limited. It is a very rare person who is really incapable of using a decent swing, easily returning a very hard hit ball, getting good pace on a serve, volleying effectively, or doing whatever else a person may assume to be beyond personal capabilities. Even inexpert players can execute nearly any stroke reasonably well in practice on a one shot basis. But when playing a match the old irrationality takes over.

Mental factors that can unhinge the sanity of a person's game include over-aggressive emotions and urges at one extreme, and inner feelings of insecurity and insufficiency at the other. When all else is in order such mental attitudes can still forestall any changes for the better. The bad consequences of being too aggressive have already been discussed in the chapter on "BLASTING". It remains to analyze some common fears so that players can avoid the opposite extreme of being too cautious.

DEFEATISM
Misgivings about lack of talent develop mostly out of repeated failure to improve. There is also apt to be a sense of defeatism stemming from the notion that nothing can be done about a game that was learned without the right amount and kind of early coaching. The net result is a belief that the existing flaws are permanent and that no new start can be made.

The inner fears need to be dealt with before, or at least along with, trying to deal with the defects in the mechanics of the strokes. This is not at all easy because for one thing inner feelings do not have the visibility of physical actions.

Fears not only inhibit attempts at mastering desired stroke patterns but sometimes induce compensations for problems and limitations that are entirely imaginary and do not exist. An imagined insufficiency generally simulates the very insufficiency feared, and the compensations generated for the imagined are likely to be the same as for the real.

THE LURE OF THE UNATTAINABLE

Paradoxically, fears sometimes develop out of trying for an over-ambitious goal, as when a person has intentions of obtaining a pace that in reality is unattainable with any technique. Players having such compulsions soon realize, but only subconsciously, that standard stroke patterns are not capable of producing the fantasy-land rewards. That is likely to lead to the adoption of desperation techniques that preclude realization of even less than ordinary level results.

Trying for a little more is quite often synonymous with playing a little worse. So then there are real problems in addition to the imaginary to contend with. A sense of athletic inadequacy sets in about being able to hit the ball with any respectable control or pace at all.

SELF-FULFILLING FEARS

An instance of insecurity of a slightly different nature occurs on the serves of some lower level recreational players. Incredible though it seems, there sometimes actually appears to be a fear of not being able to hit the ball over the net. The swing of people with this phobia becomes a desperate shove involving the whole body, something like the action in a shotput.

In most such cases the shove is not likely to have originated out of a fear of not being able to hit as far as the net, but rather out of concern about not being able to hit accurately with a free swing. The reluctance to swing freely coupled with the desire to get the ball over the net with inappropriate methods amounts to surrender to two additive and badly flawed motives.

The poor pace obtained with an unsuitable means can get to be interpreted as a personal limitation, rather than recognized as the natural outcome of deficient concepts and techniques. The expedients will not be abandoned because they have become habit, and because their use is motivated by the now enlarged fears. The embellishments that get added to the stroke in an attempt to obtain distance do not improve the prospects of reaching that objective either. Thus a continually enlarging chain of unnecessary flaws and fears is created.

A similar situation occurs when a player loses confidence and moves the hitting point more forward because a push feels safer than a free swing, and because the eye can follow the ball more easily out in front. This opens the stance, which in turn limits the forward travel of the racquet, narrows the hitting zone, and complicates the timing. Valid techniques are replaced with expedients in an attempt to cure the original and added problems, and the game is on its way to falling apart.

FEAR OF A FAST BALL

A fast approaching ball often raises an instinctive fear in the receiver that the momentum of the ball is much greater than can be handled. Such defensive attitudes can develop out of past experiences of shocks to the arm when using inappropriate means to receive very hard hits, or when the timing was not adjusted for the extra speed. So when a fast ball comes along the player reacts as if it were necessary to brace for the impact of a heavy object traveling at high speed.

Very few people consciously think that way but very many

nevertheless act that way. The body flinches backward, the arm freezes close in, the eyes are shut protectively tight, and the body makes a quick, short swivel to carry the arm into the hit. The reaction is as if it were first necessary to expend a great amount of effort merely to stop the ball and then to expend all the additional effort that by itself would produce the outgoing pace.

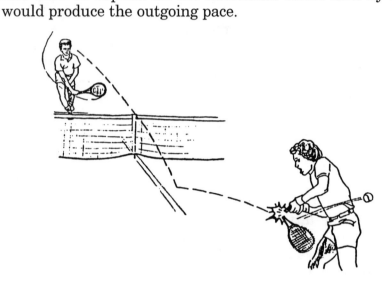

If this notion were correct the receiver would have to use more than double the effort expended by the opponent on any shot: one measure to absorb the momentum of the oncoming ball, one to provide an at least equal outgoing pace, and something extra to both make up for losses and top the incoming pace. A feeling of insufficiency for such a task would be very well founded. Such abnormal demands on a person's strength and energy would make any hard hit ball totally unreturnable.

REUSE THE MOMENTUM
But the above described notion is entirely irrational, as is obvious in the light of the earlier discussions on elasticity. The momentum of the oncoming ball is not destroyed but is first stored in the elasticities and then, with proper technique, reconverted into pace. The advantage for the

receiver is that the pace is already there. It is wrong to try to add much more. The greater the oncoming pace the less effort, not more, needed for a maximum paced return.

In case the formula for the development of pace as given in the chapter on "ELASTICITY" has been forgotten it is "BALL VELOCITY PLUS TWICE RACQUET VELOCITY". Some readers may find it advantageous to review that chapter. The mere knowledge of the theoretical formula, out of the context of the discussion about its limitations in the world of reality, is very likely to cause the formula to be misapplied.

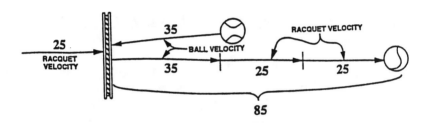

Racquet velocity has to be optimized, not maximized. If, for instance, a serve is approaching at 110 miles per hour (110 mph) it is not practical to expect the return to travel even faster. In order to be able to calculate the amount of energy that can be expended usefully in this case it is necessary to make two initial assumptions. One is that a very good speed can be achieved on the return, say 90 mph. Another is that a high level of efficiency can be attained in the recovery of energy from the elasticities, say 60 percent.

Under the given conditions the recovered ball velocity amounts to 66 mph (60% of 110). The difference between this and the desired 90 mph is 24 mph. This has to come from two sources:

1. The "carrying speed", which is 100 percent of the racquet velocity.

2. The energy recovered from racquet velocity stored
in the elasticities , which is 60 percent of racquet
velocity (not impact velocity in this case).

So the 24 mph is equivalent to 160 percent of the velocity
of the racquet. Dividing 24 mph by 1.60 gives 15 mph for
the necessary racquet velocity. This is far slower than what
most players try to use.

Making a similar set of calculations for a serve approaching
at 80 mph will show that to attain a return speed of 90 mph
the racquet velocity has to be 26.25 mph, still a modest
figure.

DIMINISHING REWARDS OF RACQUET VELOCITY
Greater racquet velocities will increase ball velocity, but the
law of diminishing returns sets in sooner or later depending
on the capabilities of the player and the properties of the
equipment. When a person tries to hit extra hard the
quality of execution often deteriorates. So the error rate
rises, conversion efficiency decreases, and the ball speed
may be lowered instead of raised.

As can be readily deduced from the above calculations, very
high racquet speeds would in theory create ball velocities
that are absolutely unattainable. In the example of a ball
approaching at a good speed of 80 mph, for instance, if the
racquet speed is raised to 60 mph the return ball speed, even
with only 60 percent efficiency, would be 144 mph.

This is far past what can be reasonably expected. Yet some
players are more likely to try to swing at 60 mph or more for
a ball speed that is not attainable, than to swing at about 26
mph for an exceptional yet realizable ball velocity of 90 mph.
Use of desperation techniques in a match degrades the pace,
interferes with timing, and multiplies the errors.
Subsequently when the same player hits with someone who
generates only moderate power the strokes return to
normal, and the comment is apt to be made: "I wish I had hit

like this yesterday. My timing was off".

The main intents in returning a fast ball should be to prepare early and execute calmly, bearing in mind that it is not appropriate to try to supply much new energy. The hitting point can be moved a trifle ahead of normal because the eye can follow the ball better there, and because a slightly forward angled arm is well braced to both counter the heavy impact and reuse the existing pace. That should be the major intent: reuse the existing pace.

The thing not to do is to assume that it is necessary to use every bit of strength and energy or that otherwise the return pace will be less than the received, resulting in a concession of inferiority and the loss of both status and the match. It invites disaster to either resort to compulsive exertions or freeze in sheer fright. Extra fast balls should not be considered to pose a difficulty as much as presenting a challenge and an opportunity.

EXPLOITING THE MISUSE OF EFFORT
An advantage that the receiver may be able to exploit is that the opponent may be off balance after using maximum effort for a very hard hit, and may be having more than normal difficulty in getting into position and being ready for the return. When a player hits a ball very hard the time available to get back to the ready position will be somewhat shorter than normal. Any fairly solid return may therefor catch him unready and off balance. But it is not something that can always be depended on because an alternative effect of a solid hit could be a more aggressive attitude and a more alert court coverage.

GETTING CAUTIOUS
Another result of insecurity is the miniature swings so commonly used by recreational players. Long, free strokes are synonymous with mastery and confidence, items in short supply wherever there are or have been problems with technique. Even expert players may suffer the qualms of

insecurity originating out of remembrances of troubles past, particularly in the case of serves.

They may then, like their inferiors, easily abandon the easy and natural way of doing things to resort to caution and compromise. Rather than that the errors will be reduced thereby there will likely be a multiplication. Caution in the swing, being an emotionally induced variation from the norm, will introduce errors in timing and execution just as surely as will the intent to be overly aggressive.

Even after a player has partially mastered an improved stroke and the time has come to use it in a game, the feelings of insecurity associated with the less familiar new methods, and the fear of making errors, usually cause quick reversion to the old habits. This is a serious predicament since those techniques that a player relies on in the more important circumstances will inevitably get to be used all the time. Not only are the errors and ineffectiveness the same as before but the repetition of the old bad habits just fixes them ever more firmly.

Of course there are apt to be problems with adopting new techniques, but no more so than with using the inadequate old. The possibility of "MIGHT NOT WORK" if done the new way is still a much better option than "WILL NOT WORK" if done the old. Hitting does not consist of merely satisfying the feelings of false security.

Quite a few players fully intend to use only smooth, expert level strokes ultimately. They nevertheless stick with the old faults during play with the reservation that these are temporary expedients to be used until the better techniques are mastered. As pointed out in an earlier chapter, this could mean that the old habits are being practiced several hundred times as much as the probably never to be adopted replacements. The logic parallels that of the old saying about not being willing to go into the water until having learned how to swim.

THE ROLE OF SUBCONSCIOUS REASONING

While the inner self can act with a high degree of practical wisdom that hidden side can also operate in a most irrational and unreasoning fashion. The conscious mind could be very rational about wanting to eliminate a mannerism or adopt an obviously better technique. But the subconscious may have reservations and may automatically force the arm to stay with what is familiar. An automatic response just happens, and so is not easily controlled by conscious decision.

The inner feelings may be equivalent to the following line of reasoning: "I tried to do exactly what the coach told me, but it didn't feel right. It is not working the way it does for other people. I can't use the coach's corrections because there is something different about me. There is no use taking chances with a swing that I know won't work for me." The above is just one possible way of thinking, and it is not being presented as a standard explanation for the many mannerisms that players invent and get addicted to with very great ease.

CHANGES FOR THE WORSE

There is an element of danger in assuming that a presumably better new technique should be used regardless of how unpleasant the feel. Some of the unpleasantness will merely be due to unfamiliarity and incomplete mastery, and will have to be tolerated for a while. But some could be due to the new methods actually being technically inferior to the old.

Any ideas that can be related to the principles of hitting can ordinarily be trusted, especially when confirmed by the satisfactions inherent in the feel. In this way the new methods, if they are really better, will come to be used because they get to be desired. In the mean time the previous habits get to be rejected because they feel decidedly inferior and unpleasant. The player realizes that the rewards were not what they were previously thought to be and that better techniques and greater satisfactions are within reach.

DEALING WITH FEARS

The three main choices available to the student in dealing with inner fears regarding the use of new methods are:

1. Reversion to the old habits (which usually happens).

2. Just trying to establish familiarity with the new via a great deal of practice of patterns (which also happens, but probably won't do much good).

3. Becoming familiar with the principles of hitting and learning to appreciate the feel and the techniques of a really smooth hit (and thereby becoming dissatisfied with the old compromises).

Ignoring fears and just imitating patterns does not address the mental and emotional sides of the problem. Fears do not, like teeth, disappear through inattention. Wherever a fear is either evident or suspected the coach can devise drills that are not very demanding on the student but yet will demonstrate that the ideas of insufficiency are nothing more than hobgoblins. In general the approach is to show that what the student may consider to be too difficult is actually very easy: returning a hard hit ball, or getting pace with an easy swing, etc.

A bonus from an understanding of the physical principles behind a good hit and an appreciation of the feel will be a growing confidence that the ideal techniques will work just as well for oneself as for anybody else. Discovering that fact and developing that confidence will go a long way toward overcoming the influence of fears.

PLAY THE BALL NOT THE OPPONENT

A player's game may fall apart when facing someone who is a level or so higher. Easy shots are flubbed, and the match becomes just an exercise in losing as quickly as possible. But a ball is a ball is a ball. It has to be respected for its own sake and not in relation to the source, which is a court's length remote and without any presence or influence on the receiver's side.

Therefor a ball with a given speed and bounce has to get the same respect and attention whether hit by a dub or a pro. Conversely, a given pace and bounce should present no more difficulty if from a pro than if from a dub. The most common mistake is to try to do too much if from a pro. Granted that the return to the pro may have to be somewhat better than ordinary, but that does not justify trying to hit impossible winners, and on every ball. In any case the player on the other side, if much better, will probably not have any more difficulty handling the occasional exceptional shot than those that are just ordinary.

Trying to hit shots beyond one's capabilities to an opponent who will be able to return the best of them with no trouble usually equates to making a variety of errors off all kinds of manageable bounces. To make matters worse, ordinary players are generally overdoing their shots to begin with. So trying to do even more merely aggravates a main existing problem.

Blasting with legitimate techniques in an attempt to win the point may be worth the chance at times, but hitting for more than attainable velocity will never work. Although moderately paced returns may not do much more than go in, making it possible for a superior opponent to take charge and win points easily, that is still much more respectable than giving points away voluntarily via unnecessary errors. Balls that just keep coming back raise the worst of all fears in the better player: the possibility of losing to an inferior opponent.

Putting something extra into a shot requires increased attention and use of energy in the preparation stage. The usual tendency is to spend even less than the normal on the preparation, and more energy than is available or can be controlled on the forward swing.

There are mental factors that relate less to techniques than to attitudes and phobias, such as the fear of losing to a lesser player, the reluctance to appear to try when playing someone considered to be of lower rank, the loss of all interest and incentive over a bad line call, etc. It can merely be noted again that a ball is a ball is a ball. Emotions have no influence on the ball, but they can interfere with execution.

The serves of most recreational players cannot honestly be described as anything better than awful. The first serve is the one stroke where most players hit as violently as possible in spite of having error rates many times greater than what is acceptable on other strokes. The problems inherent in a serve include exceptional complexity, resistance to improvement, and vulnerability to emotional execution. The difficulties provide a good test of the efficacy of some of the means that have been suggested here for the upgrading of established games.

THE EFFICIENCY OF THE SWING

It would be difficult to justify the classic service motion on the basis of efficiency and conservation of energy. While there can be some retention of momentum there is bound to be considerable loss, mostly in three up or down reversals of direction:

  a. The racquet head drops down toward the ground.

  b. REVERSES upward to a position above the head. (1)

  c. REVERSES down behind the back to below shoulder level. (2)

  d. REVERSES upward to maximum

reach and accelerates as it does so. (3)

e. Turns forward and continues to accelerate as it meets the ball.

THE EFFICIENCY OF THE WINDUP

On the classic serve many players slow the racquet motion near the peak of the first upward move to the extent of almost or even actually coming to a dead stop. When this happens all the prior arm motion merely operates to put the arm, racquet, and body into whatever form of ready posture the individual uses before the final loop of the swing.

If a person who has such a habit can place the racquet and the body into the same ready position without the help of the previous motions, and can toss the ball easily and effectively from that posture, then there is little or no physical advantage to the prior activities. But getting the whole body prepared and ready to contribute to the hitting action is not an insignificant achievement.

Even a baseball pitcher, whose actions are not complicated by the presence of a racquet, will typically go through a sometimes surprisingly elaborate and individualistic windup preparatory to the actual throw. While servers are entitled to at least equivalent preliminaries, the windups of some tennis players go past all reason with extensive rituals and a sizable expenditure of energy.

Some players introduce a halt in the motion of the body also. Of those who do not only a small percentage manage to time the body motion well enough to derive anywhere near the available benefit in the form of added racquet momentum. At the instant of the hit the big majority of players have already taken the body well past the point where it ought to be even at that late stage.

THE BIG CIRCLE

On the serve, if anyplace, the racquet travels in something

of a circle just before the hit. Since the circumference of a circle is over six times its radius, the advantages obtained by extending the arm and using wrist and arm flex to maximize the momentum of the racquet and the resultant pace of the ball can be readily understood.

Players at all levels of skill develop difficulties in their service motion because of a tendency to bring the elbow in and use at least some push instead of swing when the point is very critical. There is a feeling of security and control in pushing the ball toward the target even though that confidence is highly unjustified. In fact, in a recent year the use of push caused double fault on match point in several "grand slam" finals. The worry about accuracy is usually compounded by a desire to use an extravagant amount of strength.

A way to minimize the tendency to push the racquet is to intend to use a "swing-controlled" stroke with an extended arm. An added benefit is an enlargement of the area in the service box into which the ball can be directed. A more extensive discussion of this effect, and of the general problem of hitting the target area, is presented later on in this chapter.

THE SMALL CIRCLE

A smaller than maximum circle is not an unmitigated evil because the arm is strong close in and can provide good racquet acceleration if the motion remains a swing. However the use of a small circle is ordinarily due to uneasiness about the weakness of an extended arm, and to feelings of lack of control with a free swing. A small circle on a serve will tend to lower the hitting point, direct the ball downward instead of forward, decrease the potential velocity, and increase the probability of error.

COMPARISON TO A THROW

The classic service motion has frequently been likened to a throw. While there is considerable similarity, the serve is different from at least some throwing patterns in that for most serves a near full extension of the arm is used. In contrast, the hand travels forward at only about head height in many throwing motions. That puts the arm at considerably less than full extension. A tall person with a strong arm may be able to hit excellent serves in spite of a low toss and a throw-like swing, but for others the results are generally less than good.

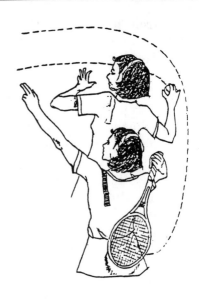

One feature of the throw that deserves to be emulated, not only in serves but in most ground strokes, is that the arm is being accelerated forward in the direction of the throw even as the ball leaves the hand. Many servers reach maximum racquet velocity before contact. And they may also hit only a glancing blow by diverting some of the forward travel of the racquet into a downward motion just before the hit.

The concept of throwing can be useful for another reason. In throwing a ball at a target there is automatic allowance for the effects of gravity. A common mistake in serves is to ignore the effects of gravity and think in terms of hitting the ball along a straight line pointed directly at a spot in the service court. The falsity of that concept will be demonstrated further on in this chapter.

THE PRINCIPLES OF THE HIT

The essential fact of a serve is that it is a hit. As such, the factors of
  recovery of energy from elasticities,
  appropriate grip and body position,

reliance on momentum rather than push,
use of a "swing-controlled" stroke,
accelerating the racquet through contact,
extending the arm to optimize the length of the arc,
straightening the arc out in the direction of the hit
    during contact (except for special effects),
using wrist and arm flex,
moving the body into the hit,
reinforcing the arm with the body,
rotating the shoulder into the hit,
avoiding rotating the shoulder or the body ahead of
    the hit,
optimizing the hitting point,
meeting all timing requirements,
keeping a sufficient amount of strength in reserve,
avoiding tensing of uninvolved muscles, etc,

must all get their due respect. But all of these actions have to happen automatically in the context of a hit and not as individual details. **How could it be possible to direct the attention to several of them simultaneously? And what would the consequence be of watching only one?**

The general requirements for the hitting point in the serve are the same as for other strokes:

where the combination of good direction, momentum,
    and attitude of racquet,
strength and freedom of the arm and wrist,
reinforcement with the body,
and availability of body motion and rotation into the
    swing

are as close to optimum as possible. More descriptively it can simply be said that the hit should occur in the good part of the swing.

RACQUET VELOCITY IN A SERVE

One of the factors that makes the serve different from most other shots is that the ball has zero initial velocity. Although this means that there is no initial momentum of the ball to be overcome it also means that there is none to augment the energies derived from the momentum of the racquet. So all the forward pace of the ball must be obtained from energy generated by the server.

Consequently a non-rigid grip and a great deal of wrist and arm flex are not only permissible but desirable as a means of increasing the amount of momentum that can be developed in the racquet. By those means the serve generates the fastest pace in tennis, in spite of the zero initial ball velocity. An unpleasant implication is that energy is not being expended and recovered as efficiently in the other strokes   On the positive side, there aren't as many errors either.

An interesting statistic that can be calculated quite easily is the velocity of the racquet. Since the ball has zero initial velocity the formula for pace reduces to: "recovered racquet velocity" plus "carrying velocity". In this case the first item can be defined as "racquet speed times the percentage of recovery", and the second as just "racquet speed". Assuming the efficiency of recovery to be 60% the pace of the ball is thus 1.60 times racquet velocity. Conversely, racquet velocity is ball speed divided by 1.60. For a 100 mph serve the racquet velocity is 100 divided by 1.6, which amounts to 62.5 mph.

DIFFICULTIES OF A SIMPLE TOSS

Besides the optimizing of the swing there is another very important element to master in a serve: a proper toss. It is surely a highly emphasized point in just about every coach's teaching routine, and is a simple enough skill to master. Among good players there is notable uniformity in the tosses. But among others there is an incredible variety of inappropriate means of placing the ball with great inconsistency into positions from which it can be hit only with difficulty, and with undependable aim and insignificant pace.

The toss presents no problem to those people who learned it

correctly initially. But it is a most formidable obstacle to those who did not. Practicing the toss can be very tedious because it is easily possible to do fifteen or more in the space of only one minute. So it is a rare individual who is determined enough to practice it for more than several minutes on more than several occasions. Such a minuscule amount of practice will not produce much improvement in spite of the simplicity of the basic skill.

COMPATIBILITY OF TOSS AND SWING
Even if perfection is achieved in the toss itself there is then the much greater problem of a lack of compatibility with the existing imperfect service motion. The imperfect swing may bring the racquet around with inappropriate timing in a path that never comes close to the ideal hitting point.

A player with a peculiar or erratic service motion has to modify the toss to suit. It is truly "swing-controlled", but with a reverse purpose. The "toss at the swing" becomes "toss at the bad swing". This has to mean good-bye perfect toss. The bad swing must be fixed before the toss can be.

"SWING-CONTROLLED" SERVE
The "toss at the swing" idea is valid only in the context of using an excellent and consistent swing. By that definition the toss is not a variable at all. A way to implement the concept is to intend to use a visualized ideal swing regardless of the location of the ball.

With the path of the racquet thus established all that remains is to get the ball to the preordained hitting point when the racquet inevitably arrives there. If the server has a firm purpose to go through the swing in that manner, without any accommodations for a misplaced toss or to feelings of insecurity, then there will be improvement in consistency in placing the ball at the appropriate hitting point at the right time. More importantly, the swing will be improved too. WHEN PRACTICING SERVES IN THIS WAY THE SWING SHOULD NOT BE

COMPLETED IF THERE IS ANY POSSIBILITY OF HITTING SOMEONE
WITH A MISDIRECTED BALL.

Since the swing should not be modified to meet a bad toss
there should be little or no attention paid to the details of
the toss while it is being made. A bad toss will only get
worse with observation. At the same time the swing will fall
apart from neglect, and old flaws will return by default. If
the ball does not get to the desired location then it is time to
examine the swing for faulty intentions and techniques,
especially violations of the rule not to modify the swing for
any reason.

PRACTICING THE TOSS

There is a common drill involving a sequence of three tosses
that can both increase the amount of practice of the toss
that a player is willing to make and facilitate the coordination of the toss with the swing. The exercise establishes the
processes by which the toss is matched to an ideal swing.

First two practice tosses are made combined with an
uncompromised swing, but with the swing stopped just
before the final forward motion into the hit. The serve
should be completely real in other respects in that the body
should participate as if the hit is to be completed. Otherwise
the exercise merely amounts to practice of improper
readiness, and a toss adapted for that condition.

When practicing tosses without going through with the
actual hit that final action must always be visualized so that
the location of the toss is determined by the intents for a
smooth, relaxed swing. This is where the slow motion type
of visualization process, SMV, can help reduce the gap
between difficulty and mastery.

When learning the toss it is advisable to also learn to vary
the swing, placement, and height slightly. The objectives
include to develop flexibility, test the advantages of swings
that have various hitting points, and remove any restrictions on the placement of the toss, and on the nature of

progressive improvements to the swing pattern. The serve is "swing-controlled" and therefor should vary only as to the type (flat, slice, or kick). The toss should still be intended to put the ball into the path of an uncompromised swing, whatever the type.

COMBINING TOSS AND SWING

On the third toss of the sequence of three a moderately paced swing can be carried all the way through in the manner visualized. If the toss is faulty the swing should either be carried out as intended without compromise or delayed a little to avoid contact with the ball.

A PRACTICE SERVE SHOULD NOT BE COMPLETED IF THERE IS ANY CHANCE OF A MIS-HIT CAUSING TOO GREAT OF A SHOCK TO THE ARM, **OR ANY POSSIBILITY AT ALL THAT SOMEBODY ELSE COULD BE ENDANGERED BY A MISDIRECTED BALL.** A good place for initial drills is against a tall backboard or wall with no windows. On all serves the requirements outlined in a previous paragraph titled "THE PRINCIPLES OF THE HIT" must be satisfied.

The swing is a big problem in itself, and an immense problem in combination with the rather simple toss. A person can easily acquire a good mastery of tossing to an ideal hitting point. But unless either the "swing-controlled" concept is used or the swing itself is perfected enough to have the racquet always pass through an ideal hitting point, there will be an automatic refusal to use an ideal toss.

The body is smart enough not to direct the ball and the racquet to different hitting points. The bad toss and bad swing at least work together. Each needs and deserves the other. So the first two tosses of the drill will be fine while the third will initially tend to go out of control.

When practicing ground strokes it is not possible to entirely avoid chasing the ball with the racquet, particularly in the case of unpredictable behavior by the ball. But there should be very few such compromises when practicing serves. If the ball is not at the hitting point when the racquet gets there the swing should not be changed to chase the errant ball. Otherwise the visualized swing is abandoned, the new ideas fail to get tested, and new bad habits are formed.

Even if the ball is missed completely the drill is still useful if the swing is carried out as intended. But a swing that is compromised to fit a bad toss, or vice versa, means that both are being practiced in a wrong way. Until the body and the subconscious become convinced that the swing will not be compromised there will be an automatic refusal to abandon the old toss.

The toss and the swing must be used at all times as described above, both in practice and as much as possible in play. When in play, though, there should not be any practice tosses except to check the wind, sun, etc. But there should be the same intent to use an ideal swing as described above, not reversion to something considered to be more suited to the practicalities involved with winning a point. It is unwise to abandon what is effective in practice for what has been proven to be unsatisfactory in play.

Coordinating the concepts of the swing with those of the toss may be facilitated by preceding the above sequence of three drills with the toss of an imaginary ball into the path of a moderate "swing-controlled" serve that contains no compromises or excesses. It should be done at slower than normal speed so as to minimize the bad habits that are a rather inseparable part of a normal-paced hit, real or imaginary. Occasionally the normal serve should be emulated also because re-experiencing it helps expose the good and bad points.

As the sequence of three or four drills is repeated there should be an attempt to improve on all the elements involved, but in the context of a "swing-controlled" stroke, not as individual details. This could include stance, grip, preparation, readiness, toss, forward travel of the racquet, shoulder turn, acceleration, reinforcement, hitting point, end position of racquet, etc. It is also necessary to be on the lookout for compromises, compensations, muscling, body ahead of arm, downward pull, emotional execution, etc. Extensive use of slow motion visualization (SMV) is advisable. The behavior of the ball after the hit <u>should not</u> be included in the visualizations. Placing the emphasis on results neglects the matters that produce the results.

TIMING OF THE TOSS

There is an old adage that on the toss the racquet arm and the tossing arm should go up together, and contact should occur just below the peak of the toss. Would that anything in tennis was that simple. The statement is only occasionally true, and so can introduce confusion if applied where it does not fit in exactly. The technique may be a good way for a beginner to learn the elements of the toss, but it may mean nothing but trouble for people whose perfectly good or even superior manner of tossing does not follow that pattern. Observation of tournament players shows that there is general disregard of that advice.

If a serve is carried exactly that way both the ball and the racquet reach the peak of the upward motion at the same time. But the racquet still has considerable to do: go down to the "back-scratch" position and then back up and forward into the hit. Meanwhile the ball does not have far to go to get to the ideal hitting point, and is not going to wait there while the racquet finishes the preliminaries.

Some players who do take the arms up together have also learned to toss high enough to re-establish correct timing for the hit. Others toss very high and then bring the racquet to a stop near the top of the upward motion So it is possible that they might be better off tossing the ball up a little earlier and then swinging as a somewhat separate, simple operation so as not to waste racquet momentum.

Tossing the ball high has several advantages:
The toss and the swing can both proceed without

interfering with each other.

Tossing the ball becomes a simple task with hardly any coordination problems.

Separating the toss and the swing reduces the complexity of the service motion, making learning easier.

At the hit the ball already has an initial downward momentum, making it easier to get the ball to curve down into the service court.

The disadvantage of a high toss is that the ball can be deflected by strong winds.

Whether or not the arms go up together has nothing to do with the successful placement or timing of the toss. In fact some of the best and most consistent servers toss the ball before the racquet arm has even started its upward move. There is nothing wrong with either <u>bringing the arms up approximately together</u> or <u>bringing them up separately</u>. In any case the toss shouldn't be on the mind while serving.

If two people of the same height and build toss to slightly different heights, and yet in each case move the tossing arm and the racquet up together, then the accommodation for the height of the toss has to be made someplace else in one of the swings. Otherwise the ball will not be at the hitting point when the racquet gets there. Additional items where variation will occur include a pause or slowing at the peak of the first upward move of the racquet, a jump during the swing, the amount of extension of the arm, the depth of the "backscratch" motion, and the velocities of the swings.

So if the adage is applied it could cause some people to try to do something other than what they normally do when serving confidently and well. Even top players with very good serves can be misled. When they are experiencing troubles with the serve they may attempt to settle down by practicing the "arms-up-together" motion. If this is not the norm, and it very seldom is, the troubles can only get worse.

Nevertheless the instruction can be useful, especially for novices, but only if the word "approximately" is used, and then only as a recommendation, not as a requirement. Children will try to use it, but most of them will quickly switch to whatever else is required to make the stroke work. Adults will assume that the closer they adhere to the rule the better will be their toss and serve. They thus become committed to something that may become a handicap instead of a help. The complex hitting process cannot be defined by a few simple rules.

THE "WINDMILL" SERVE

There are a very few people who use a circular, windmill type swing. Examples of this serve can occasionally be seen even in top tournaments, although sometimes only because the user has a shoulder injury that is aggravated by the conventional motion. The technique is uncommon enough that many players are not even aware of its existence.

The racquet is simply taken <u>down, back, up,</u> and <u>forward</u> in a largely <u>circular</u> path with no interruptions or reversals of racquet direction. The circular path is straightened during the approach to the hitting point. The intention should be to carry the forward motion of the racquet into and through contact. The racquet does come down at the end, but that should only be the result of momentum and flex, not an intention to hit downward.

There can be easy development of good racquet momentum with the "windmill" serve since it is developed gradually and continuously. By contrast, in the conventional swing most or all of the racquet velocity begins to be developed only after the racquet has reached the "back-scratch" position. This places a large and sudden strain on the muscles of the arm, back, and shoulder, and on the tendons in the elbow. When properly done the windmill serve imposes much less strain on those muscles.

The elbow should be relatively unbent, although a little wrist and arm flex can be used. If the elbow is more than slightly bent before the hit care has to be taken that it does not result in a pause at any point during the swing, especially not near the top. That would eliminate the advantages obtained with the continuous circular motion.

The arm is easily and naturally kept at full extension, so the hit generally occurs at a commendable height. All in all, there seems to be no reason why the ball cannot be hit harder with a windmill motion than with the traditional. However to accomplish that result the body must become involved. It should not just stay rigid and uncooperative while the arm travels the mainly circular path on its own.

PRINCIPLES VS PATTERNS

There is no single best serve for all people. This is by no means intended to denigrate the classic, which is really great, but to emphasize the necessity of basing the serve on the mechanics of hitting. If a motion is economical in terms of the energy required and also produces a good hit then it is fine and appropriate even when it is unconventional.

Correctly executed, but without some of the petty restrictions such as using a specific alignment of the feet, having the arms go up together, keeping the tossing arm up, or ending the follow-through in a certain manner, the genuine classic serve is synonymous with correct mechanics. Some patterns that do not resemble the classical nevertheless incorporate the correct mechanics equally effectively.

A baseball pitcher's throwing motion would be very unnatural and ineffective if it was necessary to go through precise manipulations with the glove hand, or hold it above the head, while the ball was being thrown.

An important advantage of using the basic requirements of a hit as the guide, rather than using a pattern, is that as the concepts of the serve are refined, or of any stroke, all others will share in the benefits, and all can be further improved on without any defined limit.

When ideas are open to continual expansion and improvement then what feels correct today may in the light of further experience and analysis feel quite abbreviated and inadequate. The desired game is something like the horizon, forever receding even though where it appeared to be previously may have been reached or even far exceeded.

When the serve is made to follow a pattern then that pattern represents the upper limit of achievement. Even when it gets to be mastered it may turn out to be wrong in some respects, or unsuitable, or just not as good as what is attainable through a a better application of the principles of hitting. If the hit is not as good as it can be there is something about the mechanics of the hit that is not right, whether there is conformance to an established style or not.

There is no such thing as having done everything absolutely right and yet not having obtained a correspondingly superior result. It is both possible and necessary to discover what is wrong, what is right, and what is missing. That skill is partly what this book is about.

THE HITTING POINT

The analyses of the nature of common sources of error under this and other subheadings are based on the classic serve or close variants. But the comments are nevertheless quite general in nature and have application to most other patterns as well.

The hitting point on a serve should be slightly forward of the body because the reinforcement is better and the arm is stronger out front. If the hitting point is too far forward then various problems arise, such as cutting down on the remaining forward racquet travel, slowing down of the racquet before contact, lowering the hitting point, and angling the face of the racquet both more downward and toward the side.

A consequent problem is that as the body (or perhaps the subconscious) becomes aware of incorrect direction or unpleasant feel it introduces compensations. These soon become habit. For instance, if by the time of contact the natural angle of the face of the racquet would direct the ball downward the player will learn to compensate by laying the wrist back to bring the angle up to normal. While helping the aim this does not correct the basic flaw, and will introduce new problems.

The hitting point is internal to the swing, not external and not something established by means of a definition. A "swing-controlled" stroke establishes that internal location on the basis of appropriateness.

BREAKING REINFORCEMENT HORIZONTALLY
One of the most universal of faults in serves, as in other strokes, is the breaking of the reinforcement with the body. In a serve this can occur in two directions: horizontally and vertically. In the horizontal type the body is rotated around too soon, similar to the same problem in ground strokes. When the body gets ahead in that way it puts the arm in a weak position for the forward swing.

A very common form of this fault is to go through the windup in a more or less exemplary sideways position, but then swivel the body around prematurely, or just the torso. This moves at least the upper part of the body into a face-the-net position before the arm has made comparable progress in the forward swing. The usual psychological urges behind the premature turn of the body are to use the strength of the entire physique to the utmost and to "look the ball" to the intended landing point.

The intent to maximize the use of strength neglects the fact that the body is disproportionately stronger than the arm. It must be restrained from either going all out or acting too soon. The arm should be able to push off against the shoulder and not be dragged along by it. Some body rotation should be used, but only in a manner to have the shoulder send the arm into the hit to give added force and power. A too early body turn will waste this extra power and leave the arm behind, fighting to catch up.

In some faulty serves the premature rotation is quite subtle, with the swivel of the body only partially preceding the swing. In such cases the player may find it difficult to believe that the opening of the stance occurred somewhat early, and that both the forward swing and hit occurred in an essentially face-the-net position. Yet the fault is present to some extent in the majority of serves at all levels.

Opening the stance on serves is the general custom among senior recreational level players. It is often due to feelings of insecurity about being able to aim accurately at a spot that is not in the line of vision. It also originates out of mistaken ideas about the benefits of using strength and push instead of momentum to obtain both speed and accuracy. Strength is not a factor in abundant supply among seniors, and the push is a technique with the least rewards in terms of pace and the greatest penalties in terms of strain. In its extreme the total action may begin to resemble a throw executed with the wrong foot forward.

THE FORWARD JACKKNIFE

Breaking reinforcement vertically simply means bending the body forward in a jackknife action. The arm cannot bring the racquet along as quickly as the body is capable of turning forward and downward. So although the arm continues in the forward direction it lags further and further

back with respect to the body. The racquet is then quickly dragged downward rather than swung forward into the hit. A common instruction is to hold the tossing arm up in the extended position as long as possible. This is intended to keep the head up and prevent the forward jackknife. It does have some effectiveness even though it amounts to controlling the body position by means of an artificial detail. There is at least some penalty in terms of interference with the swing. The inappropriateness can be verified by trying to throw a ball while the free arm is held above the head.

A better way to prevent the jackknife is to continually refine the concepts of the "swing-controlled" stroke and the forward travel of the racquet at the hit. Eventually the downward bend of the body, the lag of the racquet arm, and the nature of the hit will get to feel sufficiently unpleasant to cause the habit to gradually fade away.

Both the horizontal and the vertical means of breaking reinforcement overwhelm the strength of the arm. When that happens the jolt of impact created by the inertia of the stationary ball will deflect the racquet head backward with respect to the arm. The loss of pace is appreciable, and the attitude of the racquet and direction of the ball at the hit are unpredictable.

JUMPING
There often are actions that involve trade-offs between several desired objectives. Jumping into the air is one such. It extends the reach, frees the swing, enlarges the target area, can provide a quick start for an advance to the net, and can be an outlet for the urge to use every last bit of effort. But keeping at least one foot in contact with the ground

tends to maximize reinforcement, increase ball velocity, improve control, and economize on effort.

One type of motion that provides no discernible benefit or trade-off is to let the body drift sideways during the serve. The racquet is pulled away from the hit, thereby decreasing both pace and accuracy. It is never seen in tournament play but is common in recreational level tennis.

SCIENCE OF HITTING THE TARGET AREA

Hitting to a selected point in the service court is the source of an amazing amount of difficulty and misunderstanding. Many people never realize that a straight line extended in the direction of the ball as it leaves the racquet should point to an area well past where the ball is intended to land. They incorrectly assume that a racquet held over the head has an unobstructed view of a sizable part of the service court.

They also assume, with incredibly bad science, that the trajectory of a hard hit ball is a straight line. In actuality the line of travel has a decided droop, mostly toward the end.

THE STRAIGHT LINE FACTS

In the following discussions the "path of the ball" is being considered as the "path of the bottom of the ball". The center of the ball is about 1¼ inches higher up.

A little geometry will show that a straight line drawn from a point 8½ feet above the baseline, and angled down to just clear the 3 foot high point of the net, will touch ground 3.3 inches past the service line. If the straight line is raised just one inch above the net then the point where it touches ground will be 14.4 inches past the service line. So in this case one inch above the net multiplies the landing point error by more than four. Fortunately the ball does not travel in a straight line, even with no topspin.

A line pointed at the service line from a height of 8 feet will meet the net three inches below the top at the three foot high point. If it is pointed to just clear the net it will touch ground about 2 feet 5 inches past the service line. This can be confirmed without mathematics by simply climbing a stepladder at the baseline until the eye is 8 feet above the ground. A little experimentation will show that the eye has to be at a height of 8 feet 7 inches before the edge of the service line becomes visible above the three foot high point of the net. This would put the center of the ball and the "sweet spot" of the racquet at 8 feet 8¼ inches, and the tip of the racquet at about 9 feet 2 inches.

IDEAS OF THE TRAJECTORY

It is very difficult for the server to be aware of the exact initial direction of the ball. After the hit the racquet faces downward and the ball eventually travels down into the court. Those circumstances tend to create the illusion that the ball was hit downward even though the direction was actually more horizontal, or may even have been upward.

Even if a ball traveling in a straight line in the initial direction just cleared the net then the downward pull of gravity in a real trajectory would deflect the ball into the net, and there is plenty of downward motion due to gravity, as will be shown.

On the other hand, a ball travelling a real trajectory that just clears the net will normally land inside the service line by several feet, which is too far in. However for many good servers the allowance for the trajectory is more on the basis of experience than accurate observation. For them aiming just above the net can be equivalent to actually aiming so that the initial heading and the effects of gravity combine to produce the necessary clearance. Nevertheless, the number of serves that land in the net seems to be excessive, even at tournament level.

An expedient that may help with the aim is to visualize the intended curved path of the ball as being displayed by a string, or by a thin streak of light or color. The server should think of hitting out in the initial direction of that streak, not at the end point or at any location along the way. Another trick is to visualize the path as if required for a throw instead of a hit. Then there is automatic allowance for gravity. Such visualizations of the path can be useful with other types of strokes also.

SCIENCE OF THE TRAJECTORY

Be assured that the path of a serve is not a straight line. It may look straight in the case of serves hit with a good deal of pace, but it is not. Although the cumulative drop by the time the ball reaches the net may be surprisingly large it is practically imperceptible because the drop is occurring all along the path of travel, and the rate of drop is increasing continuously. At any instant the gravitational velocity is proportional to the elapsed time, but the total drop is proportional to the square of the elapsed time.

For instance, neglecting the effects of spin and air friction, a ball hit with a blazing horizontal speed of 110 miles per hour (110 mph) will have a drop due to gravity of over 11 inches by the time it travels the 39 feet to the net. And the drop will increase to a total of more than 2 feet 2 inches by the time the ball covers the additional 21 feet to the service line (Table 1).

With a more realistic but still very respectable horizontal speed of 80 mph, the drop due to gravity will be over 1 foot 9 inches at the net and over 4 feet 2 inches by the time the ball gets to the service line (Table 1). This means that for an 80 mph ball just clear the net the initial straight line path of the bottom of the ball must point at a spot 1 foot 9 inches above the net. And if the hit is made from a height of 7 feet the ball will land about 3 feet 2 inches inside the service line, which at expert level tennis is too far in (Table 2).

CONVENTIONS USED IN THE FOLLOWING TABLES

The tables on the following pages give data in feet and inches for both "REAL" and "STRAIGHT LINE" trajectories.

The path is that of the bottom of the ball. The center is 1¼ inches higher. The figures in the top line labeled "SPEED" give the speed of the ball in miles per hour (mph).

The upper line of each pair of lines relates to hits made with the bottom of the ball at a height of 8 feet, while the lower line relates to a height of 7 feet, as indicated in the column titled "HGHT" (height). Trajectories labeled "REAL" are so only in the sense of taking gravity into account, but not spin and air friction.

GRAVITATIONAL DROP AT THE NET & SERVICE LINE
In "Table 1" each number in the pair of lines titled "REAL GRAV DROP AT NET" gives the total drop due to gravity by the time the ball gets to the net. Since this particular drop depends solely on the time it takes for the ball to travel the distance to the net at a given horizontal speed, it is the same whether the ball is hit from a height of 7 feet or 8 feet, and whether the initial slant is up or down.

Each number in the pair of lines titled "REAL GRAV DROP AT SERV LINE" gives the total drop due to gravity by the time the ball travels the additional 21 feet to the service line. Again, at a given horizontal speed the drop due to gravity is the same whether the ball is hit from a height of 7 feet or 8 feet.

SPEED	110 MPH	80 MPH	53 MPH	47.5 MPH	HGHT
REAL GRAV DROP AT NET	0' 11.2"	1' 9.2"	4' 3.0"	5' 1.7"	8
	0' 11.2"	1' 9.2"	4' 3.0"	5' 1.7"	7
REAL GRAV DROP AT SERV LINE	2' 2.6"	4' 2.2"	9' 6.4"	11' 10.4"	8
	2' 2.6"	4' 2.2"	9' 6.4"	11' 10.4"	7

TABLE 1
CUMULATIVE GRAVITY DROP AT THE NET AND SERVICE LINE.

Adding 3 feet to the given drops at the net reveals that if the ball is hit at about 47.5 mph from a height of 8 feet, or at about 53 mph from a height of 7 feet, the ball would have to be aimed just about straight out initially to just clear the 3 foot high point of the net. Below those speeds, or at lesser heights, the ball would actually have to be directed upward to just get it over the net. The direction would have to be raised still more if topspin and air friction were taken into account.

LANDING POINT OF SERVES THAT SKIM THE NET

In "Table 2" the numbers in the pair of lines titled "REAL, SKIM NET LAND IN COURT" indicate the <u>distance of the landing point inward from the service line</u> under the condition of the ball just barely clearing the net while traveling a "real" trajectory. Notice that the only ball that would go long would be the one hit at a speed of 110 mph from a height of 7 feet. And it would be out by only 5.5 inches.

SPEED	110 MPH	80 MPH	53 MPH	47.5 MPH	HGHT
REAL, SKIM NET LAND IN COURT	2' 7.9"	5' 4.2"	9' 6.5"	10' 8.2"	8
	- 5.5"	3' 2.4"	8' 5.4"	9' 9.7"	7

TABLE 2
LANDING POINT MEASURED INWARD FROM THE SERVICE LINE.

NET CLEARANCE IF BALL LANDS ON SERVICE LINE

In "Table 3" the numbers in the lines titled "REAL CLEAR OVER NET" give the <u>clearances by which the ball would pass over the 3 foot high point of the net</u> in "real" trajectories that end right on the service line. Three feet have to be added to the clearances to get the height of the ball above the ground.

With any decent amount of topspin under real conditions the drops could easily be more than doubled. So the initial direction would have to be adjusted considerably more upward at all speeds to have the ball just clear the net. The slowing of the ball due to air friction has a similar but smaller effect by increasing the time interval over which gravity can act.

SPEED	110 MPH	80 MPH	53 MPH	47.5 MPH	HGHT
REAL CLEAR	0' 3.6"	0' 9.0"	1' 11.6"	2' 6.0"	8
OVER NET	- 0.6"	0' 4.8"	1' 7.4"	2' 1.8"	7

TABLE 3
CLEARANCE OVER NET OF BALLS THAT LAND ON THE SERVICE LINE.

The numbers given in the above "Table 3" have special significance. They represent the height of the "window" through which the ball can pass and go on to land within the service court. If the clearances are as indicated the ball will land on the service line, and if less the ball will touch ground closer to the net. Notice that when a ball with a speed of 110 mph is hit from a height of 7 feet the trajectory would have to pass 6 tenths of an inch below the top of the net in order to land right on the service line.

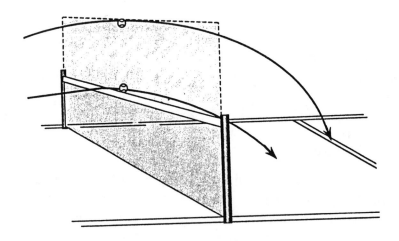

STRAIGHT LINE AIMING POINT ABOVE THE NET FOR
BALLS THAT LAND ON THE SERVICE LINE

In "Table 4" the numbers in the pair of lines titled "ST LINE CLEAR OVER NET" give the clearances by which the ball would pass over the net if it actually traveled a straight line along the initial direction of departure from the racquet, and under the condition that the corresponding "real" trajectory would end on the service line.

Three feet have to be added to get the height of the ball above the ground. Doing this for the figures given for 53 and 47.5 mph shows that the initial direction has to be upward to have the real trajectory touch ground at the service line.

SPEED	110 MPH	80 MPH	53 MPH	47.5 MPH	HGHT
ST LINE CLEAR	1' 2.9"	2' 6.2"	6' 0.0"	7' 6.2"	8
OVER NET	0' 10.7"	2' 2.0"	5' 7.8"	7' 2.0"	7

TABLE 4
CLEARANCE OF STRAIGHT LINE PATH ABOVE THE NET.

STRAIGHT LINE PATH TERMINATIONS
In "Table 5" the numbers in the lines titled "ST LINE END PAST SRV LINE" (straight line ending point past the service line) give the distances past the service line, instead of on it, where the ball would land if it traveled in a straight line in the initial direction. The corresponding "real" trajectory would end on the service line. There are no distances given for speeds of 53 and 47.5 mph because the lines would never touch ground.

A server does not need to know even an approximation of any clearance, drop, direction, or landing point as given by the data in the above tables, but must not operate with misconceptions about such things as straight line paths,

219

aiming points inside the service line, or the need to skim the net either. These are mistakes that are very common in spite of being very wrong. If any straight line aim actually points at a spot inside the service court the ball will land in the net, and that also is very common.

SPEED	110 MPH	80 MPH	53 MPH	47.5 MPH	HGHT
ST LINE END PAST	22' 11.0"	65' 9.0"	------	------	8
SRV LINE	27' 9.0"	89' 2.0"	------	------	7

TABLE 5
END POINT PAST SERVICE LINE OF STRAIGHT LINE
TRAJECTORIES EXTENDED IN THE INITIAL DIRECTION.

SERVING INTO THE SUN

Serving into the sun need not be a problem in recreational tennis. A solution seen in New York's Central Park neatly takes care of it. The side that gets the right to serve also gets the right to do so looking away from the sun. After the first game the players change courts normally and the opposition serves under the same beneficial condition, but for two games instead of only one. There is then a change of courts and the special two game service sequence is repeated, and repeated, etc.

As long as everybody holds serve each side is alternately one game down and one game up at court changes. The end result is entirely normal since neither side can win a set without breaking the opponent's service at least once. This system actually seems to be better balanced than the conventional since with the standard method there is a psychological advantage for the side that serves first: it always goes one-up when holding serve.

When used in a tiebreaker there is a disadvantage in that a change of courts is required after every two points instead of after the normal six. But this again seems more fair. In recreational tennis. a player can easily lose all three service points within the customary six point change-of-court sequence if the sun is in a location that makes serving particularly difficult.

The above system should not really be needed in expert level tennis because the serve is the one stroke where it is not necessary to pay more than cursory attention to the ball. If the swing is kept nearly ideal then the hitting point is predetermined. Experts can make the ball appear there at the right time almost automatically. So almost all of the attention can be directed elsewhere.

THE SERVE AND VOLLEY PROBLEM, THREE SOLUTIONS

At one time when balls seemed not to be as lively as today, the foot-fault rule not as lax, the racquets not as powerful, court surfaces not as fast, and the rush-the-net game not as important, the small person was considered to have an advantage because of having greater agility and stamina over long rallies than a larger, heavier person. If balls do not in fact have a better bounce they do so in effect because most of today's courts provide a higher, faster bounce than the courts of old.

So, as in many other sports, the size of a player is getting to have too much importance. In order for the game to regain its status as a sport for all people, tennis has to make some change somewhere. There have been various suggestions: go back to wood racquets, make the ball less lively, have the server stand a foot behind the baseline, and restrict the server to one serve. But these are either impractical or change the nature of the game too much.

Oddly enough, there seems not to have been any mention of going back to the old foot-fault rule. One foot had to be in touch with the ground and neither foot could be swung over or past the baseline at the hit. Now an already tall person can effectively be even taller, and be on the way to the net before the ball has left the racquet. Going back to the "one foot in touch with the ground" rule would solve much of the problem. The other part of the rule, "no foot over or past the baseline at the hit", was too difficult to observe, especially in recreational tennis, and was sensibly discarded. But someone should have foreseen the dangers involved with allowing the server to jump.

An easy solution, creating the least interference with the way player's serve, is to make the service court narrower, as in the illustration below. A space could be inserted down the middle instead of at the sides. Another alternative is to bring the service line in toward the net a few inches. This would force the players to cut back on pace, and would also restrict the angle of the serve. A big advantage with that method is that no more lines are required than at present.

But the solution that would best satisfy the needs of both the server and receiver is as shown below.

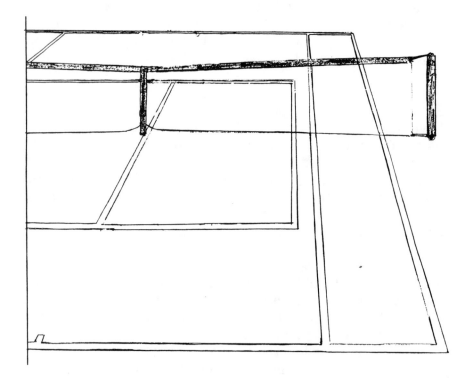

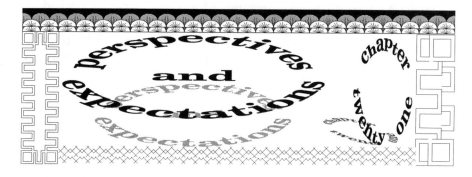

Tennis lessons concerning the basics seem to work best for young children, partly because their days are filled with a great deal of athletic activity. This pays off well in rapid development of skills in hitting, coordination, and timing. A young novice at tennis will almost surely be concentrating more on the fun of giving the ball a real whack than on whether it goes in or out.

When they are made to pay attention to such things as patterns, footwork, hitting point, follow-through, and consistency they can be expected to lose interest because then the purpose of the game conflicts with their own, which is hitting, winning, and just having fun. An important factor in their great ability to learn is that they have a knack for either not paying attention to or forgetting those ideas which do not in fit in well with their own sports experience.

Adult novices have just as much need of the basics as the children, but adults apply the information on the rational rather than the fun level. They follow the coach's advice implicitly, and believe that tennis lessons will cover every skill in all the detail necessary. They do not have day-long sports and play activities to supplement the weekly tennis lesson to provide a broad background in athletic knowledge and skill.

As a rule they defer enjoyment of the game until some time in the future when they expect to have mastered expert level

shots. Although deferring such pleasures is not a bad idea, it just so happens in tennis that there is a correlation between fun and good technique, between an enthusiastic whack and the principles of hitting, and between unpleasant feel and poor technique.

The choice for the student is therefor somewhat between "hit in a way that feels great, and win matches" or "stay with methods that feel unpleasant, and lose". It follows that even if a person elects to disregard all other considerations in favor of the practical reward of winning, that rather shortsighted objective will be best accomplished if the techniques being used have the most pleasant and satisfying feel. Rigid patterns and personal idiosyncrasies hold few such rewards, immediate or eventual.

WHAT WILL WORK IF PATTERNS & DETAILS DON'T?
Gradually succeeding in making a shot feel more pleasant amounts to devising the whole set of whatever concepts are required to master the better shot. But first it is necessary to either know or have a feel for the principles of hitting. As the effective techniques get to be the most satisfying they will begin to dominate, and the unsatisfying will be compelled to fade away. Changes required in existing habits will then be developed largely automatically, rather than that desirable new methods will be rejected because of incompatibility with the current package of expedients.

In order to be able to make changes that are enhancements, not the all too common mistakes, a player has to able to both recognize problems and to know, either consciously or intuitively, in which direction to go. The use of bad tennis habits is not often deterred solely by the unpleasant characteristics of poor hits: awkward footwork, poor preparation, inappropriate stance, faulty grip, clumsy swing, either excessive or inadequate involvement of the body, arm out of sync with the body, "arm-alone" hit, inadequate reinforcement, incomplete recovery of energy from the elasticities, deficient arm extension, inferior racquet momentum, poor

internal timing, early or late hit, accidental racquet attitude, wrong direction of racquet travel at the hit, extraneous moves, too much or too little wrist flex, jarring, tiring, off-center, jerky, hurried, pushed, cramped, stiff, hesitant, violent, roundhouse, slowed, stopped, lacking naturalness, etc.

In "CHAPTER SIX" it was shown that a single flaw and an associated compensation create at least ten obstacles to change:

Removing (or unlearning) the flaw as well as the compensation. (2)

Overcoming the feelings of deprivation of each. (2)

Learning replacement techniques for each. (2)

Overcoming the complex timing problems caused by the two removals and two replacements. (4)

The person with the more valid understandings should be able to devise the better patterns because the effectiveness of a hit is based strictly on physical principles and cause and effect. But what is assumed to be valid theory must ultimately have confirmation in satisfactory feel. Otherwise interpretation of the theory could be wrong, or the theories themselves suspect. It is unprofitable to waste attention on factors that are not important, or on consequences rather than causes.

A dependable criterion of the caliber of a shot is not the approximation to a style or the adequacy for the moment, but the quality of the experience. That is the ultimate guide to improvement because a logical or even scientific analysis of a hit can take into account only the most obvious technical factors. Even for these it is easy to arrive at incorrect conclusions. Witness the decision arrived at by reputable scientists many years ago that it is not really possible for a baseball pitcher to throw a curve, and that what seems so is merely an illusion.

APPEARANCE VS FUNCTION

The typical way both to teach the fundamentals to novices and to remedy the strokes of experienced players has been to go through the "basics": grip, footwork, stance, backswing, forward swing, etc, for forehand, backhand, and so on. It works well for beginners, but when used in the attempt to eliminate long-time bad habits these methods have proved to be ineffective. Almost all experienced players are well acquainted with the basics whether they adhere to the rules or not. So there is not much to be gained from repeated review. And even in the rare case where it does produce results, nothing has been done about the causes of deterioration. So there is nothing to prevent reversion.

In effect such learning is based on the theory that it is only necessary to mimic a selected form and then naturalness, the hit, and the elimination of bad habits will take care of themselves. But in tennis the "form" will not perfect the "function". The opposite is true: as the function is perfected the most elegant style and greatest satisfactions may also be achieved.

A POSITIVE APPROACH TO LEARNING

This book has approached the means of improvement by examining the role of many factors: physical principles, centers of control, mental processes, misinformation, urges, habits, experiences, feedback, and the satisfactions that are involved with a hit. The feel of the hit and the knowledge of

the basic principles provide reliable standards for evaluating both old and new techniques without bias, as opposed to trying to conform to conventions that are difficult to describe, open to interpretation, and uncertain as to merit.

Improvement is more a matter of recognizing, appreciating, and retaining the good, and thus crowding out the bad, than making direct attempts to discontinue the bad, impose a revision, adopt a new technique, or concentrate on a detail. Unchanged objectives will always bring back the old strokes. Removing the causes can be successful in removing the consequences, but the reverse is hardly ever true.

UNBREAKABLE CHAINS OF BAD HABITS

A very unfortunate circumstance with flawed games is that there are collections of interdependent flaws, not simple basic problems. It is thus not generally possible to eliminate or replace a wrong detail by itself, since that amounts to removing a single element from a chain of interrelated and interacting elements.

As an example, if a peculiarity in the grip was adopted to compensate for an improper hitting point then changing the subsidiary flaw, the grip, is by itself not apt to have much of a corrective influence on the controlling flaw, the hitting point. By a similar reasoning, correcting the ostensible basic flaw, the hitting point, is by itself bound to create problems with the left over peculiar grip.

A reliable way to gradually eliminate both the problem with the hitting point and the related problem with the grip is by the progressive refinement of the concepts and the intents, using visualization of a past or coming stroke, accurate recollection and evaluation of details, profiting from the satisfactions or the lack of them, etc.

Many flaws develop as a necessary compensation for another, and then progress through constant repetition into well established habits that will not quickly disappear in the

same chain-like manner of their origin. On the contrary, those that remain will tend to revive those that might seem for a time to have been successfully eliminated. A chain of flaws is thus only as weak as its strongest link.

It is therefor necessary to have some sense of priorities. Change a controlling item before changing a dependent, if the distinction can be determined. Give priority to those items that seem to promise the biggest improvement, and ignore those mannerisms that are of little consequence to the hit. Think of the hit, not the result.

LOOKING BACK TO MOVE FORWARD

When that rare perfect shot occurs it may not be easy to recognize what it was that made the stroke exactly right. In any event it is generally beside the point. Typically there will not have been sufficient savoring of the experience of the hit to make most people aware of even the most exceptional sensations and events. Not being able to recognize and evaluate good experiences is generally equivalent to not benefiting from them either.

Any abnormal swing or unexpected result deserves a moment of reflection about the cause of the variation. If a shot has a poor feel raise the question as to what went wrong, what was the basic cause, and how could it have been done better? Did emotions take charge? What did the stroke look like? The time used to occasionally mimic a good or bad stroke could be well spent.

Eventually the deliberate examinations can be replaced by a fleeting visualization that does not detract from legitimate demands on the attention. Anything that is unusual gets registered and analyzed in a fraction of the interval before the next shot. The process can be called "retrospective analysis" since the details are recalled to mind without them having been the subject of specific attention.

The suggested approach even has the important advantage

of taking the mind off extraneous matters, wild intentions, emotional urges, lazy evasions and compromises, fears of inadequacy, playing for a lucky shot, resentment of the opponent, anger over a line call, etc.

STAYING WITHIN REALISTIC EXPECTATIONS
It must be realized that not all shots can provide the same degree of satisfaction. It is a mistake to expect more than is available. A high soft bounce on the backhand generally presents such a difficulty. Satisfaction is not absolute but is relative to what is attainable under the circumstances. Demanding more assures disappointments. These in turn lead to a lack of confidence in one's own abilities, and in the value of trying to make changes.

Ordinarily a tennis match is an excuse for a steady intrusion of new bad habits as well as reversion to the old. With the approach being prescribed even a tennis match can function as an effective tennis lesson. The game can have much added interest and incentive if a principal objective is to break away from the current limitations to advance to the next level of skills and satisfactions. But the incentive will last only if there is noticeable, continual progress.

THE ROLE OF DESPERATION REACTIONS
The all-or-nothing attitude that many players have merely guarantees the development and retention of desperation techniques yielding minimal results. The better trick is to try for a lesser return, which while not winning the point outright once in a big while will not lose it outright most of the time either.

Desperation reactions cause changes in the intents, position of feet, preparation, stance, length of backswing, bend of elbow, reinforcement with the body, timing, amount of push, tensing of uninvolved muscles, etc. In short, just about everything. Since even a minor intrusion of emotion is likely to activate desperation responses and timing interactions it can easily happen that a player's strokes will

go completely haywire very suddenly with little instigation.

Examples of the effects on the serve could be that the toss gets to be a trifle off, the body is stiffened as for a huge muscular effort, a turn to face the net becomes more pronounced and occurs earlier than usual, the elbow is pulled in, the forward jackknife becomes prominent, the racquet is pushed forward and then pulled downward in a pawing motion, and the attention is totally focused on getting a very special (and unlikely) result. The odds are clearly in favor of a double fault. And even if the serve does go in it will likely be either highly ineffective or highly lucky.

THE HITTING POINT IS INTERNAL TO THE SWING
Do not think of swinging at an external hitting point. Swinging at a hitting point is usually wrong because that point is actually internal to the swing. When it is considered to be external to the swing the timing of the external elements gets to be confused with the timing of the internal. To be "swing-controlled" the stroke should be executed as if independent of external circumstances from start to finish. The trick is to time the uncompromised swing as a whole in a way to have the <u>ball meet the racquet</u> (not the <u>racquet meet the ball</u>) at the correct internal hitting point.

THE LOCATION OF THE CONTROL CENTER
There is a great deal of cumulative "know-how" stored in the conscious mind, the subconscious mind, and the muscular reflexes as a result of the many previous hits and experiences. That part of "know-how", good or bad, that is stored in the reflexes and the subconscious mind is what really constitutes a person's tennis game.

The habits operate so automatically and persistently that it seems that they have been imprinted in a control center for involuntary actions along with such things as blinking and flinching. So whatever is done to appeal to the conscious mind to gain acceptance of a change will ordinarily not have much influence on the other more hidden but more

powerful control center. A main role of satisfactions based on new knowledge, operating independently of conscious thought, is to overcome the appeal of old habits and the influence of false concepts to allow adoption of only the valid changes.

The training and habits accumulated by the racquet arm do not seem to be transferable to the free arm. When a player injures the racquet arm to the extent of having to learn to play with the other, the swing is apt to be just as clumsy and uncoordinated as when starting from scratch without any previous acquaintance with tennis. However, this limitation is much less apparent if the player's game is based on the principles of hitting, satisfactions, feedback, etc, as outlined in this book.

LEARNING TO LEARN

Each directed experience can expand knowledge and refine the process of learning just as any other skill. To the extent that a student blindly imitates patterns or constantly repeats mistakes, rather than also attempts to discover what is effective and why, the development of the ability to learn is being neglected. Merely trying again usually amounts to reinforcing the problems.

If a stroke is not being improved then it is likely to be deteriorating since there is no such thing as just standing still, and since there is always a subconscious intent to cut corners and get by without expending the required effort. So when a person's game reaches a peak, and the concepts and the horizons are no longer expanding, deterioration overtakes and surpasses improvement. Pros are more susceptible than dubs since they have many more skills to lose, and since they may develop the additional problem of expecting the ball to do more for them than for lesser players.

There are long term consequences to hitting lazy or careless shots because bad habits are very easily acquired. So even

at the start of the warm-up it is wrong to just laze the ball back instead of making a special attempt to hit ideal shots at that time. Every stroke during practice should be made with the idea of producing the best satisfactions possible, albeit perhaps not attempting to hit with heavy pace.

Given the availability of workable methods of obtaining improvement it should be of some sort of comfort to be aware of the existence of remaining bad habits since that only means that one's game has not yet reached its full potential, with a number of worthwhile changes still being achievable, and with improved results , satisfactions, and prestige as the rewards.

When you are on the court you are alone with your intentions, techniques, the ball, and the situation. You should be concerned only with them. Nobody can do so perfectly, but that is the task, and it should merely be done as well as possible. The rewards are as much in the satisfying hit and the progress toward becoming a better player as in the score. The effort to improve the strokes amounts to playing against oneself within the game of trying to win points from the opponent.

Chapter twenty-two about tennis courts

COURT DESIGN AND CONSTRUCTION MISTAKES

The contracts for the construction of public courts are often necessarily let with more regard for cost than quality. This generally means progressively declining appearance and playability after the first season. In fact playing conditions can be quite poor right from the start because some common ideas about design standards and useful features are based on myths, not on tennis requirements or even just the knowledge that comes from a little practical observation. So public or school courts excellent in all important respects are very rare.

What has been said of some of the ideas about tennis strokes can also be said of some of the ideas routinely used in the construction of tennis courts: that not enough consideration has been given to the physical principles involved. The most important penalties for this neglect are poor playability, rapid deterioration, and high hidden cost.

Once the courts are in place they are generally allowed to deteriorate quite badly before money will be spent for extensive repairs. Even minor maintenance is a very occasional item. When repairs do occur they are almost always limited to the patching of cracks, or at most to the spreading of a cosmetic layer of surfacing material.

The major flaws will probably remain as long as the courts remain. So the design, foundation, and the court itself had better be right on the initial installation. It is therefor worth the while to make an examination of what constitutes excellence. Some of it costs no more, and may even cost less. The following analysis relates only to outdoor courts since the indoor are almost always very well built, and since they have no weather problems to contend with.

FIVE MAJOR REQUIREMENTS IN COURT DESIGN

The major characteristics of good court design are:

1. A firm foundation so that the court will not settle after being built.

2. The surface laid perfectly flat without any slope in any direction.

3. No irregularities or depressions to affect the bounce, or collect and hold water.

4. No edge of the court being at either the same or lower level than the immediately adjacent outside area.

5. Good color contrast with the ball.

COURT FOUNDATIONS

There is a tendency to cut corners where it doesn't show initially: in the foundation. But this is where economy will turn out to do the most harm. So public courts are notably subject to settling and the problems it causes, which are low areas, annoying slopes, gaps between the fences and the court surface, and cracks. All of these have serious effects on playability, cost of maintenance and repair, and appearance.

Any overall settling that occurs can usually be detected by examining the fences and fence posts. The posts are imbedded in a concrete footing placed quite deep in the ground to prevent the fences from being toppled over by winds and frost. When the court itself settles the footings tend to remain in their initial positions. So the first signs of overall settling often consist of gaps between the court surface and the fence, and in paving material adhering to the fence post footings, sometimes in the form of a complete collar.

LOW AREAS AND SURFACE IRREGULARITIES

There are two types of surface irregularities: small dents that cause erratic bounces and large, shallow depressions that can hold many gallons of water. The small dents are mostly due to poor materials and workmanship. They discourage use because of the serious effects on playability. The large depressions are created by settling and/or uneven construction. Big puddles that collect in them can cause the courts to remain unusable for several days.

FREE EDGES

An often seen problem is that of an outside area being higher than the adjacent edge of the court. This is especially troublesome when occurring, as it usually does, at the low end or corner of a sloped court. Not only do large puddles develop but a thick layer of gooey mud is gradually built up from the dust that is washed down from the court surface. Sweeping or squeegeeing the puddles is difficult because of the mud, and because the water can only keep rolling back from the higher outside area instead of being able to drop over an edge and flow away.

DRAINAGE TROUGHS

A means of mitigating this improper design condition is to dig a slight trough in the ground along the affected edges, something like that on well trimmed lawns but several times as big. Regular clearing of accumulations is required. If the higher outside area is paved then a possible solution may be a small trough built into the surface just <u>outside</u> the fence. The trough bottom should have a continuous slope from one end to the other so that the water that enters does not just collect and stay there but is made to drain away.

The troughs need be no more than about two inches across, and can consist of just two sides sloped down to meet in the middle. This is a suggestion but not a specific recommendation since there may be special needs for particular installations, and since none of the construction companies and manufacturers of surfacing materials have conducted the testing needed to develop reliable standards.

The function of troughs <u>is not</u> to carry away the heavy <u>visible flow</u> that occurs while the rain is still coming down. That flow takes care of itself since water does not pile up but spreads easily and runs off rapidly. The function is to drain away the thin slick that remains after the visible flow has stopped. As the film of water at the edges seeps into the trough the rest is spread thinner and is pulled toward and into the trough also. Sometimes the troughs can have the reverse function of diverting water from flowing onto the court from the outside.

Troughs ought not be placed across entryways (where people may be caused to stumble) or inside the fences (where they can hold both water and tennis balls). In an extreme example of the latter the trough was directly under the fence, had a rectangular cross section, and was more than deep and wide enough to easily hide a football, or catch and hold barrels of water or tennis balls, or both.

A slope can advantageously be built into about the last three inches of court surface next to the fences, directed very slightly downward toward the outside. A drop of an inch per foot should be sufficient. This facilitates the seepage and helps keep balls that land next to the fence from rolling back onto the court. It is a desirable feature along the ends of all hard courts, and may eliminate the need for an additional drainage trough. Placing them between adjacent courts should be avoided because that presents a tricky construction problem. The bottom has to have a second slope toward an end of the court, otherwise puddles develop and linger along the fences, where balls are sure to land.

DRAINAGE ON SLOPED COURTS

An indoor court, being perfectly flat, radiates a comfortable feel even though the surroundings are comparatively dark and plain in appearance. By contrast, when a person steps onto a typical outdoor court there is usually an immediate and unpleasant awareness of slopes in several directions. The unpleasantness gets worse when play begins, especially when aggravated by surface irregularities, as is usual.

The misguided intent of the slopes is so that it can be claimed that "the courts will be playable a half an hour after a thunder shower". But playing characteristics have more importance than draining characteristics. And there are few areas where it rains so often, like for several hours several times every week, that it is necessary to install slopes steep enough so that no more than a half hour of play will be lost after each rain. Strangely enough, the slopes create more drainage problems than they alleviate.

A slope commonly recommended by manufacturers of surfacing materials is one-tenth of an inch drop per foot of length, but that is almost always exceeded, sometimes considerably. Even a tenth of an inch per foot means that one baseline is elevated 7.8 inches above the other. The court surface at the net is 3.9 inches above the baseline at the low end of the court, and the same amount below the baseline at the high end. In flat terrain the high end of a court with such a slope must be raised at least 8 inches above ground level. But this is almost never done. So the low end is often below ground level, and will collect and hold a small lake when it rains, a common sight.

It is very difficult to build a consistent slight incline from one end of a sloped court to the other, and the minor variations that are almost sure to occur are likely to result in shallow but sizable depressions. Flat courts are much easier to build than the sloped, and are therefor much less likely to be plagued with low areas.

Slopes do not really enhance water flow to any great extent. If the slant is increased to where it does make a considerable difference then the court becomes very unpleasant to play on, sometimes to the extent of being practically unusable. In installations where flat and sloped courts of the same materials can both be observed under the same conditions it will be seen that the flat courts drain faster than the sloped. The observation can be easily explained by theory.

For example, assume that without evaporation it takes four hours for a thin slick of water to drain off of one half of a sloped court. But after those four hours the lower half may be almost as wet as before, even though the upper half is almost dry. The reason is that although the film of water on the lower half also drained off within the same four hours it was being simultaneously replaced by water from the upper half. Draining this second accumulation could take another four hours, which means that a total of eight hours could be required.

DRAINAGE ON FLAT COURTS
A similar analysis of what happens on a flat court reveals that there is a comparative advantage for that arrangement. Let it be assumed that it takes six hours

for the water to flow off of one half of a flat court, compared to only four hours for the sloped. But in those six hours both halves of the flat court have drained since each half drains independently to the sides and to the end. There is no upper half to send its load onto the lower half. So under the assumed conditions the flat court would drain in six hours while the sloped court would take eight.

The drainage on the sloped court could be improved by installing a steeper incline, and perhaps the time required to drain the water could be reduced enough to equal or better the time for the flat. But increasing the incline to that extent would make the court essentially unusable. So then there would be a court that nobody wanted to play on even when dry.

DRAINAGE ON GRANULAR COURTS

Granular courts (improperly referred to as "clay") have a special drainage problem if sloped, which they almost always are. During a heavy rain the flow down the slope carries a fair amount of the surfacing material along too, especially the very small particles. Eventually much of what remains in the high areas needs to be scraped off and discarded because it consists mostly of the heavier particles that look and behave like loose sand. The material in low spots and at the low end, wherever water collects, requires replacement also, in this case because the very fine particles of which it consists turn into gooey, water-retaining, slow-drying mud when it rains.

DRAINAGE VS PLAYABILITY ON DOUBLE-SLOPED COURTS

A device that seems to offer a complete solution to the drainage problems is to slant the two halves of the court in opposite directions. Each half can drain both fast and independently with this arrangement. But, as might be expected, it raises other serious problems.

When a ball is hit from one point on such a court and lands on any specific point on the other side, the court surface is in effect an imaginary plane passing through those two points. The ball is unaffected by the characteristics of the terrain it passes over. But when either the hitting point or the landing point changes, the slope of the imaginary connecting plane, as well as the height of the top of the net above that plane, change also. On a baseline to baseline rally on a court with a one-tenth inch per foot slope the net is effectively 3.9 inches higher than normal for both players.

SERVING ON DOUBLE-SLOPED COURTS

The fact that the net is effectively raised above normal creates special problems for the server. On a serve the effective plane of the court extends from the baseline to the service line on the other side, sixty feet away. If the recommended slope of one-tenth inch per foot is used the service line on the other side is 2.1 inches lower than the surface at the net. And the court surface at the net is 2.73 inches above an imaginary plane connecting the server's baseline and the service line on the other side. This amounts to the net being too high by the same amount. It can be seen that double slopes increase the difficulty of getting the ball to land in the service court.

PROBLEMS WITH HITTING UPHILL OR DOWNHILL

When a ball is hit from a specific height either uphill or downhill exactly parallel to the surface of a single-sloped court the time taken for the ball to hit ground will not vary with either the velocity or the direction. As a matter of fact the time will be the same even if the ball is just dropped from the same height. However, the distance traveled will vary with the direction of the hit.

This is so because the acceleration of gravity adds to the component of velocity parallel to the surface of the court in the downhill case, and detracts from that component in the uphill case. So the final velocity parallel to the court surface, and the distance traveled, are greater when downhill than when uphill. A sly opponent can increase the variation by using suitable spin. An unobservant player affected by the variations may conclude "my timing was off".

The adjustments needed to get properly set for the hit are mostly mental: a wariness of getting too close to the bounce on the downhill side, and too far from the bounce on the uphill side. The magnitude of the adjustments are best left to instinct since the variations are small. Conscious compensation may compound the problem rather than solve it.

The hard courts currently in place at the "U.S. OPEN" tournament have slopes so small as not to be noticeable to most spectators. But the slopes on even those courts, "main" as well as "field", have been criticized by a few very prominent tournament players as creating difficulties.

COURT COLORS

Light colors, or any that do not contrast well with that of the ball, should not be used on any area in or around the playing area other than the lines. **The ball can totally vanish against such colors**. This often happens when players, linesman, or spectators are looking at the ball against the light background formed by the area outside of the court proper. Yet on two-toned courts the outside areas are almost always a lighter color than the court itself.

The error is carried to the extreme in some very major events, apparently on notions of decor rather than visibility. This is especially bad since the main TV cameras are usually located quite high in the stands. So a ball with a high trajectory will often disappear in the light color of the back-court areas.

241

If anything, **the color of those areas should be darker than the colors of the court itself, similar to the treatment of the back screens or walls**. There apparently are no instances where the screen or wall behind a court has been given one of the light colors frequently used for the outside areas.

A disadvantage is that dark surfaces absorb heat very easily, and so get hotter than the light-colored. So medium-dark colors are the best compromise, especially in hot climates. Granular courts are nicely dark, as well as cool when slightly moist as they are supposed to be. If they are not properly moist then they too become very light in color. They also get slippery, hard, and bumpy.

VISIBILITY OF LINES

The width of the lines on a tennis court are a throwback to the days when they were laid down with a white solution (originally lime) on grass or natural clay courts. They still are on grass courts, as at Wimbledon.

The nature of the process dictates that the lines have to be fairly wide. The width enhances visibility of the lines, but not that of a ball when it is viewed against a line. **In fact a ball can become almost invisible when both the line and the ball are directly in the line of sight**. On a close call a linesman or player has only a miniscule fraction of a second to judge the position after the ball reappears. If the lines are made narrow, less than an inch wide, the balls do not get lost in that way at any time.

Lines should not be at a different level than the rest of the surface, or have a different friction factor. The fact that they are several inches wide aggravates the problems caused by their comparative slipperiness. This causes the balls to skid, and occasionally even a player. Narrow lines minimize the problems of both

the view and the footing.

No lines at all would be even better than narrow lines. This could be accomplished by making the outside area a different color than the court itself, say one of the darker reds sometimes used for two-tone installations. One of the service courts could be that same color. The other could be a rather dark violet or blue. Green seems to be the best choice for the rest of the court.

A side-advantage of eliminating the lines would be that ball marks, which tend to be very indistinct on painted lines, would be easily visible when the landing mark overlapped a boundary by ever so little.

TYPES OF COURT SURFACES

Besides the mentioned five major requirements concerning the design and construction of tennis courts (good foundation, no irregularities, free edges, perfectly flat, color contrast with the ball) it is necessary to consider the relative advantages of the various surfaces. The important factors are bounce, friction with respect to the ball and with the soles of shoes, comfort under foot, appearance, glare, heat, resistance to damage, time required for draining and drying, construction costs, and ease of maintenance and repair.

The primary choice is between the granular court and the hard since grass and natural clay have all but disappeared. The selection is easily made without a detailed examination of the mentioned factors. If the high cost of a desirable level of daily maintenance and regular refurbishing of the granular can be afforded then that is the first choice. The availability of water is also an important factor since such courts should be kept slightly damp. Also, they are not suitable for year-round play in cold climates.

Almost all recreational players prefer the granular to the hard because of being cooler and softer underfoot, and because of not having as fast a bounce.   However the bounce is not as true as on the hard. It is in fact comparatively or actually quite erratic, even with good maintenance, if the players do not cooperate by continually smoothing the ridges and depressions created during play. Those dents harden and are not removed by standard brushing techniques. So it is wise to display a sign saying "PLEASE SMOOTH ANY MARKS MADE".

The perfect court has yet to be developed. It should be neither as slick and uncomfortable as hard courts nor have so much surface friction as to hold onto the ball and give exaggerated importance to spin. It should allow players the same freedom as does the granular to slide the front foot forward and move the body into the hit. The surface material should not shift or dent in normal use.

OTHER COURT DESIGN FEATURES
Fences are more of a problem than generally recognized. The mesh may have been manufactured with an eye to economizing on material. So the openings may be large enough that hard hit balls can sometimes go through if curtains are not installed. Another problem is that flimsy meshes may bulge inward at the bottom after a few years of use. This is a most serious defect since it allows balls to roll freely to the outside.

The appearance and atmosphere of public tennis courts can be considerably improved, and maintenance costs kept down, by cautioning players against a few unthinking actions. The best way is with signs. An example: "LITTERING SUBJECT TO FINE.   THIS INCLUDES CONTAINERS AND COVERS". That notice might well be put in all public areas. The court maintenance costs can be minimized with a sign saying: "DO NOT HIT THE NET

<u>CORD, NET, OR COURT SURFACE WITH THE RACQUET</u>".

A placard containing a few rules of conduct is also advisable. One that is becoming increasingly necessary is "<u>THE USE OF MUSICAL DEVICES IS NOT PERMITTED</u>". A sign needed to prevent injuries is: "<u>CHILDREN NOT ACTUALLY PLAYING TENNIS ARE NOT ALLOWED ON THE COURTS</u>". It is highly dangerous even for adults, as well as discourteous, to stray onto courts that are in use.

<u>Traditional dress codes should be strictly enforced,</u> especially in clubs and tournaments, to retain the attractive appearance and high image of the game. Otherwise the resultant unpleasant atmosphere causes many people to reject the idea of taking up the game, and the serious players to leave. Allowing the same liberties in golf wouldn't do that game much good either. It actually sounds unthinkable.

PEOPLING THE COURTS

There is a problem with tennis that doesn't relate to courts, doesn't rate a chapter of its own, is never mentioned in the books, but that ought to be brought up because it is the reason why most players quit the game soon after their school years.

It is the subject of the availability of partners, the second most important overall problem in tennis, after the inability to change established games. Some indoor clubs have partially solved this problem for their members with tennis leagues. Players just show up on the scheduled dates and the club assigns the partners, or helps to do so.

On public courts it is almost always just a matter of bringing your own. This means that in most localities there is very little mixing. Newcomers have too few chances of breaking in. Even the regulars are eventually left without suitable opponents, bad enough or good enough as the case may be.

The problem gets worse where it is possible to reserve courts in advance because then the games are all prearranged, and it is of no use for uncommitted players   to show up alone at the courts expecting to pick up a match. So reserving courts in advance should not be permitted because it eliminates mixing almost completely. Reservation systems as a whole inhibit both play and mixing, except in clubs, and so should be used only if the waiting period for a court is often an important problem.

Players easily get bored with each other if there is no mixing. There are too many chances to end a friendship over a line call, discourtesy, failure to keep accurate score, "grunting" or vocalizing (although extremely rare at the recreational level), talking during play (especially   if to people not on the same court), watching the action on other courts when the partner is   ready   to   play,   creating   distractions,   using psychological ploys, smoking or eating, playing radios, criticizing, cheating, dressing sloppily, making line calls on the other side, needlessly questioning calls, insisting that a point be played over, using an eyesore playing style, laughing at an opponent's error or distress, serving before the receiver is ready, hitting the second serve too soon or while the first ball is rolling across the court, not having a second ball in reserve when the first serve is a fault, allowing loose balls to remain on the playing   area, returning loose balls while the server's back is turned, rolling loose balls to the server or hitting them at the fences rather than returning them with a convenient bounce, not retrieving wayward balls when changing courts, hitting in a way to create maximum annoyance for the opponent during the warm-up, hitting volleys into the corners or at sharp angles during a warm-up, hitting passing shots or lobs when the other player comes to the net to practice volleys, hitting hard toward the opponent's head or body, not furnishing a fair share of new balls, being consistently late or even failing to show up, etc. Even if these actions do not end a friendship they may cause partners to quit tennis because of not finding it to be fun anymore.

A few years ago a newspaper published a report describing a computerized match arranging system used in a large city. The list of registrants went to over seventy thousand, which amounted to about one out of every ten residents. Players elsewhere have talked about the desirability of setting up the same system in their own areas. But so far there has been no subsequent mention of it , or of any other plan that may be equally successful, being made available to the fans at other locations.

So most experienced tennis players eventually have to quit because of the lack of suitable partners. About the only commonly provided community arrangements are group lessons and court reservation systems. They have been around for quite awhile.

An alternative could be to just arrange and announce something like "open tennis hours" to be held several times a week at public or club courts in other than prime time periods. Players interested in taking part would just show up. All matches could be set up on the spot by one or two knowledgeable coordinators, volunteer or not. The system would work best if lessons and prearranged matches were not permitted.

Tennis, like just about all recreational activities, operates mostly on an age category basis. It also operates on a rather strict peer basis, admittedly somewhat necessarily. During the great tennis boom of the 60's many high level players would readily hit with any reasonably capable player who happened to be around, including those rated several levels lower. The custom faded, and so did tennis.

In order to keep getting new partners to replace those who inevitably drop out, players at any level have to occasionally invite those at lower levels to just rally. And the less skilled players have the obligation to improve their games so that it becomes a pleasure for others to hit with them.

It is not desirable to have players who are unequal in style or skill play each other regularly, or to have equal partners play each other exclusively. So almost all recreational tennis operates best on a pickup or other rotational basis. Everybody hopes to not only have dream strokes themselves someday but to be in a club and go to vacation spots where all others do so also.

The match arranging system, the suggested alternative "tennis hours", and this book are not really intended to "promote" tennis but just to make better tennis and better partners available to those who are committed to the game.

This appendix contains two lists of "boost grips" to be applied with the "free" or "boost" hand, one list for forehands and one for backhands. Most of the practical possibilities are listed, but only a few will become part any particular individual's game. The grip used by the racquet hand can be whatever is currently used on one-handed shots. But a player can also take the opportunity to switch to another grip as seems desirable.

The initial reading of the lists of "boost grips" should be in the nature of a quick survey, rather than as a means of remembering them. It is useful to apply each grip lightly during the reading. Use any convenient "application point". If the "DOUBLE-FORCE" strokes are being self-taught it is necessary for the player to have read the first ten pages of "CHAPTER TWO", titled "DOUBLE-FORCE TECHNIQUES".

Following the two lists of "boost grips" is a set of "going-through-the-motions" drills. All of the "grips" and "application points" should be tried so that an intelligent preliminary selection can be made of those which might be used either regularly or just in special situations. The steps are mainly for familiarization and need be used only on a one-time basis.

It is advisable to go through all the options also, even those that seem to be unsuitable. If a player does not examine those alternatives there can be unwise selection of the regularly used grips. Or the player may be unaware of the one most suitable for an unusual circumstance. "Grips" and "application points" are just <u>tried</u> not <u>chosen</u> in these initial drills. The final choices are made gradually with subsequent drills and during play, and are forever subject to change.

Then there is a second very similar set of drills intended as preliminary practice of "DOUBLE-FORCE" swings, not for just "going through the motions". Here it is probably best to use only those "boost grips" and "application points" that were found to be promising in the first set of drills. "APPENDIX B" and the others that follow contain drills designed to apply to the entire game, whatever the style and whatever the grip: one-handed, two-handed, or "DOUBLE-FORCE".

The "DOUBLE-FORCE" techniques should be tried with each type of stroke. That means forehand, backhand, volley, and even the serve and overhead. For the latter two the term "<u>end of backswing</u>" should be taken to mean the "<u>beginning of the final upward and forward move of the racquet</u>".

The applicable "grips" for the serve and forehand overhead are forehand grips "A", "B", "E", and "F" and all backhand grips except "E". <u>All backhand "grips" except "E" can be used with the backhand overhead.</u>

LIST OF FOREHAND "BOOST GRIPS"

The "grips" available for use with the forehand are:

**A. Grasp the racquet arm lightly with the "boost hand", thumb ON TOP of the arm. Use just the fingers or the entire hand, as desired.

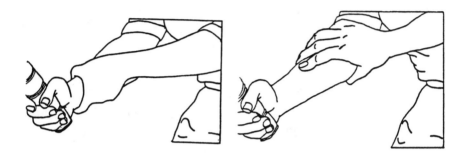

**B. Grasp the racquet arm lightly with the "boost hand", thumb BELOW the arm instead of on top. Use just the fingers or the entire hand, as desired.

C. Position the "boost hand", PALM UP, UNDER THE RACQUET ARM. Bend the fingers up against the BACK OF THE RACQUET ARM to be able to exert a FORWARD PULL on it. Use the entire length of 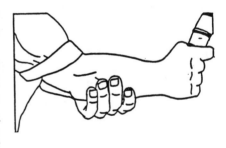 the fingers on the "boost hand" or just a part, as works best. Do not use a grasp in this drill.

D. Same as grip "C" except use just two or three fingers against the back of the racquet arm instead of all of them.

E Position the "boost hand", PALM DOWN ON TOP OF THE RACQUET ARM. Bend the fingers down against the BACK

** *Denotes usability on both the forehand and the backhand.* **251**

OF THE RACQUET ARM so as to be able to exert a FORWARD PULL on it. Use the entire length of the "boost hand" fingers or just a part, as works best.

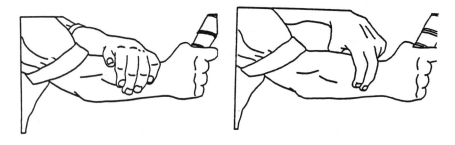

F. Same as grip "E" except use TWO OR THREE FINGERS against the the racquet arm instead of all of them.

G. Position the "boost hand", PALM DOWN, UNDER THE RACQUET ARM. Place the BACK OF THE HAND BEHIND THE RACQUET ARM to be able to exert a FORWARD PULL on it. The wrist of the "boost hand" is bent back slightly.

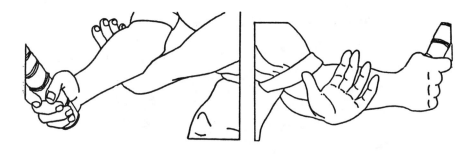

H. Position the "boost hand", PALM DOWN, UNDER THE RACQUET ARM. Extend the fingers and PLACE THE BACKS OF THE FINGERS BEHIND THE RAC-QUET ARM so as to be

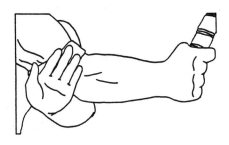

able to exert a FORWARD PULL on it. The wrist is bent back slightly.

J. Position the "boost hand" UNDER THE RACQUET ARM put the "V" FORMED BY THE THUMB AND FOREFINGER BEHIND THE RACQUET ARM so as to be able to exert a FORWARD PULL on it. The other fingers can be anything from being extended and bent back to being closed in a loose fist. Another variation is to place just the thumb behind the arm.

LIST OF BACKHAND "BOOST GRIPS"
The "grips" available for use with the backhand are:

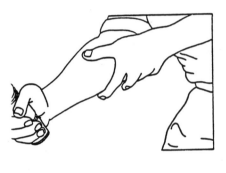

**A. Grasp the racquet arm lightly with the "boost hand", THUMB ON TOP OF THE ARM. Use just the fingers or the entire hand, as desired.

    1. "Grips" "A" and "B" make transition easy from standard two-handed grips.

**B. Grasp the racquet arm lightly with the "boost hand", thumb BELOW the arm instead of on top. Use just the fingers or the entire hand, as desired.

C. Place the TIPS or the faces of the tips of the fingers against the racquet arm so as to be able to exert a PUSH against it. As many of the fingers as desired can be used.

    1. Experiment with having the palm facing up or down, or anywhere in between.

    2. When the faces of the tips are used the pressure bends the fingers back slightly. This

gives a springy action that helps prolong the "boost" through the contact interval. The greatest reach for applying the "boost" is obtained with the fingers extended.

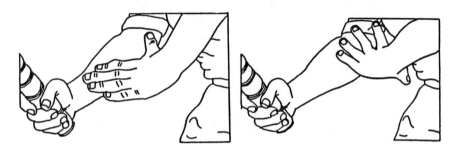

D. Place the BACKS OF THE FINGERS AGAINST THE RACQUET ARM so as to be able to exert a PUSH against it. As many of the fingers and as great a portion as desired can be used.

    1. Experiment with having the palm facing up or down, or anywhere in between.

E.   Position the "v" FORMED BY THE THUMB AND THE INDEX FINGER AGAINST THE RACQUET ARM so as to be able to exert a PUSH against it. The "V" can be along or across the arm depending on which works best at the location.

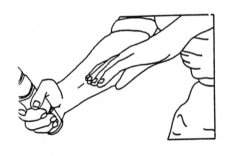

F. Place a closed or loose fist (try both) against the racquet arm to be able to exert a PUSH against it.

    1. Experiment with having the palm facing up, down, or anywhere in between. This "grip" is useful when an extra hard push or strong

reinforcement is to be transmitted to the arm via a large application area.

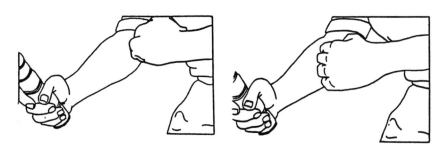

2. Another means of getting resistance against impact is to lower the "application point". Any method used for that purpose tends to reduce the reach of the "boost hand".

G. Place the palm against the racquet arm so as to exert a PUSH against it. The fingers can be above, below, or along the racquet arm. This grip provides good resistance against impact.

All backhand "grips" except "E" can be used with the back-hand overhead.

APPLYING FOREHAND AND BACKHAND "DOUBLE-FORCE GRIPS" AT "APPLICATION POINTS"

1. Select "boost grips" sequentially from the above two lists. Assume the end of backswing position. (Use the "back-scratch" position for the serve). Apply the selected "grip" to the racquet arm at an "application point" that seems to be about right when the racquet is at the end of the backswing. The location could be on the arm, wrist, or even the hand. (In actual play the "grip" may be applied during the forward swing instead of before the start of it.)

    a. Move (not swing) the racquet arm forward through the hitting point while applying light force with the "boost hand" through and just past contact. Get the body as well as the racquet arm involved in the action.

2. Maintain the hitting posture attained in the Step above and place the racquet at the <u>hitting point</u>. Reapply the selected "grip" to the racquet arm. But change the "application point" to what seems to be comfortable when the racquet is at the <u>hitting point.</u> The location will in all probability <u>not be the same</u> as for the <u>end of backswing</u>.

    a. Move (not swing) the racquet back and forth through the hitting point a few times. Apply the "boost force" only during the forward motion. Adjust the "application point" as seems necessary.

3. Bring the racquet arm to the end of the backswing position. Select a "grip" location that seems suitable for the needs of both the end of the backswing and the hitting point. In actual play the needs for the hitting point take preference, but there has to be compromises.

    a. Move (not swing) the racquet from <u>the end of the backswing</u> through the <u>hitting point</u> several times, readjusting the location of the "application point" as necessary. Reflect on the feel.

4. Repeat exercises one through three with the hitting point at about knee level and also at about shoulder level. The "grip" preferences may change with the level. (This step is skipped for the serve and overhead.)

5. Repeat exercises one through four with the opposite of the currently used stance, closed or open. If the customary stance is in between "open" and "closed" it may be desirable to experiment with a

variation in each direction

DRILL NOTES

Since the appropriateness of a "grip" used by the "boost hand" at an "application point" depends to some extant on the grip used by the "racquet" hand it may be advisable to experiment with that grip also. A further complication is that the grip on the racquet may vary with the bounce, velocity, type of shot, etc. So when several types of shots are being practiced it is up to the player or coach to evaluate the need for associated experiments with the "boost grip".

A "grip" that works well at one "application point" may not do so at the others. Do not try to decide on optimum "grips" and "application points" at this time. The above drills are for familiarization only, not final selection. They are used just to develop background information. Even preliminary selections are made later on.

The fleshy "application points" do not transfer the "boost force" to the bone structure, and then to the racquet, as efficiently as the firmer locations. On the other hand they are not as apt to transmit as much torque to the arm either. Ultimately a player will be able to both select the best location automatically and to compensate for any resultant torque.

However "torque" and "transfer of force" should not be the major influences in choosing the location of the "application point" for a particular shot. The decision should be based mostly on being able to apply the "boost force" effectively through the hitting point, and over as much of the previous swing interval as can be done conveniently. In other words, one of the important considerations is the REACH OF THE "BOOST HAND" just before and through the contact interval.

Reach improves as the "application point" is moved upward on the racquet arm but the effectiveness of the"boost force" decreases correspondingly. The amount of decrease is not significant unless the "application point" is well above the elbow. Any loss is undesirable when extra bracing against impact is needed. This could include heavy pace, late backswing, uncomfortable height, etc.

THE FOLLOWING "SWING" DRILLS ARE INTENDED FOR POSSIBLE REPEATED USE. THEY CAN BE USED EITHER IN SEQUENCE OR ON A SELECTIVE BASIS.

FOREHAND AND BACKHAND "DOUBLE-FORCE" SWINGS

Select a "grip" from the *FOREHAND* or the *BACKHAND* list to use with any or all of the following exercises. Use the most likely grips as determined by the previous drills.

1. Get into the WAITING position (not the hitting). Hold the racquet in front of the body in the customary manner. Turn and make the backswing in any way that seems comfortable and natural.

    a. At any time before the forward swing apply the selected "boost grip" to a location on the racquet arm that seems comfortable when the racquet is at the <u>end of the backswing.</u> Make a moderate forward swing at an imaginary ball, gradually accelerating the racquet through the hitting point.

        1. Assist the racquet arm with an easy force applied by the "boost arm".

        2. Release the "boost grip" and discontinue applying the "boost force" <u>just past</u> the hitting point, <u>not before</u>.

        3. Do not try to control the follow-through. Let it take care of itself. It is the consequence of the swing, not the cause of it.

        4. In actual play the "grip" may be

applied during the forward swing instead of before the start of it.

2. Maintain the hitting posture attained in the Step above and take the racquet to the hitting point.
    a. Reapply the selected "boost grip" to the racquet arm. But change the location to a point that seems to be comfortable when the racquet is at the hitting point. The location may not be the same as for the end of the backswing

    b. Take the racquet back a very short distance, not to the end of the backswing. Make a small swing maintaining the "boost" through the hitting point. Repeat a few times. Apply the "boost force" only during the forward motion. Adjust the "application point" as seems necessary.

3. Maintain the hitting posture attained in Step 1. Bring the racquet arm to the end of the backswing position.
    a. Select a "grip" location that seems suitable for the needs of both the end of the backswing and the hitting point. In actual play the needs for the hitting point take preference. But there may have to be compromises.
        1. Make an easy swing through the hitting point several times, readjusting the location of the "application point" as necessary. Accelerate the racquet through the hitting point.

        2. Do the same for a few moderate and a few hard hits of an imaginary ball, but always with an easy swing.

    b. Reflect on the suitability of the "grip" and

"application point". Try alternatives as seems desirable.

4. Repeat Step 3 making a few moderate hits off of easy bounces of a real ball. Make adjustments to the "application point" as seems desirable.

   a. These hits are intended for <u>preliminary familiarization</u>. The "grips" and "application points" have to be used with quite a few exercises in the following appendices before much hitting is advisable. The swings have to be reconciled with the revised "hitting planes", "swing distances", hitting points, etc, that will be established in the next appendix.

5. Repeat the above four exercises with the hitting point at about knee level and then at about shoulder level. Omit serves and overheads.

6. Repeat the above five exercises using the opposite of the currently used stance, closed or open. If the customary stance is already between open and closed then it may be desirable to experiment with one or more variations in either direction.

Reflect on the feel, arm extension, ease of applying the "boost" to the racquet arm, the amount of torque associated with the "application point", freedom of the swing, use of acceleration in developing momentum, nature of the follow-through, effort used, suitability of stance, naturalness, etc.

Check for enough reach by the "boost arm" to apply the "boost force" effectively through the contact interval. But as a rule do not think about such details during the swing. Concentrate on the idea of making a good, "swing-controlled" hit.

"Grips" and "application points" not only have to be compatible with each other but also with the stance. These initial exercises form a background for determining which combinations of stance, "grip", and "application point" are compatible and which are not. The "grip" can be rotated, modified, or even invented as desired.

For most people the "DOUBLE-FORCE" methods work best with a closed stance because it allows the best transfer of the "boost force" and the best reach by the"boost arm". The stance is considered to be defined by the orientation of the upper part of the body regardless of the position of the feet.

The many variations and return loops in the above exercises can take quite a bit of time, particularly if these "DOUBLE-FORCE" basics are being self-taught. And after these drills are finished then the new techniques have to be used in connection with the more numerous general drills in the following appendices.

So it is obvious that the exercises cannot all be done in just a few sessions. They have to be spread out over a relatively large number of sessions as convenient or necessary. The fact that a large amount of time is required is actually an advantage because the practice sessions can all be different. They do not all have to follow the same format and repeat the same routines.

The exercises in this and the following appendix can be particularly useful in tennis camps on rainy days. Many of them can be used indoors with or without racquets, and in a relatively small space. When the above exercises are used for group lessons it is advisable not to use racquets except for actual hits. This is purely for safety considerations. If the group is small, say four people, then the players can spread out so that racquets can be used as specified without danger.

MISCONCEPTIONS ABOUT HITTING POINTS, ETC

There is considerable reference to "hitting point", "hitting plane", and "swing distance" in this book. In spite of being very important. they are just details The swing is likely to deteriorate badly if attention is wasted on a detail, particularly if the concept of it is not one hundred percent correct. Details are more properly discovered and evaluated than defined and prescribed. Even top players sometimes apply "cures" that are worse than the problems.

A perfect hit establishes the perfect hitting point, etc, for a particular person, style, and shot. But the converse is not true: the hitting point does not establish the perfect swing and hit. That is a "tail-wags-the-dog" type of approach. The often heard advice in regard to the hitting point to "hit well out in front" has that flaw. And in fact more people already hit farther out in front than is advisable. It is generally a sign of deterioration rather than progress.

The terms "hitting point", "hitting plane", and "swing distance" should be regarded as applying only to a particular shot or set of circumstances, not as pre-set, inviolable standards.

Some of the factors affecting the location of the hitting point are the stage of the bounce, height at which the ball is hit, velocities of the ball and racquet, stance, style, and the type of shot (hard, soft, flat, spin, volley, etc). The appropriate hitting point is contained in the path of the swing, and so is internal to the swing. External timing merely arranges to have the ball appear at that point at the right time.

The first step in correcting a timing problem, internal or external, is to be able to recognize it. A fault in one merely becomes compounded by making corrections or compensations in the other. That perpetuates the original bad habit and produces others in the form of associated compromises.

ESTABLISHING THE "HITTING PLANE"

1. Stand the approximate hitting distance behind any line and assume the preferred hitting stance (not the "ready"). The line should be considered as parallel to the net. and forward of the body, not alongside. Make a few easy swings, making contact with an imaginary ball directly above the line.

   a. If the swing seemed to be compromised because of improper distance from the line (the "*hitting plane*") adjust the position and repeat.

2. Without moving from the position established above make an imaginary hit without regard to the line.

   a. If this swing and associated "hitting plane" were not nearly the same as those in Step 1 go back to Step 1.

   b. When the swings in Steps 1 and 2 agree note the position of the body with respect to the line. This is the "*hitting plane*

distance". It is a variable.
1. On an actual hit this distance should be as much "swing-determined" as above, whether the shot is made from a set position or on a dead run.

3. Without a racquet, and with the arms just hanging loosely at the side, emulate the motion of the body in the swing in Step 2. (Such emulations can be used in connection with other drills also.)
a. This exercise is just to familiarize the player with the role of the body in the currently used techniques. There should be no attempt to observe or control the behavior of the body during an actual hit. The action should just happen as a result of the intents for the hit.

b. Reflect on whether the participation by the body was as appropriate as it had been assumed to be.

4. Repeat the above Steps with an imaginary ball at about knee level and about shoulder level.
a. The "hitting plane distance" may vary with the height of the ball.

5. Repeat the above Steps with the stance a little more open than normal, and with a stance a little more closed.

Let the body participate naturally without conscious control. Otherwise the "hitting plane" will not be correctly determined. Evaluate its location on the basis of such things as comfort, absence of compromises in the wrist angle, direction of racquet travel, quality of swing, arm extension, reinforcement, etc. If the wrist is more than slightly angled back at the hit, or if the arm is constrained from moving in the direction of the hit, the location may be too far forward. The distance of the line from the body is usually described as the distance from the front foot. But actually it is a concept of the position of the body, not the foot, relative to the "hitting plane". The main use is in providing the answer to the question: "Am I making contact too early, too late, or about right?".

Some inexpert players have unsound ideas, or practically none at all, about where the "hitting plane" should be. Even when it is both inappropriate and variable it simply doesn't register. Using this drill to establish and evaluate the location of that plane creates awareness of its general location, and of its importance to the hit.

The location of the "hitting plane" should be reviewed periodically because there is a common tendency to move it farther and farther forward of the optimum. That is one of the important causes of deterioration in games at all levels. As a result even great players may get to look somewhat ordinary a few years after quitting tournament play.

ESTABLISHING THE "SWING DISTANCE"

1. Imagine a ball coming down a line (a sideline can be used). Get into the hitting position approximately the right distance from the line (path of the ball). Execute an easy swing meeting an imaginary ball directly above the line. Involve the body.

   a. If the swing appears to be compromised due to being at an improper distance from the line adjust the position and repeat.

SWING DISTANCE

2. Without moving from the position

established above, execute an easy swing without regard to the line.

    a. If this "hit" was not directly above the line make adjustments and go back to Step 1.

    b. When the "hits" in Steps 1 and 2 both occur above the line note the distance from the line. This is defined as the "*swing distance*".

        1. On an actual hit this distance should be as much "swing-determined" as above, whether the shot is made from a set position or on a dead run.

3. Repeat Steps 1 and 2 with a stance a little more open than normal, and a stance a little more closed.

4. Repeat the above Steps with swings at an imaginary ball at about knee level and about shoulder level.

    a. The "swing distance" will probably vary with the height of the ball.

Observe the stance, arm extension, and the position of the body with respect to the line. Do not worry about footwork at this time, only about establishing the "swing distance".

Moving closer than optimum to the path of the ball is a major cause of deterioration in established games, and of lack of progress in general. It is usually done because a compact swing gives a sense of security compared to a free swing with a comfortably extended arm. The distance to the path of the ball is partly established by the arm extension. For most players the most effective swings generally occur when the arm is at a near full but comfortable extension.

Players who have respectable form nevertheless occasionally improvise a swing rather than exert effort to get into proper position. In that case the arm extension is determined by the happenstance position. Each compromise in getting set to make a shot, whether in practice or in play, generates compensations which easily become permanent bad habits.

ESTABLISHING THE HITTING POINT

1. Stand in position inside the corner formed by two intersecting lines. The position should be the "hitting plane distance" away from the line parallel to the net and the "swing distance" away from the line perpendicular to the net. So the corner can be considered as the general location of a whole stack of suitable *hitting points*. Make an easy swing meeting an imaginary ball directly above the corner.

  a. Involve the body. Use the preferred stance.

  b. If the swing was modified because of improper distance from the hitting point adjust the position and repeat.

2. Make a moderately paced imaginary hit using a free swing without trying to conform to the lines. Use an adequate backswing, maintaining a gradual acceleration past the hitting point. Involve the body.

  a. Reflect on the location of the hitting point. If it was not directly above the corner, or if the swing at a ball above the corner now seems to have been unnatural and uncomfortable, adjust the positioning and go back to Step 1.

  b. When the hits in Steps 1 and 2 are both above the corner note the locations of the lines

with respect the body.
1. On an actual hit the hitting point should be as much "swing-determined" as above, whether the hit was made from a set position or on a dead run.

3. Repeat Steps 1 and 2 with a stance a little more open than normal and one a little more closed.
   a. Reflect on preferences.

   b. If the stance is changed it may be useful to repeat Steps 1 and 2 with the new stance. Step 3 need not be repeated because everything is subject to continual adjustment.

4. Repeat Steps 1, 2, and 3 with swings at an imaginary ball at about knee level and about shoulder level.
   a. The hitting point will probably vary with the height of the ball.

Some of the causes of variation in the hitting point are the opening of the stance, shortening of the backswing, bringing the arm in for a quick swing, letting the body swing around faster than the arm, tensing normally relaxed muscles, etc.

EXPERIMENTING WITH INAPPROPRIATE "SWING DISTANCE" AND "HITTING PLANE DISTANCE"

1. Stand in the hitting position inside the corner formed by two intersecting lines. Get the "hitting plane distance" away from the line in front and the "swing distance" away from the line alongside.
   a. Carry out a few "swing-controlled" strokes at an imaginary ball. Adjust the position until the "hit" occurs exactly at the corner.

2. Vary the distance to each line separately, closer and farther than normal. Then swing at an imaginary ball exactly at the corner. Have the sweet spot of the racquet travel roughly above the line (path of

the ball) as it approaches the corner (hitting point).
   a. Alternate each swing with a free swing not restricted to the lines. Compare these swings with the swings made exactly at the corner. Evaluate on the basis of feel, "swing distance", "hitting plane distance", "hitting point", etc.

Varying the distance to the "hitting plane" gives the FEEL OF HITTING EARLY OR LATE. Varying the "swing distance" gives the FEEL OF REACHING OR CROWDING. The object is to become familiar with the feel of appropriate and inappropriate distances. A major cause of poor pace, and also of deterioration of the game as a whole, is hitting early (being too far back of the "hitting plane"). Not being able to associate a disagreeable feel with the cause makes it very difficult to devise or accept corrections.

EVALUATING ARM EXTENSION AND ARM ANGLE

1. Put the racquet aside. Move as if getting ready to hit an easy paced oncoming ball with an open hand, but just meet it and hold on to it.   The   arm   must   be comfortably   extended   at about the same angle as for a hit, not held forward or to the side as for a catch. The ball should be in easy reach so that no expedients or difficult moves have to be used.
   a.   Repeat   until meeting   the   ball with the hand at an appropriate point can be done naturally.

2. With a racquet, get into position to hit an easy paced oncoming ball, but just block it with the rac-

quet as was done with the hand in Step 1.

    a. Repeat until meeting the ball with the racquet at an appropriate point can be done naturally.

    b. If the overall execution was not similar to that in Step 1 go back to that Step. Modifications can be made in either Step or both as seems fit.

Many people learn wrong techniques because of having the arm at an improper angle and extension, and the body in an inappropriate position. Catching the ball forces the player to move into reasonably good position for the hit since using the hand is a very natural action. Hitting with a racquet is not.

It is futile to practice strokes without using a suitable "arm extension" and "arm angle" because they determine the "swing distance". The :"arm angle" is the angle of the arm with respect to the body. Maximum angle is obtained with the arm held out at shoulder level Minimum angle occurs when the arm is held close to the side. The "HITTING PLANE", "SWING DISTANCE", and ARM ANGLE determine the hitting point.

One of the reasons why the games of all players, even tournament, inevitably deteriorate is the tendency to resort to compensations in the swing to make up for not being in optimum hitting relationships with the ball. Compromises are especially common during practice, where bad habits are as likely to originate and become permanent as in play.

VERIFYING THE "SWING DISTANCE" AND HITTING POINT WITH "DEFERRED SWINGS"

1. Get into the hitting position, make the backswing, and get ready to hit an oncoming ball. Delay the forward swing and just watch the ball go by while visualizing the completion of the hit. Switch the attention from the ball to the "hitting plane" just before the ball goes through it.

   a. This is a better alternative to "watch-the-ball". It makes provision for meeting the ball at the "hitting plane" instead of just watching the ball in isolation from any other action or requirement.

2. After the ball has gone by complete the swing exactly as imagined in Step 1. Do not make changes or corrections. This is defined as a *"deferred swing"*. It is restricted by the path of the ball but is free of the complications involved with the "external timing" involved in an actual hit.

   a. Reflect on and analyze the appropriateness of the positioning and techniques.

   b. Did the positioning and preparation allow for a free, normal swing using continuous acceleration to develop momentum? The more difficult the shot the poorer is the preparation likely to be. Two important conditions are:

      1. Be the optimum distance from the path of the ball and the "hitting plane".

      2. Get ready for a good hit, not in terms

of "get the racquet back", but in getting completely ready, including the mind, arm, body, feet, and racquet.

3. Without changing location, swing normally at an imaginary ball without reference to the path of the last ball.

    a. Did the hitting point coincide with the one used in Step 2? If not, keep adjusting the position and repeating the swing at an imaginary ball until the points do coincide. Note the difference in the final positioning from that used in Step 2.

VERIFYING TIMING, "SWING DISTANCE", AND "HITTING PLANE" WITH "TIMING SWINGS"

1. Time a moderate swing with the arrival of an oncoming ball. But use a path higher or lower than that of the ball. Use a comfortable arm extension <u>whether or not that puts the racquet vertically in line with the ball.</u> This is a *"timing swing"*.

    a. Reflect on whether the racquet and ball passed through the correct "hitting <u>plane</u>" at the same time? (External timing)

2. Without changing location, swing at an exactly similar imaginary ball using whatever compromises are necessary to make a "hit" of the last ball.

    a. Were the arm extension and "swing distance" approximately the same as for the

273

uncompromised swing in Step 1? If not, adjust the position and repeat the swing at the same imaginary ball. Note any difference in the final positioning from that used in Steps 1 and 2.

b. Reflect on the reasons why the swings are not always, or never, the same.

VERIFYING TIMING, "SWING DISTANCE," AND "HITTING PLANE" WITH "SHADOW SWINGS"

1. Prepare carefully for an oncoming ball and complete a moderate swing, but for a *"shadow"* rather than actual hit. This means a hit of an imaginary ball directly above or below the real ball. So if the positioning is poor the swing will have to be compromised to suit.

a. Reflect on whether the hitting point and the "swing distance" were approximately correct.

b. Was the positioning far enough from the path of the ball? Was the backswing long enough? Any cramping of arm? Hitting point feel right? Any push in the contact zone? Getting set too early or too late? Any hurrying of the swing?

2. Without changing position, make a moderate imaginary hit at the same level as the previous but not restricted to being vertically in line with the path of the last ball.

a. If the hitting point was not approximately the same as in Step 1 adjust the positioning and repeat the imaginary hit. Note any differences in the final positioning, arm extension, and arm angle from those used in Step 1.

b. Note any other differences in the nature of the swings for the "shadow" and imaginary hits, such as in stance, use of the body, arm extension, naturalness, etc.

3. Carry out a moderate "swing-controlled" stroke to meet an oncoming ball rather than to swing to miss as in Step 1.
   a. Reflect on whether there was bracing for the impact and\or compromises in the swing, "swing distance", hitting point, arm extension and angle, etc.

"Timing" and "shadow" swings combine the requirements of "external" timing (which determines where the ball will meet the swing) with the requirements of "internal" timing (which controls the coordination of the activities internal to the stroke). Ideally, external timing should not affect the internal timing, the hitting point, or the velocity of the swing. The hitting point is internal to the swing. But it becomes external and less than ideal if the swing is compromised to accommodate to the position of the ball.

For many people swinging at a real ball will be accompanied by reversion to many bad habits. Such reversions cannot be corrected in a few practice sessions. The process is gradual. It is likely to be continual also if the player is familiar with the ideas developed in this book. One of the main objectives of the current drills is just to develop awareness. That is the first requirement for any change.

An oncoming ball seems to travel faster and is harder to follow as it comes closer, and particularly so when it is passing alongside the body. That is one reason why players tend to move the hitting point (or "hitting plane") forward from where it should be. If the hitting point is moved forward of the optimum location there will be a corresponding loss in pace and accuracy. And occasional use is likely to develop into consistent use on all shots.

It is only necessary to see the outline of the ball, not to be able to "read the print", to have a sufficient idea of its location, direction, pace, and spin. It is a mistake to intend to "keep your eye on the ball" because that one external detail then monopolizes not only the view but also the attention, and for too long an interval. It is more important to be concerned with the hit. In doing so the ball, as well as other factors, will each tend to get as much attention as warranted. "Time the momentum of the swing" or "switch the attention to the "hitting plane"" are much better slogans than "watch the ball".

COMPARING MERITS OF VARIOUS ARM EXTENSIONS

1. Try elbow-in, normal arm extension, and full arm extension on moderate hits off easy bounces while trying to maintain the initial arm extension.

   a. Note the effects of the various extensions on feel, power, effort, control, shock, roundhouse, interference with the body, etc.

   b. Note the pull on the arm required to counter the centrifugal force of the racquet and arm. The pull creates an unpleasant feel, is tiring and is a cause of variation in direction. The feel is even more pronounced if the elbow is pulled in during the late stages, a habit occasionally seen even at tournament level.

2. Using the preferred arm extension established in Step 1, try moderate hits of imaginary balls holding the arm at smaller than normal, normal, and larger than normal angles with the body This is experimentation with the "ARM ANGLE", a generally unexamined element of stroke production.

   a. Note the effects of the various arm angles on

reach, feel, power, effort, control, shock, roundhouse, interference with the body, etc.

b. The nature of a swing is determined not only by the "extension" (amount of bend of the elbow) but also by the position of the arm with respect to the body, tight in or comfortably but not artificially out. The position of the arm affects the radius of the swing as much as does the bend of the elbow.

Although the angular velocity of the swing can increase when the racquet is held close in, the velocity of the racquet in the direction of the hit is likely to decrease. And the reach and length of the arc of the swing are considerably less than when the arm is held further out.

During warm-ups it is wise to hit with <u>preferred or greater than normal arm extension</u>, not with cautious, elbow-in techniques. The first strokes must be in full compliance with the rules and best concepts of hitting, even more so if anything than for subsequent hits.

EVALUATING THE RESULTS OF INCREASING THE ARM EXTENSION DURING THE FORWARD SWING
1. Make a moderate hit of an imaginary ball having the elbow in a little more than normal at the start of the swing and then gradually letting it out to normal or greater than normal extension as the racquet progresses toward the hitting point.
a. Evaluate for the effects on feel, power, effort, control, shock, roundhouse, interference with the body, involvement of the body, etc.

2. Repeat Step 1 with hits off of easy bounces of real balls.

This method combines some of the advantages of the bent-elbow and extended-arm swings. And the problems created when hitting with a bent elbow, such as centrifugal pull, roundhouse, erratic control, etc, are avoided. It is usually combined with the "elbow-first" backswing, and is actually a much used technique, especially at the higher levels.

Values are established for the "hitting plane", "swing distance", and "hitting point" in the above drills. They are not defined as fixed quantities but in terms of positions within the swing. The process involves experiment, knowledge, feel, satisfactions, feedback, awareness, visualization, emulation, results, evaluation, etc. Details should not determine the stroke, or even be the subject of direct observation. They should just happen, not be made to happen or be given control over what does happen.

CENTRIFUGAL   CENTRIPETAL

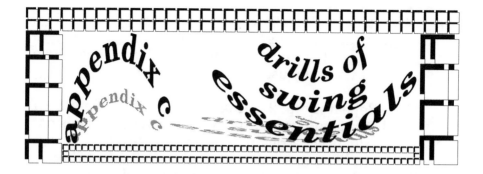

EVALUATING THE LENGTH OF THE BACKSWING

1. Take the racquet to the end of the backswing several times in the normal manner. Try using both one hand and two hands just for comparison sake. The second hand can be placed anywhere convenient. On succeeding drills use whatever seems best.

2. Make the preferred backswing and then bring the racquet forward about a foot several times to check the effects of the length of the backswing on the start of the forward swing.

   a. Do the same but complete a moderate paced forward swing at an imaginary ball using normal arm extension.

   b. Evaluate for feel and ease of development of forward momentum.

3. Repeat Step 2 with shorter than normal and longer than normal backswings.

   a. A short backswing may cause the hitting point to be moved forward to where the swing begins to degenerate into a push.

   b. The intent here is not to try to decide on a particular length of backswing but merely to create awareness of the effects of the length on the nature of the stroke.

4. Repeat Step 2 with <u>higher</u> and <u>lower end of</u> <u>backswing positions</u>, and also with the <u>racquet face</u> <u>open</u>, <u>closed</u>, and <u>vertical</u> at the end, whichever two are not normally used.

5. Repeat Step 2 using the preferred length of backswing and trying the two backswing methods not normally used: <u>straight, loop,</u> or <u>elbow-first.</u>

a The methods were only briefly described in the chapter on the "BACKSWING" since they are adequately covered in the standard texts.

b Reflect on the influence, if any, of the type of backswing on the stance, hitting point, the nature of the swing, etc.

6. Execute moderate hits off easy bounces. Use the preferred backswing method and arm extension.

a. Experiment with <u>normal, shorter,</u> and <u>longer</u> backswings to get comparisons of associated feel, power, effort, consistency, hitting point, etc.

b. Experiment also with <u>higher and lower end</u> <u>of backswing positions</u>, and with various <u>open</u> <u>and closed racquet attitudes.</u>

c. At a later stage, on three successive hits intend to send the ball in three different directions. Think of the direction of the ball as it leaves the racquet, but do not worry about whether it actually goes that way. Otherwise the compromises introduced to get control invalidate the development of the stroke.

7. Repeat Step 6 making hits at about <u>knee</u> and <u>shoulder</u> levels, first with an imaginary and then with a real balls.

8 Repeat Step 6 with the opposite of the currently used stance, open or closed. first with an imaginary ball and then with a real ball.

The backswing is important mainly in the sense of providing for sufficient length so that easy development of momentum is possible in the forward swing. Trying for adequate length in the backswing could also help remedy wrong stances, techniques, swings, hitting points, and the consequent poor results.

If it is decided to change the length of the backswing as a result of these drills it may be desirable to repeat the drills in APPENDIX "B" titled "ESTABLISHING THE "HITTING PLANE"", "ESTABLISHING THE "SWING DISTANCE"", and "ESTABLISHING THE HITTING POINT". The processes of re-examination and refinement should never end because the interactions never do.

ACCELERATION AND THE FOLLOW-THROUGH

1. Hit an easy shot in the normal way without trying to influence the end of the follow-through.

   a. Emulate the stroke as closely as possible with a hit of an identical <u>imaginary</u> ball. Do not pretty up the stroke in any way or the purpose of the drill is defeated.

   b. Reflect on the path of the entire forward swing and follow-through. Reflect on the area and nature of acceleration. The principle objective of the drill is to obtain awareness of the current techniques, and of the nature of the follow-through.

2. Repeat Step 1 trying to have the racquet <u>point in the direction of travel of the ball</u> at the end of the follow-through. Notice whether there is general improvement or deterioration

   a. This was formerly regarded as a requirement. But the rule was gradually abandoned

281

as it became apparent that it was seldom observed by expert players. It can still have use for initial lessons and as a means to create awareness of round-house in the regularly used strokes.

3. Repeat Step 1 trying to have a <u>circular follow-through so that the racquet points backward</u> at the end of the stroke.

    a.   Reflect on whether round-house in the fol-low-through actu-ally started before contact.

    b. Reflect on the differences be-tween the regu-larly used follow-through, straight, and circular as experienced in Steps 1, 2, and 3.

4. Hit an easy shot trying to <u>accelerate the racquet gradually in the forward direction through contact</u>. After that it can go anywhere as seems most natural.

    a. Do not worry about form, grip, positioning, direction of the hit, follow-through, etc, only about the acceleration.

        1. It is necessary to learn whether the normally used acceleration is about right, excessive, or deficient. In actual

play it is unwise to pay conscious attention to a detail.

    b. Emulate the above stroke as closely as possible with a hit of an imaginary identical ball. Do not pretty up the stroke in any or the purpose of the drill is defeated.

        1. Reflect on the direction of racquet travel through contact (not follow-through) as compared to what happened in the circular follow-through in Step 3, where there was no emphasis on accelerating the racquet through contact.

5. Repeat Step 4 with <u>moderately</u> hard hits.
    a. Note the nature of the follow-through, especially any tendency to deviate from the forward direction, compared to what happens in a moderately paced hit. An unusual follow-through could be a sign of a bad swing.

6. Repeat Steps 4 with both <u>easy</u> and <u>moderately hard</u> hits at about <u>knee</u> and <u>shoulder levels</u>.

There is no need to standardize the endings of strokes. For one thing the finish varies with the circumstances, spin, spin, etc. It is a result of the swing and the hit, not the producer of either. For maximum efficiency and accuracy the general direction of racquet travel during contact should be forward.

The body tends to turn faster than the arm can follow as the pace is increased, breaking reinforcement and pulling the arm into roundhouse. This reduces the forward racquet velocity, as well as reinforcement and strength in that direction. Reinforcement is critical in countering the momentum of the ball, otherwise racquet momentum is wasted for the purpose.

The conscious control and observation specified here are for familiarization purposes only. During play the follow-through should be automatic, and should intrude on the attention only when unusual in some respect.

GETTING THE FEEL OF RACQUET ATTITUDE AND HORIZONTAL MOMENTUM

1. Extend the racquet sideward at waist level on the forehand side, face at any convenient attitude. Use whatever grip is normal on the forehand. Make a slow horizontal swing to the backhand side. Have the body get into the rhythm slightly. Accelerate slowly and continuously through midpoint, but without swinging fast, or with muscle instead of momentum. A little wrist flex is advisable, but no arm flex.

    a. The only restriction on the attitude of the racquet is that at midpoint it should be faced as for a normal hit. But don't think about it.

2. Change to whatever grip is used on the backhand and swing the racquet back slowly to the forehand side. Go back and forth without any strain. Try to get the swings to resemble and feel like the slow sweeps of a pendulum.

3. Repeat Steps 1 and 2 with the racquet face open or closed initially and in the opposite condition at the end of the swing.

4. Repeat Steps 1and 2 with swings at about <u>knee</u> and <u>shoulder</u> levels.

EXPERIENCING VERTICAL MOMENTUM

1. Extend the racquet sideward at about shoulder level on the forehand side, racquet face pointing up at the start. Use whatever grip is normal on the forehand. Swing the racquet up and around in a slow vertical half-circle to the backhand side. Keep the face of the racquet vertical to the path of the swing.

Stop the swing at a level a trifle lower than the shoulder. The face of the racquet that was up now faces down.

2. Change to whatever grip is used on the backhand and swing the racquet back to the forehand side. Go back and forth without any strain trying to get the swings to resemble and feel like the slow motions of an inverted pendulum. If there is a feeling of strain then too much force is being used to accelerate the racquet.

This drill is primarily intended as remedial for those who have had little experience in sports and don't have a feel for accelerating the racquet, developing momentum, and controlling the attitude of the racquet.

DEVELOPING AND TIMING RACQUET MOMENTUM
1. Alternate four swings at four similar, easy-paced oncoming balls in the order shown below. Try to accelerate the racquet in a way to develop the same momentum in the same way on the first four swings. It shouldn't be as if swinging at a feather on the first three and bracing for the crash of a bowling ball on the fourth.
   a. Use a "deferred swing".
   (The forward swing is delayed until after the ball has passed by. The hitting point must be what would have been used had the swing not been deferred.)

   b. Use a "shadow" swing.
   (A swing at an imaginary ball directly above or below the real ball.)

   c. Use a "timing swing".
   (A swing at an imaginary ball in a path higher or lower than that of the real ball, but at a comfortable arm extension. The imaginary

285

ball is not restricted to being vertically in line with the real ball.)

d. Use a moderate actual hit.

1. The strokes must still be "swing controlled" even if it means that the ball is not met at the correct hitting point, or on the sweet spot of the racquet, or met at all. It is necessary to expose deficiencies in order to overcome them.

a. Do not complete a hit if there is any chance of anybody getting hit by a misdirected ball.

e. For contrast, hit balls maintaining a constant racquet velocity, instead of using continuous acceleration. Compare to the preferred method in the previous steps with respect to feel and results.

In Steps "a", "b", "c", and "d" was the acceleration of the racquet through the hitting point and the development of momentum about the same on all four swings? Racquet velocity should vary inversely with ball velocity and with difficulty. The natural tendency is to increase racquet velocity as that of the oncoming ball becomes greater. One purpose of this drill is intended to minimize the tendency to mask insecurity with fast swings.

Check for and try to eliminate differences in techniques and feel. Continually refine the positioning so as to minimize the differences between the four swings.

On the actual hits was the arm extension and the length of the backswing about the same as for the other three? Was the stance no more open, the hitting point no more forward? Was the shot muscled or momentum-powered?

On all the swings except the "deferred" was the nature of the stroke adversely affected by the need to pay attention to external timing? Was the hit early, late, or just right? Were either the backswing or forward swing started too late and then hurried?

Early or continuous application of maximum effort does not provide either good control or power. Yet all-out effort is what most players resort to in pressure situations. Impulsive acceleration of the racquet causes changes in the hitting point, attitude of racquet, arm extension, etc.

The "deferred" swing amounts to practice of internal timing independent of the external. The "shadow" and "timing swings" combine internal and external timing without the complications and consequences of an actual hit. The actual hits are influenced by anticipations of the shock of impact.

Internal timing can be defined as the proper coordination of the internal activities with each other. It determines the nature and appearance of the stroke and the location of the hitting point within the swing. Correct external timing coordinates an unmodified stroke with the arrival and behavior of the ball. It is not basically the most important of the two. Errors in either one require compensations in the other.

The external timing must be adjusted to the swing, not vice versa. Once the swing starts it should proceed independent of external timing and everything else. That is what makes it a "swing-controlled stroke". The intent is to eliminate compromises of internal timing (nature of the swing).

USING THE FREE HAND TO INFLUENCE THE SWING
1. Swing the free arm some-what parallel to and in sync with the racquet arm. This can be done with any type of hit: imaginary, "shadow", "deferred", "timing", or real.

2. At a later stage try to have the free arm not only

move with the racquet arm but also mimic its actions.

The free arm does not use and therefore does not learn either the skills or the bad habits, compensations, and compromises used by the racquet hand. So it tends to operate per the person's basic concepts. These could be quite different from what the racquet arm does. The free arm also does not have to engage in compromises imagined to be necessary to take up the shock of impact, steer the ball, kowtow to urges and feelings of insecurity, etc.

Since each hand coordinates with the other the actions of the free hand will influence the swing and the location of the hitting point. It will also improve awareness of what is happening with the racquet hand. Awareness is the first step to improvement.

EXPERIMENTS WITH REINFORCEMENT

1. Stand at the end of a fence or wall. Assume the hitting position and stance. Hold a tennis ball against the surface with the racquet. The arm should be at the normal hitting extension and angle.

2. Press the racquet forward

lightly so as to just keep the ball from falling, not so hard as to require a bent elbow. Reflect on the feel of the arm being backed up by the body, and the sense of being able to swing (not push) the racquet through the rest of a stroke.

3. Experiment with the forward angle of the arm by changing the position of the body slightly to the left and to the right. This simulates hitting early and late. Experiment also with the stance and arm extension. Reflect on preferences.

4. Just meet moderately paced balls attempting to use the most suitable stance, arm extension, angle of the arm, etc, as experienced in Steps 2 and 3.

During a swing the arm should gain on the body from being way behind to becoming a little ahead by about midpoint of the forward swing. Some common flaws are weakening, breaking, over-achieving, or not achieving reinforcement of the racquet with the arm and body.

Improper reinforcement is one of the reasons why seemingly unaccountably weak shots occasionally occur even for good players. And it is most apt to happen as the result of a hard run, or some special circumstance such as extra difficulty, caution, abandon, etc.

For many people there is likely to be too much reinforce-ment (the arm angled too far forward) rather than too little. One effect is that the freedom to swing the racquet in the direction of the hit becomes limited. The problem can origi-nate out of a short backswing, lazy footwork, a desire to watch the other court, insecurity, getting the body too close to the path of the ball, hitting too far out in front where the ball is easier to see, etc.

EXPERIMENTS WITH WRIST FLEX
1. Alternate hits of very easy paced oncoming balls in

the following manner:
    a. Hit the first with an almost stiff wrist.

    b. Hit the next by laying the wrist back slightly and letting it flex easily forward during the hit.

Reflect on feel, shock, results, preferences, etc. A shot made with a rather firm wrist is fine for just blocking the ball back, as for most volleys. But for normal hits there is sacrifice of pace, control, naturalness, disguise, etc.

In this drill the oncoming ball should have very easy pace because the wrist can be easily injured if angled back when impact occurs. The swing should be very moderate for the same reason.

Conscious control of wrist flex should only be used for drills such as this. In other situations it should occur automatically as a result of the intentions for the hit. There is no need to try to get more flex than happens naturally.

EVALUATING THE GRIP AND RACQUET ATTITUDE
1. Have the racquet face either very open or very closed at the end of the backswing. As the racquet comes forward turn it so that it arrives with appropriate attitude for the hit of an <u>imaginary</u> ball.
    a. In addition to going forward the racquet can be traveling upward, downward, or sideward to obtain the type of spin desired.

    b. Experiment with the grip to <u>obtain a suitable racquet attitude at the hit</u>.

2. Repeat Step 1 alternating "<u>timing swings</u>", "<u>shadow</u>

swings", and real hits off easy bounces. On the real hits note the type of spin that results, but just let the spin happen without trying to influence or exaggerate it.

a. Topspin can be achieved with either an initially closed or open racquet face by moving it at a moderate upward angle. The attitude of the racquet at the hit is best established by experiment rather than definition.

b. A closed racquet face at the end of the backswing is commonly used on the forehand. Conversely, an open racquet face is used more often than a closed on the backhand. There is no requirement or objection to using either on either side.

c. The troubles that many players have in hitting topspin backhands are often due to the combination of a high "end of backswing", an initially open racquet face, and a hitting point that is too far forward.

3. Repeat Step 1 with hits at both knee and shoulder levels, and hits of both real balls and imaginary balls.

4. Repeat Step 3 with a stance more open and a stance more closed than the preferred.

This drill familiarizes players with the techniques, feel, applications, pluses, and minuses of an initially open or closed racquet face.

TESTING THE "VERTICAL RACQUET FACE" THEORY
1. Return balls, either against a wall or across the net, with the only requirement being to have the racquet face exactly perpendicular at contact.
   a. Vary the path of the racquet, velocity, follow-through, etc, as desired or necessary to try to get the spin, pace, control, trajectory, or depth desired.

The vertical racquet face is not a workable option and is not being recommended. The purpose of the drill is merely to have the student test the validity of the theory and become acquainted with the consequences of that action.

CONTROLLING THE DEPTH OF SHOTS
1. Hit oncoming balls aiming alternately at the baseline and the service line. The specific techniques to be used are:
   a. Change only the racquet attitude.

   b. Change only the outgoing pace.

A common mistake when trying for accuracy is to increase the pace as the target gets smaller. This is because the straight line trajectory seems to offer more security than a looped trajectory. So there is a great temptation to rely exclusively on a bullet type trajectory when trying to pass an opponent at the net, or to hit very close to a line. As a consequence even tournament players use a surprising and undesirable lack of variety on passing shots, or when trying to hit very close to a line.

ESTABLISHING THE REQUIREMENTS FOR HITS OF HIGH BOUNCES

1. Get into position to hit a high imaginary ball with the hitting point located above a corner or mark on the court. Complete the backswing, but hold up the forward swing. Make adjustments and note the final end-of-backswing position.

    a. Bring the racquet forward to the visualized hitting point. Back the racquet off about a foot and then return it to the hitting point again.

        1 Back it off several times in that way, increasing the distance a few inches each time until it reaches what seems to be a suitable end point of backswing. Make adjustments in the positioning if required, in general in the direction of a closed stance.

    b. Repeat the complete forward motion from the end of backswing through the hitting point several times. Swing slightly faster than slow motion at first, then at half-speed, and finally at a moderate speed. Make adjustments in the positioning as required.

        1. Do the positioning and preparation seem adequate? Is the stance mostly sideways? The length of the backswing and follow-through sufficient? Feel of the swing right? Use of momentum instead of push? On high balls the answers are usually all "no".

    c. Repeat Step "b" with both a longer and shorter backswing than the preferred.

        1. Note any difference in the ease of developing momentum between the three lengths of backswings. Note the unpleasant feeling associated with a short swing and insufficient momentum.

d. Repeat Step "b" with both a more open and a more closed stance than the preferred.

While most drills in this book do not indicate a preferred technique, here it is advisable to use the "DOUBLE-FORCE" methods.

If the "application point" is above the elbow the "boost" force will probably be applied to fleshy areas. So for efficient transfer of force the contact area has to be maximized by using the palm or fist.

Inexpert players tend to open the stance and move the hitting point forward for hits of high bounces. This can be due to feelings of insecurity. But on high bounces it is advisable to use a stance more closed than normal.

Make extensive use of "slow motion visualization" (SMV). Try to base the hit on the momentum developed via a swing. If the racquet seems to have insufficient momentum when it reaches the hitting point the most likely reasons are poor positioning and insufficient length in the backswing.

Often the worst feature of hits off high bounces is the backswing. Inexpert players may use just about none at all. The racquet is then started from a position close to the hitting point, and pushed forward and downward from there with a sway of the body and an almost frozen arm. The stance and follow-through tend to be very inappropriate also.

CHECKING THE REQUIREMENTS FOR HITS OF HIGH BOUNCES USING REAL. BALLS

1. Get in position for a moderately high-bouncing oncoming ball. Complete the backswing, but hold up the forward swing.

    a. Bring the racquet forward to what would have been the hitting point. Adjust the positioning if the "hitting plane" and "swing distance" do not seem to be correct. The path of the ball will tend to be closer to the body than with hits at lower levels because the reach is diminished as the height increases.

b. Take the racquet to the end of the backswing again and bring it forward about a foot in a slow swing. Repeat several times increasing the racquet travel by four or five inches each time.

1. Continue lengthening the swing up to and past the hitting point until a moderate follow-through is achieved. This is normally less for a high bounce than for an ordinary bounce.

c. When the length and direction of the forward swing seem satisfactory repeat the swing several times, a little faster than slow motion at first, then at about half speed, and then at almost normal velocity.

It is not possible to make a decent hit of a high bounce if the positioning is not right, the stance is inappropriate, or the backswing is inadequate. On the other hand, a full swing is usually inappropriate also.

If the "DOUBLE-FORCE" methods are used (as is advisable) the "application point" of the "boost force" should not only be reachable but must be effective during contact. So the "application point" is usually above the elbow to make it possible to maintain the "boost force" through the hit.

Evaluate the backswing, hitting point, stance, and the feel and direction of the forward swing. The stroke should be based on good use of momentum, not muscle. There should be participation by the body but very little forward sway.

The procedures in the above two drills, working backwards from the hitting point and forward from the end of the backswing, can be useful with other types of strokes also. The reverse can also be true: some other drills may be effective with high bounces. It is desirable to make repeated use of previous drills because there is a good deal of cross-application, and because the lessons get to be forgotten.

PRACTICING REAL HITS OF HIGH BOUNCES
1. Alternate "shadow", "timing", and real hits off easy high bounces.
   a. At first use a length of about one foot for the backswing. Accelerate the racquet slightly from there and just bring the racquet barely past the hitting point. Increase the length of the backswings until the appropriate end-of-backswing position is reached. The follow-through increases also, but not by very much.

Common tendencies on high hits are to open the stance, use almost no backswing, freeze the wrist and arm, use a push generated by a sway of the body, and meet the ball more forward than normal. This is a very ineffective combination. It has led to the mistaken idea that the arm has inadequate strength on high hits. But the arm loses strength even at ordinary levels if a similarly short backswing and advanced hitting point are used.

DROP-HITS   (ALSO KNOWN AS BOUNCE-HITS)

Any practice can be worse than nothing if not done properly. The drop-hit is an example. It is frequently used by individuals practicing alone, sometimes even a pro. But the techniques are seldom taught. The consequence is that the compromises that are inadvertently used for drop-hits inevitably invade the regular strokes. So new errors are being practised in the process of trying to get rid of the old.

GETTING A SUITABLE BOUNCE FOR A DROP-HIT

1. Assume the <u>hitting</u> stance (not the "waiting"). Visualize where contact with the ball should occur. Take the racquet there to check the arm extension and the feel. Re-evaluate and adjust as necessary.

2. Drop the ball from a high enough level, or toss it up slightly, trying to get it to bounce to the point established in Step 1. (Do not throw or push the ball down.)

a. At the same time take the racquet to the end of the backswing but hold up the forward swing. Evaluate whether the ball bounced as intended. Repeat until consistency is obtained.

b. Move the racquet forward to where the hit would have occurred with that bounce. Then take the racquet back and execute a swing through that point. This is a modification of what was previously defined as a "deferred

swing" (APPENDIX B).

c. From the same position execute an easy swing-controlled hit of an imaginary ball at the same height but without regard to the location of the bounce.

    1. Note any differences between the swings in Steps "a" and "b" as to backswing, arm extension, acceleration, feel, hitting point, etc.

    2. If there are differences reflect on what should be done in the preparation and the drop to make the swings in "a" and "b" essentially the same.

COORDINATING THE SWING WITH THE DROP

1. Assume the <u>hitting</u> stance (not the waiting). Drop the ball trying to get a bounce slightly <u>lower than the preferred</u> and make a hit of an imaginary ball directly above the real ball ("shadow swing").

    a. Analyze for adequacy of the backswing, acceleration through contact, proper positioning and arm extension, timing, feel, appropriate moderate swing, hitting point, etc.

    b. From the same position make an easy "swing-controlled" hit of an imaginary ball at <u>the same height</u> as before but without regard to the location of the real ball.

        1. Note differences between the swings in Steps "a" and "b" as to backswing, arm extension, acceleration, hitting point, feel, etc.

2. Repeat Step 1 using a "<u>timing swing</u>". In <u>Step 1-b</u> swing at the <u>same level</u> as the ball instead of at a different level.

    a. A "timing swing" is at a different level than

the ball and not restricted to being vertically in line with the ball. It amounts to a "swing-controlled" stroke.

3. Repeat Step 1 but with a <u>normal bounce</u> and a <u>real hit</u> instead of a "shadow" hit.
    a. Reflect on similarities, differences, preferences, and good and bad points in the swings in Steps 1 and 2.

On a drop-hit it is quite common for players not to have any awareness of the bounce, length of the backswing, stance, swing, racquet attitude, hitting point, etc. A common tendency is to drop the ball too close to the body, or too much toward the net, or both. That makes it necessary to introduce expedients and compensations into the swing. That is why drop-hit practice, which can be very beneficial, is often detrimental to a player's game.

EXPERIMENTING WITH THE "SWING DISTANCE" AND "HITTING PLANE" ON DROP-HITS

1. Assume the <u>hitting</u> stance. Drop a ball <u>too close to the body</u>, hold up the forward swing slightly ("deferred swing"), and then complete the swing as it would have occurred with that particular bounce.
    a. From the same position hit an imaginary ball at the same level but without regard to the location of the last bounce.

    b. Compare the feel and nature of the swing, arm-extension, backswing, wrist angle and flex, acceleration, hitting point, follow-through, etc, of the two swings.

2. Repeat Step 1 with a ball dropped <u>too far away from the body</u>
    a. Steps 1 and 2 help establish the feel of inappropriate distances. It is not desirable to

practice drop-hits without an awareness of the typical flaws that can develop.

3. Repeat Step 1 with a ball dropped <u>too far toward the net</u> of the body.

4. Repeat Step 1 with a ball dropped <u>too far back</u> toward the back fence.
    a. The exercises in Steps "3" and "4" help familiarize players with the feel of inappropriate "hitting planes".

5. Drop the ball trying to get a decent bounce.
    a. <u>If it is good</u> make a moderate hit with a swing-controlled stroke. Do not worry about direction or results, only the swing.
        1. Reflect on the feel and nature of the swing, stance, arm-extension, backswing, wrist angle and flex, acceleration, hitting point, follow-thouing, etc.

    b. If the bounce is unsatisfactory complete the stroke as a "timing swing". (Defined on the previous page)

One purpose of the drills is to be able to recognize the feel of swings at good and bad bounces. Part of knowing what to do and what to avoid is being able to recognize the feel of each.

DROP-HITS USING A SINGLE STEP

1. Assume the <u>hitting</u> stance. Do a drop-hit of an <u>imaginary</u> ball dropped far enough out so that it is necessary to take a single step into the hit. Use more than one if necessary. Try making the initial step with each foot to find out which seems preferable.
    a. It may help to make small movements of the feet before dropping the <u>imaginary</u> ball and then letting the feet do the rest on their own.

2. Repeat Step 1 making moderate hits of real balls if the positioning is good.

    a. After each hit mimic the swing with all its faults and then make an imaginary hit as in Step "b" below.

    b. If the positioning does not put the ball at the correct "hitting plane" and "swing" distances defer the forward swing. Then swing at an imaginary at the same height as the bounce but at corrected distances.

Evaluate the strokes for stance, backswing, arm extension, timing, proper development of momentum, moderate swing velocity, reinforcement, etc. Was the racquet chasing a straying ball? For the majority of people the arm should be no more than slightly bent (arm extension), and the upper arm should be held comfortably away from the body (arm angle), but not artificially so.

If the positioning is not right a protective reflex is to swing much faster than necessary. This not only provides practice of wrong distances but degrades the timing and creates new problems. The swings have to be kept moderate to expose the flaws, not disguise them or compensate for them.

GETTING INTO POSITION FOR DROP-HITS

1. Move from the standard face-the-net waiting position in any way convenient to get into the normal hitting position for a hit. At the same time drop or toss the ball and make the backswing, but hold up the forward swing. In the process make additional positioning adjustments if necessary.

    a. Make a slow "deferred" forward swing so as to have the racquet pass through what would have been the hitting point, good or bad.

    b. From the same position, mimic the swing with all its faults.

c. Execute an <u>imaginary</u> hit at the <u>same height</u> as the last bounce but without regard to the location of the bounce.
  1. Note the differences in the strokes, hitting points, arm extensions, etc.

2. Repeat Step 1 but with a <u>real hit</u> instead of a "deferred swing".
  a. If the bounce is unsatisfactory hold up the swing and finish the procedure as in Step 1.

The pattern of this drill is "deferred" or "shadow" or "timing", followed by mimicked and corrected imaginary. Another is real hit, mimicked, and corrected imaginary. They involve a good related set of learning procedures that can be profitably used as a standard pattern for other drills.

No specific rules are being proposed for footwork on drop-hits. The main thing is to end up in something like the appropriate stance and position. In good footwork the feet do whatever is necessary, not act out an arbitrary pattern.

CONSISTENT POSITIONING FOR BOTH THE DROP-HIT AND THE HIT OF THE RETURNS

1. Drop-hit a ball against a wall with moderate pace trying to use exactly the right positioning. Make a "timing swing" at the return off the wall trying to be in a similarly good position. ("Timing swings" are defined on the third page of this chapter.)
  a. Check for differences in the preparation and execution of the two swings. They often are very different.

2. Repeat Step 1 with a <u>hit of the return</u> instead of a "timing swing", but only if the preparation and positioning are reasonably close to what they should be, making allowance for the skill level of the player.
  a. <u>Continue hitting returns as long as those requirements are met.</u> When the preparation

is not acceptably good hold up the forward swing. Then adjust the position and make a corrected "deferred hit" of the same ball.

Stopping the swing when there is awareness of deficiencies in the readiness magnifies the infractions in the mind. It also averts practice of expedients and helps motivate the player to make better preparation on following shots.

It is quite common to see players use an almost completely different stroke for the hit of the return off the wall than for the initial drop-hit. The beneficial effects of a good drop-hit will be far outweighed by the bad effects of the more numerous subsequent poor hits of returns off the wall.

DROP-HITS FOR PACE & REASONABLE ACCURACY

1. Hit returns off the wall trying for a moderately strong pace. Accelerate the racquet through contact. After that the racquet can go where it will.

   a. Do not make a hit if the preparation is not reasonably correct. In that case hold up the forward swing. Then adjust the position and make an imaginary hit of the same ball as it should have been done. A "timing" or a "shadow" swing can also be used.

   b. Do not try to increase the pace to where there are compromises in the techniques, or where the accuracy deteriorates noticeably.

   c. If there is variation in the "hitting plane" and "swing distance" cut back on the pace. Another choice is to switch the view to the "hitting plane" just before the ball gets there.

2. Alternately hit a ball intending a hard yet manageable pace and then hit a ball with easy pace using a "swing-controlled" stroke.

   a. Reflect on any differences in feel and pace in

the two types of strokes, and on the reasons.

b.   The swings for hard and moderate hits
should be fairly similar. Among good players
they   are,   but   among   poor   players   the
techniques used for a hard hit may be far
worse than those used for a moderate hit.

The idea of the drill is to learn to keep the power level
within the limits where legitimate techniques work, and
below where counterproductive embellishments are used.
Even   top   tournament   players   can   sometimes   be   seen
reverting to common faults and questionable techniques
when intent on hitting a winner.

Reflect on any prominent elements or characteristics: backswing, arm extension, acceleration, racquet momentum,
hitting point, follow-through, feel, stance, wrist flex, shock,
jumping, roundhouse, steering, tensing, etc. The habit of
being aware of various factors without specifically observing
them is a skill that also has to be developed.

These drills are among the few in which the balls are to be
hit hard. Ordinarily a rather slow pace should be used
because hitting hard can cover up minor or even major
flaws. For instance, the hitting point can be too far forward
and the racquet will still have enough momentum to
disguise the fact that it is not up to the possible, or even the
normal. On a moderate hit the fact that contact occurred
near the end of the forward reach would be much more
easily detected.

While it is fine to practice power shots against a wall, the
pace and techniques used must be suitable for use in play.
The intent to produce pace that cannot be risked in games
may introduce comparably unreal bad habits, timing
problems, and error rates.

appendix e

creating and receiving pace

HITTING HARD WITHOUT SWINGING FAST

1. Gradually increase the pace on the returns of moderate speed oncoming balls to a comfortable maximum. Do not try to increment the pace past the point where any of the following compromises begin to appear:

    a Less than normal extension of the arm.

    b. Shorter than usual backswing.

    c. Lack of steady, easy, forward acceleration through contact.

    d. Lack of reinforcement resulting from the body turning or staying ahead of the arm.

    e Convulsive effort in the forward swing.

    f. Using push in the swing.

    g. A muscular rather than "swing-controlled" shot.

    h. Violent use of body, especially if it adversely affects the direction, velocity, or reinforcement of the swing.

    i. Tensing or stiffening the wrist, arm, or body.

◇⟨XXXXXXXXXXXXXXXXXXXXXXXXXXXXXXXXXXXXXXXXXX⟩◇

j.   Changing the nature of the swing (compromised internal timing).

k. Meeting the ball at a wrong hitting point (compromised external timing).

l.   Roundhouse before the end of contact.

m. Turning too soon to observe the results. It results in the ruin of many shots that would otherwise have been good. Almost all players turn sooner than necessary or advisable.

n. Using a more than usually open stance.

o. Jumping in a way to adversely affect the results.

p. Getting poor results, feel, or accuracy.

The items in the above list can be used to evaluate problems and techniques, and as restrictions to be observed during practice. Ease up when they are observed to have occurred. During play they should not be on the conscious mind. Deliberately not doing something is an inefficient way of improving strokes, and in fact can result in the opposite.

The reader can augment the list by analyzing personal deficiencies, and by studying the strokes of those players who cannot hit with good pace. The converse is also useful: careful observation of those who do hit well.

A primary purpose of the above list of expedients is to develop awareness of problems rather than provide guidelines for hitting hard. The techniques to be used for hitting are covered in the discussions in various chapters in this book. The specific means of hitting hard are covered in "CHAPTER 17" on "BLASTING". The major categories are:
        1. Increase racquet velocity, acceleration, and rein-

forcement.

2. Conserve racquet momentum.

3. Improve the length and timing of the swing.

4 Augment the swing with body motion and wrist and arm flex.

5. Lengthen the contact interval.

COMPARISON OF PACE OBTAINED WITH FLEX OR REINFORCEMENT

1. Hit moderately paced returns while keeping the arm very loose. This should result in more than normal flex in the wrist and elbow.

  a. Gradually increase the pace on the returns of oncoming balls to a comfortable maximum.

    1 Hit the ball in the desired direction of departure from the racquet. Intend to hit with the good part of the strings.

    2. Accelerate the racquet gradually. Concentrate on using racquet moment-um for the hit. Avoid using muscle

  b. Evaluate for feel, control, effort, pace, etc, compared to when the hits are made with less wrist and arm flex.

2. As the ball approaches apply the preferred "DOUBLE-FORCE grip" ("APPENDIX A"). Gradually increase the pace on the returns of oncoming balls to a comfortable maximum. (If the "DOUBLE-FORCE" drills in "APPENDIX A" have not been used yet select any likely "grip" from the lists in "CHAPTER TWO" or "APPENDIX A" and apply it to the racquet arm near the elbow.)

  a. Accelerate gradually and apply the "boost" force through the hitting point and as much of the previous swing interval as convenient.

b. Evaluate for stance, arm extension, feel, control, effort, pace, etc, compared to strokes not based on the "DOUBLE-FORCE" techniques.

There should be sufficient length in the backswing to provide room to develop good momentum in the forward swing. Pace is obtained with forward direction, acceleration, momentum, and reinforcement, not with roundhouse. The "elbow-in" stroke tends to go into roundhouse more easily than an extended arm swing.

It is difficult to erase feelings that super results require special techniques and violent exertion. But extra pace can best be obtained with the help of valid techniques, not the handicap of counterproductive embellishments.

VARYING RACQUET VELOCITY INVERSELY WITH ONCOMING PACE
1. Receive slow and fast balls using the same normal arm extension and pattern of swing on each shot, but varying outgoing pace inversely with oncoming ball velocity. This means making a slow swing if the oncoming pace is fast and a fast swing if the pace is slow. Do not turn too soon to observe the results.
   a. The major purpose is to break the habit of varying racquet velocity directly with oncoming ball velocity. Another is to get a feel for making changes in racquet velocity.

2. Receive slow and fast balls using the same normal arm extension and swing on each shot, but vary the swing velocity inversely with oncoming pace. In addition, try to get the same fixed moderate pace on each return.
   a. Keep the grip, swing pattern, reinforcement, etc, as constant as possible. Control the pace only by varying the racquet velocity. Do not

turn too soon to observe the results.

b. Although in this drill racquet speed should vary oppositely to the change in oncoming ball speed it should do so only by about half as much. This is because return velocity, which is to be kept constant, is equal to "ONCOMING BALL VELOCITY PLUS **TWICE** RACQUET VELOCITY".

c. That formula can be used to calculate racquet velocities. The diagrams below show how two equal final velocities of 75 mph are obtained with two different oncoming ball velocities (25 and 41). However the formula doesn't account for losses. So adjustments are still more a matter of feel than formula.

ONCOMING BALL VEL	RAC'T VEL	OUTGOING PACE
25 MPH	25 MPH	75 MPH

ONCOMING BALL VELOCITY	RAC'T VEL	OUTGOING PACE
41 MPH	17 MPH	75 MPH

Note that when oncoming ball velocity increases by 16 mph (25 plus 16 = 41) then racquet velocity must be decreased by half as much, or 8 mph (25 minus 8 = 17), to keep the outgoing pace constant.

3. Receive slow and moderate paced balls using the same arm extension and swing on each shot, but varying swing velocity directly (and wrongly) with oncoming ball velocity. This means making a moderate swing if the oncoming pace is moderate and a slow swing if the oncoming pace is slow.

a. Reflect on the appropriateness of the racquet velocity in comparison to what was developed in Steps 1 and 2. Reflect on the predictability of the direction of the ball. The drill creates awareness of the feel of improper responses to the speed of the ball.

b. Do not use fast swing with fast oncoming pace. The wrist can be injured by swinging hard when receiving fast balls. During practice it may be wise to let unusually fast balls go by if the required skills are beyond the current capabilities, or if either the backswing or forward swing is late.

An unfortunate result of the usual tendency to vary swing velocity directly with ball velocity is that the problems created by a fast oncoming ball are compounded by a corresponding increase in the risks taken with the return. In these drills the compensation for oncoming ball speed must be made only by varying the racquet velocity.

A DISCUSSION OF THE TIMING INTERACTIONS
ASSOCIATED WITH CHANGES IN SWING VELOCITY

One of the specified conditions in the above drills is that the nature of the swing should not change, only the velocity. If the swing is slowed when the oncoming pace is fast (as it should be) the duration of the swing is increased. So for a fast approaching ball the start of the stroke has to be advanced (made to occur earlier) for a double reason:

1. There is less time available for the racquet to reach the hitting point (due to the fast ball),

2. The time required by the racquet to get there is increased (due to the slow racquet velocity).

For a slow oncoming ball the conditions are reversed. The start of the stroke has to be delayed for a double reason:

1. There is more time available for the racquet to reach the hitting point (due to the slow ball).

◇▽▽▷

2. The time required by the racquet to get there is decreased (due to the fast racquet velocity).

Not taking into account the additive nature of the timing shifts is partly responsible for the many gross errors made off of easy bounces, even by tournament players. Everybody is aware about the need for timing adjustments, but not in the detail given above. So it is not surprising that adjustments to racquet velocity relative to ball speeds can easily be either inadequate, overdone, or in the wrong direction.

Awareness of theory helps prevent irrational responses, or at least makes it possible to recognize them if they are present. But the adjustments, with the correct direction and magnitude, have to be made automatically. These exercises provide practice in selecting appropriate racquet velocities, and in adjusting both internal and external timing correctly.

VARYING RACQUET VELOCITY INVERSELY WITH DIFFICULTY

1. Alternately return easy bounces and difficult bounces by hitting the easy bounces moderately fast and the difficult bounces less fast.

2. Mark adjacent one foot and six foot squares on the other side of the court. Direct balls alternately to one and then to the other.
   a. Hit moderately fast at the large target and hit less fast at the small. Do not resort to expedients with either target, such as racquet manipulations, push, elbow in, turning too soon, keeping the eyes on the target, etc.

Think of hitting in the direction of the required trajectory of the ball as it leaves the racquet. That trajectory points beyond the target. Hit the ball moderately but freely. Very small targets tend to bring out faults at their worst. Fast swings are often unconscious compensations for unsound or insecure techniques.

◇◇

HITTING UNDER PRESSURE

1. Practice playing under pressure by trying to better the previous record of the <u>number of good shots in a row</u>, or it could be the <u>number of good out of a fixed number of shots</u>.

    a. Various definitions could be used for "good shot". It could mean hitting a target area, varying racquet velocity inversely with ball velocity, hitting freely, making use of momentum, getting fast but controllable pace, etc.

    b. A variation is to count only the number of bad shots. This works best if a very few specific transgressions are defined.

Pressure may be just what is inadvisable for some players at times. The sense of insecurity increases with the need for accuracy. And it increases still more as the count reaches a critical point. At such times players are likely to abbreviate the preparation, backswing, and forward swing, start all of them late, bring the elbow in, tense normally unused muscles, stand closer to the path of the ball than normal, swing faster, use a more forward hitting point, etc. The difficulty of the shot is thus compounded by a corresponding increase in the use of expedients.

So if the strokes deteriorate as the pressure increases it is quite a job to determine the cause.

Good techniques will work for one's self just as well as for anybody in any situation if given a chance. Direction of departure, pace, and spin are the only factors available to control the path of the ball. It is wrong to augment the valid means of obtaining accuracy with embellishments. That amounts to doing more than enough, and with invalid means.

appendix F

anticipating positioning footwork timing

EXPERIMENTS WITH FOOTWORK AND STANCES

1. From a normal <u>waiting</u> position turn and walk toward either side while preparing to make a hit of an <u>imaginary</u> ball. Start with either foot and count each step. <u>At the count of four be at the end of the backswing</u> and be making the last step. Hold up the forward swing. Evaluate the backswing, stance, and position of feet.

    a. <u>Move the racquet to the likely hitting point using preferred arm extension.</u> Observe the reach. Are the racquet and body in good position for the hit?

2. <u>Repeat Step 1 starting with the other foot</u> from the same location. Compare the reach with that obtained in Step 1. Reflect on preferences for the stances and the hitting points obtained in the two Steps.

3. Repeat Steps 1 and 2 <u>using five steps</u>.

The drill is for familiarization with the alternatives as to footwork and positioning so that eventually preferences will be built up based on experiences, evaluations, and satisfactions. This is a much sounder procedure than adopting a set pattern, such as "step out with the near foot" or "cross over with the far foot".

Ending up in the open or closed stances by starting out with either foot and using various numbers of steps develops footwork preferences that will help to produce the preferred stance in any situation. Tournament players almost always end up in the preferred stance without seeming to make any special effort to do so.

The length of the reach obtained with a given number of steps may be a deceptive statistic. There is also the matter of the time required to make the steps. Differences are measured in terms of small fractions of a second. So footwork is more a matter of art and experience than definition.

EXPERIMENTING WITH FASTER FOOTWORK
1. From a fixed <u>waiting position</u> about ten feet from a sideline turn, step out with the preferred foot, and walk easily to make a hit of an <u>imaginary ball</u> traveling down the line.
> a. Start the <u>forward swing</u> and the <u>last step</u> as the correct "swing-distance" to the sideline is being reached.
>> 1. Try both having completed the last step at the hit and having the foot still in the air. Reflect on which feels natural and which does not.
>>
>> 2. Reflect on whether the stance, "swing distance", and general readiness were approximately correct when the racquet reached the "hitting plane".

2. Without moving from the <u>hitting position</u> make a moderate, <u>"swing-controlled"</u> hit of an <u>imaginary</u> ball using the preferred arm extension whether that places the hit above the sideline or not.
> a. Did the "hit" occur directly above the sideline? If not adjust the position and repeat the swing until it does. Reflect on the final positioning.

3 Repeat Steps 1 and 2 <u>starting out with the other</u>

foot.
   a. Reflect on suitability and preferences.

4. Repeat Steps 1 and 2 at a fast walk and then at a slow run. Let the feet take off on their own without mental decision as to which to use. Check for any deterioration of the techniques as the speed of the foot movements increases.

5. Repeat the entire test from a fixed starting position about five feet further from the sideline.

COORDINATING FOOTWORK, POSITIONING, AND SWING ON IMAGINARY WIDE BALLS

1. From a normal waiting stance at the baseline step out with the preferred foot, walk without slowing or stopping, and make a hit of an imaginary ball coming down a sideline. Keep moving during the hit and take one step after the hit to simulate a wide run.
   a. Complete an easy backswing before arriving at the hitting location, and start the forward swing while arriving. Use a comfortably extended arm.
      1. Do not compromise arm extension or speed of swing to compensate for not coordinating the footwork, positioning, and swing correctly. It is necessary to learn how to arrive in the right way at the right time, not learn how to compensate.

      2. Reflect on whether the swing was hurried, early, late, or on time. Was the "hitting point" too far forward? The acceleration correctly gradual? The stance proper? The body involved? Reinforcement of the arm adequate? Etc. On a wide run the hit depends more on racquet momentum and less on

reinforcement than on normal shots.
2. Repeat Step 1 but make the first step with the other foot.

3. Repeat Steps 1 and 2 at a faster walk and then at a slow run.

4. Repeat Steps 1 and 2 with swings at about knee and shoulder levels.

The backswing must be completed before arrival at the hitting location to allow for development of good racquet momentum without hurrying the swing. On hits of very wide balls even tournament players can be seen making a late backswing and yet hitting early because of shortening the backswing, hurrying the forward swing, and making an earlier forward turn of the body than desirable. The result of any one of these can be an ineffective and undependable hit.

Movement type drills <u>should not be a test of endurance</u>. Combining practice of skills with tests of stamina is usually a mistake. When fatigue sets in the player has to use all kinds of expedients to compensate for not having enough energy to make the necessary preparation for a decent stroke. And expedients become permanent habits very easily.

Note that specific types of foot movements, such as skipping or sidestepping, are not included in these drills. Players should become acquainted with those techniques via the standard "how-to" drills. Whether or not the movements are applicable or are to be used in a particular drill is up to the student. Experimentation is advisable.

EXTERNAL TIMING & FOOTWORK ON WIDE BALLS
1. <u>Walk without stopping</u> from a fixed position at the baseline toward and through the path of an easy-paced wide ball. Use a full backswing and <u>bring the</u>

racquet forward in a "timing swing". Keep moving during the hit and take two steps after the hit to simulate what happens on a dead run.

    a. A "timing swing" is one timed with the ball but at a different level, and with the racquet not necessarily vertically in line with the ball.

    b. The ball can be made to be nearly out of reach by timing the footwork so that it is necessary to reach out with more than normal arm extension and/or body bend.

    c. The "timing swing" allows making "swing-controlled" hit without the compromises involved with actual contact, or the compensations made necessary by poor positioning. But the timing requirements must be observed.

    d. Use a lazy motion at the end of the backswing and the start of the forward swing, not a hasty slap or a short push. Accelerate the racquet gradually.

2. Repeat Step 1 but make a "shadow" hit instead of a "timing swing". Keep walking during the hit and take two steps after the hit to simulate what happens on a dead run.

    a. A "shadow hit" is a hit of an imaginary ball directly above or below the real ball.

    b. Next, repeat the swing at the imaginary ball at the same level but at the correct "swing distance". This eliminates the need to use compensations for positioning errors. Note any improvements over the previous swing.

3. Repeat Step 1 but make an actual hit using a "swing-controlled" stroke instead of a "timing swing".

    a. Do not modify the normal arm extension or

swing to compensate for poor positioning, or in anticipation of the shock of impact. The player is thus made to use adjustments in the footwork and preparation instead of compromises in the techniques.

1. The ball may not be met squarely, or may even be missed completely. THEREFOR THE HIT SHOULD NOT BE COMPLETED IF ANYBODY COULD BE AT ALL ENDANGERED BY A MISDIRECTED BALL.

2. Hard drives should not be attempted at this time because a mis-hit could cause damage to the arm or wrist.

The sequence of "deferred swing", "timing swing", "shadow hit", and "swing-controlled" hit, interspersed with repeats using an ideal imaginary hit, can be used in many situations. One of the purposes here is to outline a variety of procedures. The "deferred" swing was not used in this drill because it is not suited for hits made while in motion.

ANTICIPATING THE DIRECTION OF THE OPPONENT'S SHOT

1. Stand in the waiting position at the baseline, or the net, or whatever other spot is selected for the drill. Have the coach hit with moderate pace to various easily reachable locations.

2. Watch the coach very closely so as to be able to anticipate the direction of the shot. At the moment of the hit, or at a signal such as "go", move without delay toward the anticipated hitting location. Do not wait until the ball is on its way. The "go" signal, if used, can be delayed a bit to adapt to the skill level of the receiver.

a. The coach has to hit the shots with consistent form, not necessarily standard, so that the receiver has some chance of anticipating the direction of the ball from the preparations for the hit. For the same reason the coach should decide ahead of time where to hit and should not change that decision just before the hit.

b. Score can be kept if desired, but mainly on the basis of both a prompt start and the right direction. At a later stage the receiver can also be required to make the hit.

BACKING AWAY FROM THE PATH OF THE BALL

1. Stand in the waiting position (not hitting position) less than the "swing distance" from a line. Back away to make a hit of an imaginary ball coming down the line.

a. Make sure that the backswing is early enough. It should usually start simultaneously with the backing-away move. The normal tendency is to get to the hitting location and then make a hurried backswing and forward swing.

b. Try starting out with either foot. At a later stage do not try to control the footwork.

c. Experiments can be made with backing away more than enough and then stepping into the hit in the normal manner.

2. Repeat Step 1 making the initial move with sidesteps instead of a backing-away move.

3. Repeat Step 1 with actual hits of real balls, and letting the feet do whatever they want without mental interference.

Evaluate items such as stance, length and timing of backswing, footwork, positioning, hitting point, nature of swing, arm extension, inadequacies, compromises, etc.

RUNNING AROUND A SHOT

1. Stand close to a line representing the path of an imaginary ball (a sideline can be used). Then swing around to make the hit from the other side. Practice the move to each side, strong and weak.

    a. Experiment with starting out with either foot, and with the distance from the line. At a later stage do not plan the footwork.

    b. Repeat the sequence with "timing swings", "shadow hits", and actual hits of real balls.

    c. Reflect on the feel and quality of the shot.

2. Walk toward a line representing the visualized path of a moderately wide imaginary ball. Switch to sidesteps upon reaching the vicinity of the line, complete the turn, and take the ball on the other side.

    a. Practice the move to each side, strong and weak.

    b. Repeat the sequence with "timing swings", "shadow hits", and actual hits of real balls.

    c. Reflect on the feel and quality of the shot.

3. Repeat Step 2 at a slow run.

Running around to take the ball on the weak side may have advantages at times. For instance, a backhand could be used on the forehand side as a means of variation, or to hit down the line better, or to be positioned to cover the wide open court right after the hit.

MOVING IN FOR A SHORT BALL

1. Move in to hit an imaginary ball at a mark about fifteen feet in from the baseline. The move should be to a hitting position to the side of the mark, not to the mark (hitting point), or to a position directly behind

the mark.
   a. Experiment with starting out with either foot.

   b. Experiment with going in to either side of the mark, going in at various angles, taking the ball at various heights, using a half-volley, etc.

2. Repeat Step 1 with actual hits of real balls, letting the feet do whatever they want without any mental interference.

3. Move in to hit a real ball about fifteen feet in from the baseline. Try for topspin by having the racquet face either closed or open at the end of the backswing and then turning to whatever attitude is appropriate for the hit. The racquet has to move forward at an upward angle.

Evaluate items such as position, stance, timing of backswing, readiness, arm extension, hitting point, nature of swing, body involvement, etc. Do not worry about results. The positioning and the swing have been mastered first.

EMERGENCY HITTING TECHNIQUES
1. Stand at the baseline and make a good hit at the correct "hitting plane" regardless of the location of the bounce of the oncoming ball. Sideways moves can be made to obtain the best possible "swing distance". But no forward or backward moves to adjust to the bounce should be made, as would ordinarily be required.
   a. Repeat each shot with an imaginary identical ball, trying to improve on the techniques used.

2. Move in five feet and repeat Step 1 under the same restrictions.
   a. Experiment with topspin approach shots by

having the racquet face <u>closed at the end of the</u> <u>backswing</u> and then <u>turning to whatever</u> <u>attitude is appropriate</u> for the hit. The racquet has to move forward at an upward angle. Repeat with an initially open racquet face.

Evaluate for anticipation, positioning with respect to the path of the ball, readiness, stance, appropriate and timely backswing, no intrusions of unnecessary expedients like hurrying the swing, hitting too far out in front, etc. Avoid desperation type techniques like freezing or swinging wild.

The ball may have to be taken at odd heights, or with a volley, half-volley, etc. If it is not possible to make decent contact on a particular ball a "timing swing" should be used.

A prime purpose of the drill is to develop the ability to adapt. It also promotes opportunism: moving up when there is an opportunity and then at least coping with any unexpectedly effective response from the opponent. A danger is that it may encourage the tendency to use whatever expedients are necessary to avoid having to move the feet.

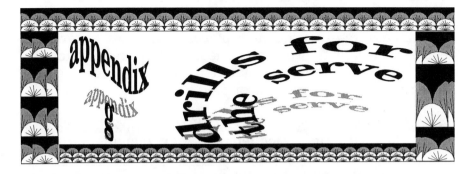

ESTABLISHING THE HEIGHT & POSITION OF THE TOSS

1. Toss a ball for a serve alternately <u>higher than</u>, <u>lower than</u>, and <u>to</u> the preferred height. At the same time go through the service motion but stop the swing just before it turns forward into the hit. Just <u>visualize going through the rest of the stroke</u>. Think of remaining in a mostly sideways stance through the hit. "Lift" rather than "flip" the ball.

    a. For basic or group lessons this drill is best done without a racquet.

2. Repeat Step 1 alternately tossing to the preferred location and then a little to each side of it.

3. Repeat Step 1 alternately tossing to the preferred location and then a little to the front and back of it.

In each case evaluate the preparation for the serve in respect to readiness, balance, stance, strain, potential power, likely hitting point, likely direction of the hit, being "swing-controlled", etc. Reflect on the body attitude at the hit. Is it mostly sideways or facing too much toward the net?

The optimum height of the toss is an individual matter rather than something that can be defined by a standard formula. Many top servers use an exceptionally high toss. Most of them have the tossing arm going up considerably sooner than the racquet arm. But there are a few who use a low toss, with the arms going up more nearly together.

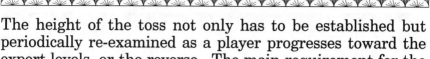

The height of the toss not only has to be established but periodically re-examined as a player progresses toward the expert levels, or the reverse. The main requirement for the toss is for it be "swing-controlled": it must place the ball into the path of an uncompromised swing.

AWARENESS OF ARM & BODY INVOLVEMENT IN SERVES

1. Without a racquet, serve an imaginary ball at moderate pace with the normally used techniques. Do not pretty them up in any way. Then visualize going through the same serve as it actually happened. In other words, emulate the serve mentally.

2. **Without a racquet**, close the eyes, toss an imaginary ball, and go through the normally used service motion again, but this time only with the body. Let the racquet arm just hang at the side because the intent here is to discover how the body is used in the personal manner of serving.
    a. Do not worry about ideas of correctness at this time, just awareness. Bad servers usually have a very inadequate awareness of the actions of the arm or body, or the lack of them.

3. Repeat Steps 1 and 2 while thinking of making a moderate "swing-controlled" serve. Do not use either a pattern or the regularly used stroke (unless it already is "swing-controlled").
    a. Evaluate for differences in the use of the body or arm, attitude of body, etc, from that in the normal serve in Steps 1 and 2.

4. Without a racquet, go through the motions of a moderate serve. Apply a "DOUBLE-FORCE grip" with the tossing arm as soon as the tossing arm is free. Stop the racquet arm when it is above the head and do not finish the forward swing.
    a. The "DOUBLE FORCE grip" can be "A", "B", "E", or "F" in the forehand list or all except "E" in

the backhand list, "CHAPTER 2" and "APPENDIX A". Grips "A" and "B" are the same in both lists.

VISUALIZING & ACTING OUT THE SERVICE MOTION

1. Use "Slow Motion Visualization" (CHAPTER 5) to picture the first part of a serve. The motion ends with the racquet at about shoulder level ready to go up and forward into the hit. Stance is sideways. If a "DOUBLE-FORCE" serve is being used apply the "boost grip" as soon as the tossing arm is free.

   a. The purpose of this portion is merely to optimize the conditions for the final portion.

2. Do an <u>exact emulation</u> of the stroke as visualized in the above Step, using an <u>imaginary ball</u>.

   a. Evaluate for flaws, especially an early turn toward the net, and for means of improvement.

3. Repeat Steps 1 and 2 but with the <u>last part of a serve</u>. Stance is sideways and the racquet starts at about shoulder level ready to go up and forward into the hit. Imagine the <u>racquet floating up</u> and <u>accelerating steadily to about the full reach forward</u>.

   a. On a real hit the momentum of the racquet will carry the racquet down. The intent should still be to carry the racquet out, not down.

4. Combine the first and final portions of the swing as developed in Steps 1 and 3. Use the same types of visualization and emulation techniques as in Steps 1 and 2 to develop a picture of the complete swing.

   a. Reflect on the complete swing. The picture will be used to try to avoid reversion to the old compensations and idiosyncrasies when the toss is included. The **toss** is the **dependent** factor. The **swing** is the **independent** factor.

5. Repeat Step 4 with a racquet.

   a. On each serve MAKE SURE THAT NOBODY WILL BE

IN THE WAY OF THE SWING. All precautions are primarily the responsibility of the server.

Check for flaws such as the forward "jackknife", statue like aloofness, body rotation before the forward swing, sidesway, bent elbow, etc. Reflect on whether a forward bend of the body encroached on the swing by moving or pulling the racquet downward during contact.

Is the racquet arm at about full extension through the hit and into the follow-through? Does the body participate? Does it reinforce the arm? Some players hardly involve the body during a serve, but most involve it far too much, and in unproductive ways. Do not turn the body too soon, or turn the head to follow the path of the imaginary hit.

COMBINING THE SERVICE MOTION WITH THE TOSS

1. Use "Slow Motion Visualization" to picture the last part of a serve. The motion starts with the racquet at about shoulder level ready to go up and forward into the hit. Stance is sideways.

2. With both racquet and ball, take the racquet back to the same initial position and make an unhurried toss of the ball into the path of the visualized swing. Have the racquet poised but do not actually swing.

3. With the ball out of the way, take the racquet through a slow "swing-controlled" finish, emulating the visualized swing of Step 1, not as necessary to have met the toss. Use full body involvement. MAKE SURE THAT NOBODY IS IN THE WAY.
   a. Reflect on the compatibility of the toss with the uncompromised swing.

4. Repeat Steps 1and 2 but start the racquet from the usual place instead of from about shoulder level. Then do the complete serve without a halt.
   a. Use a normal speed toss but a slow swing.

This means that the ball will have dropped away before the ball gets to the hitting point.

b. Do not modify the swing in any way to accommodate the toss.

One of the main objectives of this drill is to develop the proper set of intents for a "swing-controlled" serve. It is difficult for a person to conceive of swinging independent of the location of the ball. Here the task is simplified by avoiding the complications involved with an actual hit.

COMPATIBILITY OF TOSS & SWING ON REAL HITS
1. Visualize a complete "swing-controlled" serve as developed above. Assume that the toss will put the ball into the path of the racquet at the right time.
a. Think of hitting with moderate momentum, holding a fair amount of strength in reserve.

2. Carry out two unhurried serves as visualized in Step 1, the first <u>with an imaginary ball</u> and the second <u>with a real ball</u>. **Swing absolutely every time without fail <u>unless somebody is in the way</u>**, and absolutely **do not modify the swing** regardless of the position of the ball.

3. <u>Without a racquet</u>, emulate the serve of Step 2, but close the eyes as the swing goes forward into the hit. Open the eyes <u>after</u> a swing ends. In the same way, repeat the swing the way it should have occurred.
a. Do not think about the toss. Just intend to make an uncompromised swing and hit.

b. DRILLS LIKE THIS SHOULDN'T BE USED IF ANYONE IS STANDING, OR MOVING TO, WHERE THEY COULD BE HIT BY A WAYWARD BALL. THE SERVER IS PRIMARILY RESPONSIBLE FOR ALL PRECAUTIONS.

4. Repeat Steps 1, 2, and 3 with a <u>stance a little more</u>

closed and a stance a little more open than normal. Evaluate the feel, effectiveness, strain, pleasure, etc.

5. Repeat Steps 1, 2, and 3 trying for a little greater than normal arm extension and for a little less. Do not pull the elbow in as the swing progresses, but let it float out and forward. Evaluate feel, effectiveness, strain, pleasure, etc.

Initially a "swing-controlled" hit may be far off the "sweet spot", and may even be with the rim, throat, etc of the racquet. Do not make any changes to the swing to correct the problem. When there is a firm intention both not to modify the swing and to complete it every time, the toss will adapt to the swing, and with correct timing. Otherwise the converse is true: the swing will adapt to the toss, and there will be progress in the wrong direction.

It is neither necessary nor advisable to think of the nature of the toss, or of the height, or of whether or not the arms go up together. In other words, the swing is the constant. The serves are then "swing-controlled", not "toss-controlled". It is not easy to do because habits are strong, and urges, emotions, and fears are hard to control.

The arm should be slanted slightly forward at the hit so that there is a feeling of the arm being reinforced by the body. Use of SMV to resolve difficulties is advisable.

A common mistake is to accelerate the racquet downward in the follow-through because of the desire to hit down into the service court. Hitting directly into the court is an impossibility, as discussed under "THE SCIENCE OF THE TRAJECTORY" in the chapter on the "SERVE".

EXPERIMENTS WITH WRIST FLEX
1. Dangle the racquet in front so that the head is pointing downward and the hand is at about shoulder

level. Pull the racquet up from there, let it loop behind the back, and bring it forward into the final hitting stage of a serve. Keep the wrist loose. Send the racquet out to the full reach forward. The swing should be only a little faster than slow motion.

    a. Visualize making a free swing on each attempt. Do not think about using wrist flex. Whatever is needed occurs naturally here, and nothing extra should be added.

2. Repeat Step 1 gradually increasing the speed of the motion until an easy, momentum-powered swing is achieved. Accelerate the racquet forward through the "hitting plane". Do not substitute strength for swing.

3. Repeat the easy swing of Step 2 but make a toss of an imaginary ball into the path of the swing.

4. Repeat the easy swing of Step 2 but lift a real ball into the path of the swing. Do not think of the nature of the toss, or the height, timing, etc. **Do not modify the swing regardless of the location of the toss.**

    a. Use a low level of exertion. Do not turn to watch the ball until well after the hit. DO NOT MAKE THE HIT IF THERE IS ANY CHANCE OF ANYBODY BEING HIT BY A MISDIRECTED BALL.

EXPERIMENTS WITH THE DIRECTION OF DEPARTURE OF THE BALL

1. Toss an imaginary ball and hit a moderate serve in a straight out direction as it leaves the racquet.

    a. Let a free swing send the ball outward in a forward direction. Do not worry about the path of the racquet, just the direction of departure of the ball.

2. Repeat Step 1 with a real ball. Do not think about the landing point, only about the straight out initial direction. Do not steer the ball with a push or try to influence it with post-contact coercion.

329

a. Consider whether the ball was sent outward as it left the racquet. Reflect on how any problems could be corrected without violating the "swing-controlled" concepts.

b. Do not turn to soon to watch the path of the ball. It may be advisable to combat that habit by looking at the path of the racquet at the hit instead, or the hitting plane.

3. Repeat Steps 1 and 2, but with the idea of <u>having</u> the ball leave the racquet at a <u>slight downward slant</u> as it leaves the racquet. <u>Do not aim at a target</u>, such as the net. Think only of the prescribed <u>initial direction</u>. Do not worry about where the ball lands

4. Stand about ten feet in front of a fence. Repeat Steps 1 and 2 hitting into the fence and intending a <u>slight upward slant</u> for the direction of departure.
a. Some players find it difficult hit upward. Downward is what most intend to do. Upward is what actually happens on all spin serves, and on most flat serves that are not very fast.

At a later stage allowance must also be made for the effects of pace and spin. Accuracy depends on being able to control the direction of the initial part of the trajectory.

When players double fault at critical times the serves usually end up in the net rather than past the service line. This is the result of either giving the ball a downward direction of departure, slowing the forward swing, or pulling the racquet down during contact. The intent of the pull is to influence the ball to skim the net and then curve downward, both of which events are made unlikely to happen. Of course some people think, erroneously, that it is possible to aim the ball directly at a spot on the service court.

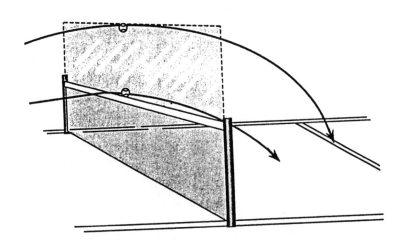

EXPERIMENTS WITH NET CLEARANCES OF SERVES

1. Picture the height of the <u>slightly curved trajectory</u> of a serve that lands right <u>on the service line</u>. Visualize a "window" above the net having the same height. Alternate hitting <u>imaginary and real balls</u> with the idea that the direction of departure produces a <u>trajectory</u> that goes <u>below the top of the "window"</u>. Use a "swing-controlled" stroke. Allow for gravity.

    a. The drop due to gravity of a ball hit with high pace does is not large until after the ball has reached the net. The reason is that the downward velocity <u>increases at the rate of 3.2 feet each tenth of a second</u>. At one hundred miles an hour a ball takes 4 tenths of a second to reach the service line on the other side, and 5.2 tenths of a second to reach the baseline.

2. Repeat Step 1 with a trajectory that passes through the bottom of the "window" (just above the net). The ball should land well inside the service line.

The vertical size of the "window" is not fixed. It depends on the height of the hitting point, pace, and spin. It is wrong to aim straight at a spot in the service court or at the service

line because such straight line trajectories go below the "window" into the net.

Do not "steer" the ball but keep the serve "swing-controlled". Swing the racquet out, not down. Do not open the stance by turning to watch the travel of the ball. Use a moderate racquet velocity in this drill to fight the normal tendency to over-exert on the serve.

STAYING WITH A "SWING-CONTROLLED" SERVE WHEN UNDER PRESSURE

1. Hit serves with reasonable compliance to the concepts of the toss, swing, direction, etc as developed in these drills and in the other chapters in the book.

   a. Mimic each serve, first using visualization and then actually, but with an imaginary ball. Consider how it could have been done better.

   b. Evaluate each serve and keep score of the good or the bad.

   c. The count could involve the number of good serves out of a fixed number of attempts, or the number of good serves in a row. Or count one for each good serve and minus two for each bad. Try to better the best previous score.

In this drill the definition of a "good" serve is that it must not contain any pre-specified deviations from a "swing-controlled" stroke. Specify a single taboo or a few, whatever can be managed at the current stage of development. The taboos should be general in nature and concerned with principles and problems, not patterns. At a more advanced stage an added requirement could be that the ball must at least land in the service court.

Restricted actions could be: impulsive effort, bending in a forward jackknife, bringing the elbow in, compromising the swing to accommodate the toss, opening the stance, using

push, using downward pull, stopping or slowing the swing before completion, inadequate or over-zealous involvement of the body, not hitting freely, emulating a pattern, etc. It should be remembered that the proper way to correct the toss is to refuse to modify the swing.

At critical times just about everybody <u>tries to do something extra</u> to get the first ball to land in the service court. But the act of <u>doing something extra amounts to doing more than enough</u>. So by that definition the <u>added measures are almost always a mistake</u>. Allowing any compromise of good technique, whether in the direction of extra abandon or extra caution, merely increases the chances of an error.

AWARENESS OF THE NATURE OF THE HIT
1.   Hit a serve, using an <u>imaginary</u> ball,with reasonable compliance to the current concept of good technique, but <u>close the eyes at contact</u>. Do not close the eyes before contact.

   a. Reflect on the nature of the swing and the "hit", the behavior of the body, the direction of racquet travel, presence of compulsiveness in the action, premature turn to watch the ball, modification of the swing to meet the toss, etc.

2. Repeat Step 1 with a real serve.

   a. **MAKE SURE THAT NOBODY IS APPROACHING, OR IS IN THE WAY ON EITHER SIDE OF THE COURT.**

Closing the eyes in this way <u>promotes awareness of the</u> **processes** involved in the stroke. It prevents concentration on the destination. The player experiences the feel of the hit in isolation from the results. When players are concerned about results they are often unaware of the techniques that produced those results, good or bad.

MAKE SURE THAT THERE IS ABSOLUTELY NO POSSIBILITY OF ANYBODY BEING IN, OR MOVING TOWARD, A LOCATION WHERE THERE IS ANY CHANCE OF BEING HIT, EITHER BY THE BALL OR BY THE RACQUET. ALL PRECAUTIONS ARE THE RESPONSIBILITY OF

THE SERVER.   THE BALL SHOULD NEVER BE RETURNED.   THE
SERVER MAY BE UNAWARE OF ITS APPROACH.

THE MATTER OF TAKING CARE NOT TO ENDANGER A BYSTANDER,
OR THE OPPONENT, APPLIES TO ALL TYPES OF STROKES. IT
COULD BE A MATTER OF LIFELONG REGRET TO HAVE INFLICTED,
OR SUFFERED, PERMANENT DAMAGE TO EYE, EAR, NOSE, TEETH,
THROAT, ETC, BECAUSE OF A SINGLE WRONG HIT OF A TENNIS
BALL. IT DOES HAPPEN, USUALLY AS THE RESULT OF A HARD HIT
AIMED AT OR NEAR SOMEONE'S HEAD AT CLOSE QUARTERS.

It is an unwritten rule that hard hits toward the vicinity of
someone's head at close range should not be made under any
circumstances. When it happens in tournaments it can be
considered suspect because professionals seldom have that
much lack of control.

THE WINDMILL SERVE

1. Without a racquet, assume the service stance,
arms in the normal position. Visualize the racquet
travelling in a circle whose plane points in the
direction of the serve. Let the racquet arm drift
around slowly and continuously in the visualized
circle at near full arm
extension.   Do not use
muscle or push. Close the
eyes at the start and open
them after the "hit", when
the arm is pointing
forward at about shoulder
level.   Involve the body
slightly.

    a. Reflect on both
good and bad im-
pressions, nature of
the swing, and on
ways of making any
improvements.

b. If the motion is unsatisfactory adjust the concepts, positioning, stance, etc, as necessary and repeat Step 1. In general, a mostly sideways stance will work best, causing minimum strain on the arm.

2. With a racquet, repeat Step 1 simulating a toss to meet an uncompromised swing. Close the eyes at the start of the swing and do not open them until when the racquet is pointing forward at about shoulder level.

    a. The racquet should be accelerated gradually and continuously, but not to the extent that the racquet will be carried below about the shoulder level.

    b. The arm and wrist should be loose, but there should be no pause in the motion of the arm or racquet.

    c. SWINGS OF THIS TYPE SHOULD NOT BE MADE, OR COMPLETED, IF THERE IS ANY CHANCE OF ANYBODY GETTING HIT BY THE RACQUET. ALL PRECAUTIONS ARE PRIMARILY THE SERVER'S RESPONSIBILITY.

3. Repeat Step 2 <u>with both racquet and ball</u>. Use a swing-controlled motion and do not modify it for any reason. <u>Unless someone is in the way</u>, **swing absolutely every time** regardless of the position of the ball, and **absolutely do not modify the swing to accommodate a bad toss.**

<u>*PRACTICING THE OVERHEAD*</u>
1. <u>Without a racquet</u> just move into position and catch the ball with the free arm held in front of the head at about full extension. At the same time hold the racquet arm in the ready position above the head, but do not swing.

    a. Visualize completing the swing with the arm

at about full extension.

b. Reflect on the suitability of the position, stance, hitting point, intended direction of the overhead, etc. Unlike the serve, the stance may or may not be fairly open, mainly because only a moderate swing is needed.

2. <u>Without a racquet</u> catch the ball as in Step 1, but make a short forward swing with the racquet arm after the ball has been caught. The arm should be at about full extension
   a. Use a low level of effort, much less than in a serve. <u>Since a racquet is not being used there is no racquet momentum.</u> So the follow-through <u>should go out, not down.</u> This is generally true even with a racquet since the effort is not very great.

b. Repeat Step 2 several times, experimenting with the ready position of the racquet until a comfortable location from which to start the forward swing is found.

c. If the "DOUBLE-FORCE" method is used, discard the ball toward the net after catching it. Move the free hand immediately to the racquet arm, apply the "boost grip", and make the forward swing.

3. With a racquet repeat Step 2. The momentum will usually carry the racquet below shoulder level. On a serve the racquet will go considerably lower. But on an overhead there is a much lower level of effort.

4. Repeat Step 2 making actual hits instead of catching the ball. Be very conservative with the effort. Try to get into the same position as in the previous Steps.

a. If the position, stance, or timing does not appear to be right delay the forward swing a bit, correct the flaw, and then execute a deferred "swing-controlled" hit as it should have occurred. The purpose of the delay is to avoid practicing the improper position, stance, and hitting point, as well as the associated compensations.

The most common mistakes made by inexpert players are:

1. Using almost no backswing and then just pushing the racquet at the ball with a forward sway of the body.

2. Bending the elbow so as to hit at only a little above head height rather than at arm extension.

3. Using either the extreme of swinging as if to demolish the ball or of just patting it into the middle of the service court with little pace.

4. Being out of position, too far back or forward.

5. Jackknifing the body forward and down.

6. Hitting downward. Even tournament players make the inexcusable error of hitting an easy overhead into the net from a position very close to it.

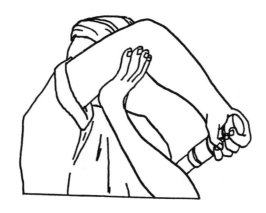

SELECTING AREAS FOR INVESTIGATION

There are other areas for experiment and investigation besides those dealt with in the previous drills. So if any difficulty is being experienced in an area that has not been covered it may be possible to resolve the problems using one of the techniques prescribed for other situations.

A useful device is to vary an element in each direction from the normal, as the stance, backswing, footwork, turn of shoulders, wrist flex, arm extension, hitting point, etc. The value of trying variations derives from the fact that good modifications will generate satisfying feel and results, while the poor will not. It is as important to discover the ideas do not work as those that do, and why.

But the feel of some actions can be somewhat misleading. As an example: a technique that produces maximum pace may not give that impression because of not producing as much shock to the arm, not requiring maximum effort, and therefor not satisfying the irrational urges, or providing the customary misleading sensations.

TRACING COMPENSATIONS TO CAUSES IN ORDER TO ELIMINATE BOTH

When solutions to problems turn out to be elusive a good alternative approach is to analyze the stroke for the presence of compensations, expedients, idiosyncrasies, and enhancements.

    1. Suppress them one at a time, but leave everything

else in the stroke unchanged. The undesirable event that the now suppressed action was intended to prevent must be allowed to occur, let the ball go how and where it may.

2. Analyze any undesirable consequence to try to identify the responsible flaw. Typically this could be the direction of racquet travel, stroke production, stance, body rotation, internal or external timing, arm extension, "swing distance", "hitting plane", urges, breaking of reinforcement, etc. It doesn't do any good to try to eliminate a compensation if an underlying flaw creates a need for it.

LEFTOVER TIMING HABITS

There is a great deal of interaction among the elements of a swing, especially timing-wise. So the addition or removal of a detail, flaw, or compensation can create timing problems for seemingly unrelated items. Even an apparently harmless idiosyncrasy has to be timed to fit in with everything else, good or bad. If it is removed or just mistimed it may cause disaster by directly or indirectly upsetting the timing sequence of other elements that are useful.

Added to this is the fact that the force of habit and feelings of deprivation will exert a pull to restore flaws that have been successfully removed. And even when the removal or replacement of an obviously undesirable element has been accomplished the timing of the rest of the elements tends to remain unchanged, in spite of the changed environment. Therefor the strokes may not work as efficiently as before. So direct removal is not as effective as educated experimentation and evaluation. With the latter approach the new satisfactions will gradually crowd out the old. Techniques are adopted, not imposed.

Conformance to patterns is not a cure. For one thing it involves changing many elements instead of just a few. It is undesirable to clean out the good with the bad in a player's natural way of hitting. And it is difficult enough to work on one or a few items at a time. Tackling a whole set at once just hasn't worked. Also, patterns do not deal with the origins of bad habits, or the forces that cause reversion.

When a player seems unable to get rid of a habit, say a slice backhand, there ought to be manageable drills to show that what is difficult can become fairly easy if legitimate techniques are used, and if realistic rather than impossible results are expected. In the case of the slice backhand the most usual cause is lack of confidence in the strength of the arm. So a possible approach would be to learn to depend on momentum. Solutions are never to be considered final since the process is automatic and continuous for all aspects of all strokes.

ANALYZING A COMPLICATED PROBLEM

Suppose that a player needs help in solving the problem of erratic control. Say that the most prominent quirk in the strokes is a sudden forward tilt of the racquet at the end of the hit. Also, the hitting point may be somewhat too far forward. Neither of these is necessarily wrong since similar quirks can be seen in the strokes of top players.

Suppressing the forward tilt of the racquet, and changing nothing else, reveals that the ball then goes up at an unwanted angle. The easily recognized cause is that the racquet attitude is now slightly open at the hit. A simple case of cause and effect. Slow motion emulation and visualization of a shot show that the grip may be incompatible with a somewhat laid back wrist, although neither is unusual in itself.

A noticeable trait of the player is lack of confidence. But this could be the result of the problems, not the cause of them. In either case the result would be a tendency to favor techniques that provide a sense of security. These could be standing too close to the path of the ball, shortening the

backswing, opening the stance, and advancing the hitting point.
The advanced hitting point could be the result of standing too close to the path of the ball, or vice versa. At any rate it would require laying the wrist back at the hit in order to keep the racquet facing forward. And that compensation could result in an open racquet attitude, even if the grip and the stance being used would ordinarily produce a closed racquet face.

That explanation seems to be the most plausible since there is close correspondence to the player's habits. It doesn't answer everything, particularly the important question of which came first, the lack of confidence, the improper positioning, or the too far forward hitting point? One clue is that the grip appears to have been adopted for use with both a different hitting position and hitting point.

Here the trail ends since it is not advisable to attribute everything to a single assumed cause. There usually are combinations of causes. But at least the scenario eliminates unlikely solutions, like changing the follow-through so as to conform to a pattern. Counterfeit "solutions" can only introduce new complications, while covering up clues that could lead to cures. It may be possible to develop a skill, like control, but not to banish a nothing, like lack of control.

If the most important mechanical flaw is corrected, in this case the location of the hitting point which eventually results in the rotation of the racquet face, then the forward tilt of the racquet at the end of the hit should gradually disappear of its own accord because of being unnecessary. The drills pertaining to the "swing distance", "hitting plane distance", and hitting point should be reviewed periodically to upgrade the concepts and restore compatibility as the game changes.

THE USES OF VISUALIZATION

Visualization can be used in play both before a shot and

after. It can also be used as a non-physical practice session. The format of the latter might be to spend say five minutes, or much more or less as necessary and profitable, visualizing a particular item or sequence. The choices would depend on the proficiency of the student, the area being worked on, difficulties being experienced, etc.

The purpose might be to master something new, examine and refine an old, work on a persistent flaw, study timing problems, review tennis lessons, evaluate the hitting techniques, experiment with various options, determine the origins of compensations, find explanations for poor and erratic results, associate good or bad feel with causes, etc.

Typical items that could be chosen for visualization are positioning, footwork, preparation, backswing, path of swing, hitting point, follow-through, use of wrist flex, effects of a bent elbow, involvement of the body, coordination of body rotation with the swing, the timing of the opening of the stance after the hit, direction of departure of the ball as it leaves the racquet, behavior of the racquet as to attitude, acceleration, momentum, manipulation, etc.

MENTAL DRILLS

1. Execute a shot normally. Do not attempt to hide the deficiencies. Analysis of problems is difficult enough without the handicap of a conscious effort to disguise the real shortcomings.

2. Visualize the stroke, or just a part, as it did occur, not trying to exaggerate the flaws or disguise them either. Then go over and over the total action mentally, trying to improve the shot by just making it feel better. Do not try to make it conform to a concept of what constitutes good or bad.

3. Visualize how the stroke should have occurred. Compare the actual shot with the visualized hit as corrected. Try to identify the biggest flaw or flaws in

both.

a. <u>A strange but fortunate feature of ordinary visualization is that the techniques used in a visualized shot are identical to those used in the actual shot. All the bad habits are there.</u> It is very difficult to picture a shot done in other than the customary manner. So, expect a struggle in trying to introduce revisions. Progress will be gradual but certain.

b. The drill must be entirely mental since this is an attempt to change the mental pictures that control the physical actions. "Slow Motion Visualization" (SMV) should be used at times, especially when no headway can be made at normal speed. Remember, most flaws seem to be automatically eliminated in Slow Motion Visualizations. <u>So using SMV and gradually working up to moderate speed shots can promote change in the pictures and carry-over into the real strokes</u>.

1. Visualizing how a stroke should look can also be used when learning new techniques instead of just as a means to correct the existing.

4. Execute the shot as visualized, slowly at first, and with an imaginary ball. Make use of "deferred", "shadow", and "timing" swings. If the progress seems to be nil, as is often likely, go back to the visualizations in Step 2, but just for a few tries, not forever. Expect to have to put up with "deferred solutions".

5. Eventually a series of connected actions should be practiced mentally, preferably at less than normal speed. The following is a complicated sequence similar to actual drills often employed in standard coaching procedures.

a. Visualize making a down-the-line hit from the right-hand corner.

b. Visualize an approach to within six feet of the net to cut off the return. Make a volley to the left-hand corner off of a low or other difficult return.

c. Visualize a hard run to your own left-hand corner to retrieve the opponent's down-the-line response. Make a soft drive, desperation shot, or lob somewhat close to a corner or sideline.

1. Make sure that the racquet is back soon enough, hitting point is not moved forward, swing is not hurried, etc.

2. A standard recommendation for a lob is to hit toward the middle to cut down the angles available on the return. But against expert opponents the percent of success is very small. In the big majority of cases at tournament level the down-the-middle lobs turn out to be not high or deep enough, and the opponent has no difficulty in putting them away.

3. A cross-court or down-the-line lob may open the available angles on the return, but the defender is not right under the ball without having had to move. A player at the net has good reach on passing shots but almost none at all on a lob. It is necessary to get directly under it. So a lob to a corner increases the difficulty of making an overhead. Another little used option with the same advantage is a soft, deep, down-the-line drive.

WORKING ON FAULTS USING VISUALIZATION ALONE

The fact that visualized strokes have the same flaws as the actual is evidence that physical skills may reside mostly in the mind, not the muscles. Developing a physical skill can really amount to establishing a set of automatic mental commands that tell the muscles what to do. So practicing tennis, or any physical skill, or doing therapy to regain or develop a physical skill, etc, can be conducted mentally.

The storage area for physical skills is not in the depths of the untouchable subconscious. It can be accessed and modified by the ordinary thinking and picturing processes. If a new technique, such as "DOUBLE-FORCE", is demonstrated or explained a player can practice it via visualization, and can acquire a little mastery before ever trying it with a racquet.

The mental approach has the advantage of making it possible to look at a shot in a variety of ways: as if executing the shot in reality, watching it as a spectator while one's own body executes the shot, or watching it being executed by somebody else. And in each of those three cases the player can also sort of experience the feel of the shot. This is understandable since in both the physical and the visualized shots the same set of mental controls is used. The physical muscles do not get to be exercised or developed, but those of the mind do, which also happens to be the general aim of education.

The Index

◆◆

◆▼

❖❖❖❖❖❖❖❖❖❖❖❖❖❖❖❖❖❖❖❖❖❖❖❖❖❖❖❖❖❖❖❖❖

◆▼◆

❖❖

◆▼◆

❖❖❖❖❖❖❖❖❖❖❖❖❖❖❖❖❖❖❖❖❖❖❖❖❖❖❖❖❖❖❖❖❖

◆◆◆◆◆◆◆◆◆◆◆◆◆◆◆◆◆◆◆◆◆◆◆◆◆◆◆◆◆◆◆◆◆◆◆◆

◆❤◆❤◆❤◆❤◆❤◆❤◆❤◆❤◆❤◆❤◆❤◆❤◆❤◆❤◆❤◆❤◆❤◆❤❤

◆◆◆◆◆◆◆◆◆◆◆◆◆◆◆◆◆◆◆◆◆◆◆◆◆◆◆◆◆◆◆◆◆◆◆

❖❖❖❖❖❖❖❖❖❖❖❖❖❖❖❖❖❖❖❖❖❖❖❖❖❖❖❖❖❖❖❖❖❖❖❖❖❖

◆◆◆